Twenty-four Common Open-Position Chords

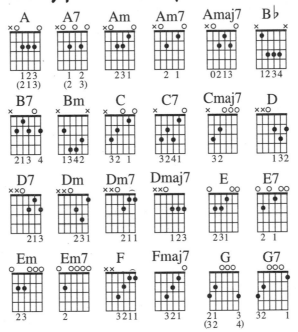

Six Common Moveable Chord Forms: 6th-String Root

Six Common Moveable Chord Forms: 5th-String Root

Six Other Moveable Chord Forms: 5th-String Root

Rock Guitar For Dummies®

Cheat Sheet

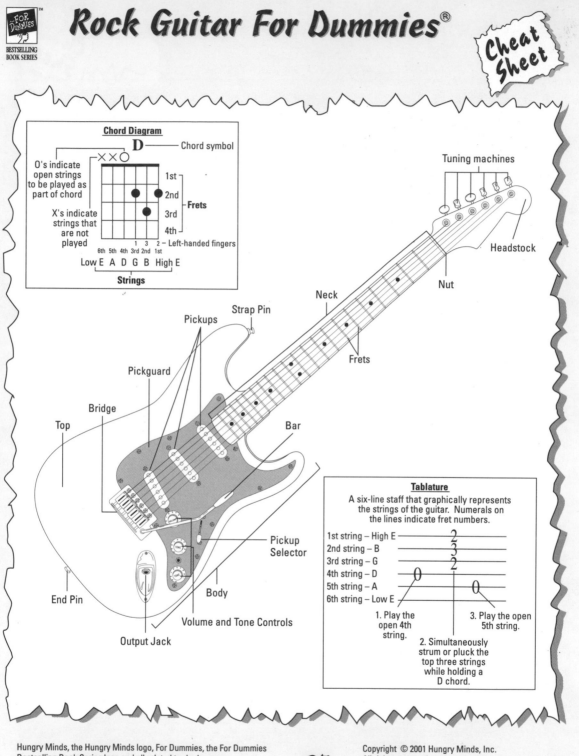

Chord Diagram

D — Chord symbol

O's indicate open strings to be played as part of chord

X's indicate strings that are not played

1st
2nd — Frets
3rd
4th

1   3   2 — Left-handed fingers
6th 5th 4th 3rd 2nd 1st

Low E A D G B High E

Strings

Tuning machines

Headstock

Nut

Neck

Frets

Pickups

Strap Pin

Pickguard

Bridge

Bar

Top

End Pin

Output Jack

Body

Volume and Tone Controls

Pickup Selector

Tablature

A six-line staff that graphically represents the strings of the guitar. Numerals on the lines indicate fret numbers.

1st string – High E	2
2nd string – B	3
3rd string – G	2
4th string – D	0
5th string – A	0
6th string – Low E	

1. Play the open 4th string.

2. Simultaneously strum or pluck the top three strings while holding a D chord.

3. Play the open 5th string.

Hungry Minds™

For Dummies: Bestselling Book Series for Beginners

Rock Guitar FOR DUMMIES®

by Jon Chappell

Foreword by Carl Verheyen

Hungry Minds™

Best-Selling Books • Digital Downloads • e-Books • Answer Networks • e-Newsletters • Branded Web Sites • e-Learning

New York, NY ◆ Cleveland, OH ◆ Indianapolis, IN

Rock Guitar For Dummies®

Published by:
Hungry Minds, Inc.
909 Third Avenue
New York, NY 10022
www.hungryminds.com
www.dummies.com

Library of Congress Control Number: 2001092880

ISBN: 0-7645-5356-9

Printed in the United States of America

10 9 8 7 6 5 4 3 2 1

1B/RY/QZ/QR/IN

Distributed in the United States by Hungry Minds, Inc.

Distributed by CDG Books Canada Inc. for Canada; by Transworld Publishers Limited in the United Kingdom; by IDG Norge Books for Norway; by IDG Sweden Books for Sweden; by IDG Books Australia Publishing Corporation Pty. Ltd. for Australia and New Zealand; by TransQuest Publishers Pte Ltd. for Singapore, Malaysia, Thailand, Indonesia, and Hong Kong; by Gotop Information Inc. for Taiwan; by ICG Muse, Inc. for Japan; by Intersoft for South Africa; by Eyrolles for France; by International Thomson Publishing for Germany, Austria and Switzerland; by Distribuidora Cuspide for Argentina; by LR International for Brazil; by Galileo Libros for Chile; by Ediciones ZETA S.C.R. Ltda. for Peru; by WS Computer Publishing Corporation, Inc., for the Philippines; by Contemporanea de Ediciones for Venezuela; by Express Computer Distributors for the Caribbean and West Indies; by Micronesia Media Distributor, Inc. for Micronesia; by Chips Computadoras S.A. de C.V. for Mexico; by Editorial Norma de Panama S.A. for Panama; by American Bookshops for Finland.

For general information on Hungry Minds' products and services please contact our Customer Care department; within the U.S. at 800-762-2974, outside the U.S. at 317-572-3993 or fax 317-572-4002.

For sales inquiries and resellers information, including discounts, premium and bulk quantity sales and foreign language translations please contact our Customer Care department at 800-434-3422, fax 317-572-4002 or write to Hungry Minds, Inc., Attn: Customer Care department, 10475 Crosspoint Boulevard, Indianapolis, IN 46256.

For information on licensing foreign or domestic rights, please contact our Sub-Rights Customer Care department at 212-884-5000.

For information on using Hungry Minds' products and services in the classroom or for ordering examination copies, please contact our Educational Sales department at 800-434-2086 or fax 317-572-4005.

Please contact our Public Relations department at 212-884-5163 for press review copies or 212-884-5000 for author interviews and other publicity information or fax 212-884-5400.

For authorization to photocopy items for corporate, personal, or educational use, please contact Copyright Clearance Center, 222 Rosewood Drive, Danvers, MA 01923, or fax 978-750-4470.

Hungry Minds™ is a trademark of Hungry Minds, Inc.

About the Author

Jon Chappell is an author, writer, and award-winning guitarist. He began his serious musical life as a multi-style guitarist, transcriber, and arranger, attending Carnegie-Mellon University where he studied with guitarist Carlos Barbosa-Lima, and then earning his master's degree in music composition from DePaul University.

Jon has served as editor-in-chief of *Guitar Magazine* and *Guitar Online,* technical editor of *Guitar Shop Magazine,* and musicologist for *Guitarra,* a classical magazine. He has played and recorded with Pat Benatar, Judy Collins, Graham Nash, and Robert Cray, and has contributed numerous musical pieces to film and TV. Some of these include *Northern Exposure; Walker, Texas Ranger; All My Children;* and the feature film *Bleeding Hearts*, directed by actor-dancer Gregory Hines.

In 1991, Jon became associate music director of Cherry Lane Music, where he transcribed, edited, and arranged the music of Metallica, Joe Satriani, Steve Morse, Steve Vai, Bonnie Raitt, and Eddie Van Halen, among others. He has 20 method books to his name, which have sold in excess of 500,000 copies, and is the author of *Guitar For Dummies, Blues Rock Riffs for Guitar,* and *The Recording Guitarist — A Guide for Home and Studio.* He has published pieces in the *New York Times, Rolling Stone, Spin, MacWorld,* and many other publications. Jon is currently online publisher of the Music Player Network, and lives in New York with his wife and four rock-and-roll children.

Dedication

To Mary —

My north, my south, my east, my west;

My working week, my Sunday best.

Author's Acknowledgments

This book was a journey, and many people helped guide this weary traveler toward his destination by offering direction, hospitality, and generosity. I'd like to take a moment to thank just a few of them.

Special thanks to my project editor, Linda Brandon, who kept me going with wise counsel, expert advice, and good cheer, and who showed conspicuous bravery and uncommon valor in the face of the most dire of deadlines. You go, girl!

Then there's a big thank you to "the brain trust," my cadre of trusted advisers whose sage wisdom and patient forbearance helped me untangle my thoughts and get them onto the page: Corey Dalton, Jeff Jacobson, Rich Maloof, Emile Menasché, and Pete Prown.

As well, I'd like to thank the artistic crew: Woytek and Krystyna Rynczak, of WR Music Service, for their beautiful and elegant music typesetting; Miriam Lorentzen for her expert photographic work and direction; and Matt Brewster and Ned Brewster of 30th Street Guitars, NYC, for providing all the cool gear in the photos.

I'd also like to extend a grateful thank you to "the believers": Kathy Nebenhaus and Tracy Boggier of Hungry Minds, Inc., who backed this effort and didn't flinch once (at least that I could see!) as the scope grew and grew.

And, finally, thanks to these folks, all of whose direct influence (whether they know it or not) is tucked somewhere inside the pages of this book: Craig Anderton, Nick Bowcott (Korg USA), Leslie Buttonow (Korg USA), Tara Callahan (Roland Corp. US), Addison Chappell and David Chappell (my guitar playing brothers), Jen Chappell, Katie Chappell, Lauren Chappell, Ryan Chappell, Robbie Clyne (Neilson/Clyne), Phil Sanchez (TASCAM), JC Costa, Rusty Cutchin, Steve De Furia (Line 6), Doyle Dykes, Andy Ellis, Paul Gallo, Chris Gentri, Tim Godwin (Line 6), Rory Gordon, Mike McGee, Michael Molenda, Mike Myers, Gil Parris, Mark Phillips, Marty Porter, Marsha Vdovin (Steinberg), Allen Wald, Kellie Wilkie (Roland Corp. US), Tom Wilson, Alex Wright.

For the recording of the CD, special thanks to these manufacturers, who lent expertise and technology: Line 6, whose POD Pro supplied all the killer guitar sounds, effects, and a lot of the inspiration; Roland Corp. U.S., whose JS-5 JamStation served up the impeccably played backing tracks; and Steinberg, for Cubase VST/32, and TASCAM, for the US-428 control surface, who together helped create a seamless and stellar digital recording.

Publisher's Acknowledgments

We're proud of this book; please send us your comments through our Online Registration Form located at www.dummies.com.

Some of the people who helped bring this book to market include the following:

Acquisitions, Editorial, and Media Development

Project Editor: Linda Brandon

Acquisitions Editor: Tracy Boggier

Copy Editor: Corey Dalton

Technical Editor: Rich Maloof

Media Development Specialist: Marisa Pearman

Editorial Manager: Christine Beck

Editorial Assistant: Jennifer Young

Cover Photos: © Mitchell Gerber/Corbis

Production

Project Coordinator: Dale White

Layout and Graphics: Jackie Nicholas, Jill Piscitelli, Brian Torwelle, Jeremey Unger

Proofreaders: Andy Hollandbeck, Marianne Santy, TECHBOOKS Production Services

Indexer: TECHBOOKS Production Services

General and Administrative

Hungry Minds, Inc.: John Kilcullen, CEO; Bill Barry, President and COO; John Ball, Executive VP, Operations & Administration; John Harris, CFO

Hungry Minds Consumer Reference Group

Business: Kathleen Nebenhaus, Vice President and Publisher; Kevin Thornton, Acquisitions Manager

Cooking/Gardening: Jennifer Feldman, Associate Vice President and Publisher; Anne Ficklen, Executive Editor; Kristi Hart, Managing Editor

Education/Reference: Diane Graves Steele, Vice President and Publisher

Lifestyles: Kathleen Nebenhaus, Vice President and Publisher; Tracy Boggier, Managing Editor

Pets: Kathleen Nebenhaus, Vice President and Publisher; Tracy Boggier, Managing Editor

Travel: Michael Spring, Vice President and Publisher; Brice Gosnell, Publishing Director; Suzanne Jannetta, Editorial Director

Hungry Minds Consumer Editorial Services: Kathleen Nebenhaus, Vice President and Publisher; Kristin A. Cocks, Editorial Director; Cindy Kitchel, Editorial Director

Hungry Minds Consumer Production: Debbie Stailey, Production Director

◆

The publisher would like to give special thanks to Patrick J. McGovern, without whom this book would not have been possible.

◆

Contents at a Glance

Cartoons at a Glance

By Rich Tennant

"That's the third time tonight that's happened. They start out playing the blues, but by the end, everyone's playing a polka. I blame the new bass player from Milwaukee."

page 319

"So you're attempting to learn how to play rock guitar, but your wife hates rock music. Go on...."

page 7

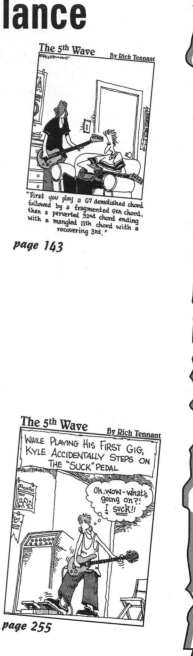

"First you play a G7 demolished chord, followed by a fragmented 9th chord, then a perverted 32nd chord ending with a mangled 11th chord with a recovering 3rd."

page 143

"Okay- I'll front the band. But I want someone other than Dopey on lead guitar."

page 67

"Now this little plant is called Emma. Emma blooms best to the scathing guitar riffs of Ted Nugent and Eddie Van Halen."

page 177

WHILE PLAYING HIS FIRST GIG, KYLE ACCIDENTALLY STEPS ON THE "SUCK" PEDAL

Oh, wow- what's going on?! I suck!!

page 255

Cartoon Information:
Fax: 978-546-7747
E-Mail: richtennant@the5thwave.com
World Wide Web: www.the5thwave.com

Table of Contents

· ·

Foreword

*B*y the end of 1971 my high school band was pretty hip. We played most of the Hendrix and Cream staples, and we were very successful at the local dances. My bass player, drummer, and I had devoured *Wheels of Fire* and we were still wading through *Electric Ladyland* when Jimi died. We had even gone to see Led Zeppelin on their first U.S. tour, after which I proudly proclaimed, "Yeah, I'm as good as Jimmy Page!"

But that was the year they released "Stairway to Heaven," and using a fake sore throat as an excuse, I stayed home from school to figure it out. My naive, schoolyard boasting quickly withered away as I realized that rock guitar had changed on that record. There were layers of carefully crafted acoustic and electric parts woven together in a tapestry of power and mystery. And it rocked. The blues-based illegitimate child of Chuck Berry had turned a corner; from now on anything was possible.

These were the early years, and sitting in my room with my guitar and record player, I never would have guessed that someday all this would spawn detailed transcriptions in books, magazines, videos, CD-ROMs, and all over the Internet. But then I couldn't foresee some of the brilliant rock guitarists to come, like Larry Carlton, Joe Walsh, Steve Morse, Eddie Van Halen, Steve Vai, David Gilmour, and Eric Johnson. The required listening and essential repertoire is as deep as the classical guitarist's, and is constantly expanding. A book such as *Rock Guitar For Dummies* could never have been possible 30 years ago. We are so lucky to have this history we can now draw from.

The *Dummies* format is perfect for presenting the many facets of rock guitar — its history, personalities, and techniques. *Rock Guitar For Dummies* takes you into the passionate world of the most creative musicians ever to strap on a six-string, and presents everything you need to get the music under your hands. Jon Chappell understands the legacy and the mission, and guides you through the essentials of the music, its chords and riffs, and the different rock styles. I know of few authors/musicians as qualified or uniquely suited to bring together all these varied aspects of rock guitar. As the editor of *Guitar Magazine,* and as a performer, teacher, and writer on all things music, Jon has surely heard it all and seen it all. And as a player, his well-rounded abilities are matched only by his deep love of the instrument and all its amazing potential. Enjoy this book and enjoy playing the guitar!

Carl Verheyen

Introduction

*F*ace it, being a rock and roll guitar player is just about the coolest thing you can be — next to a secret agent with a black belt in karate. But even if you were a butt-kicking international person of mystery, playing rock and roll would still be cooler because it involves art, passion, power, poetry, and the ability to move an audience of listeners. Whether "moving your listeners" means mowing down crowd surfers with your stun-gun power chords or making the audience cry with your achingly wrought melodies, no other art form allows you to wreak such devastation and look so sensitive doing it. And playing the guitar is also a heck of a lot safer than hanging upside down from the helicopter of your nemesis as he tries to drop you into a shark tank.

Whatever rocks your world, *Rock Guitar For Dummies* will help you to bring the message out through your fingers, onto the electric guitar you've got slung so insolently around your neck, and piped through that turbo-charged amp you've got cranked up over in the corner. All you have to do now is learn how to play. And for that, you need only your eyes to read the text, your ears to hear the CD, a set of willing digits (that would be your fingers), and a little time and patience. *Rock Guitar For Dummies* will handle the rest.

About This Book

Rock guitar is a specific subset of the larger world of guitar playing. If you find you need some help in the real basics of guitar, irrespective of rock or any other genre, I recommend picking up my other *Dummies* book, *Guitar For Dummies*. Now before you think I'm just shamelessly plugging my wares, consider that while *Rock Guitar For Dummies* was written not as a sequel, it *is* a very specific and focused look at a single genre: rock. As such, *Rock Guitar For Dummies* assumes a slightly higher level of guitar literacy ("literacy" is a funny word to use when discussing any genre that includes the band KISS, but there you go). It doesn't mean that I launch into arcane discussions of music theory or demand you perform acrobatically advanced techniques, but I tend to condense issues such as syncopation and forming barre chords with the left hand. If you find you want more information on those issues *Guitar For Dummies* may provide the solution. Besides, the only thing better for your musical education than owning a *For Dummies* book on guitar is owning two. End of "shameless plug" section.

If anything breaks the mold of a traditional approach to learning, it's the pursuit of rock guitar. I present to you many ways to learn the material in this book, and I don't recommend any one way as superior to another. Here are some ways in which to take advantage of the different means offered:

✔ **Look at the photos:** Photographs are purely visual and require no text to explain them. Simply look at the photos of the hand positions and the shots of the gear to get a purely visual read on what's going on.

✔ **Read the tab:** In true guitar fashion, I present guitar notation in a system designed exclusively for showing music on the guitar: tablature ("tab"). Tab isn't your one-stop-shopping solution for all your notational needs, but it's really handy for seeing exactly which string to play and on what fret. Plus, it works really well when accompanied by standard music notation.

✔ **Listen to the CD:** Some old-fashioned teachers don't like you listening to the piece you're supposed to learn. Not so here. I want you to internalize the music in this book through every means possible. Also, I want you to hear the different tone and signal processing represented in the examples — and that just can't be communicated in the notation.

✔ **Read the music:** You know that expression "As a last resort, read the manual"? It's meant as a joke, because often the info you need is right there in the written documentation. And the same is true with *Rock Guitar For Dummies.* Although you don't *need* to read music to play any and all of the exercises in this book, doing so will help you understand better what's being asked of you and may speed up the learning process.

Not-So-Foolish Assumptions

You don't need to have *any ability to read music or previous experience with the guitar* to benefit from *Rock Guitar For Dummies.* All you need is an electric guitar and some sort of means to amplify it (either through a guitar amp, a small headphone amp, or even a spare input on your home stereo or boom box). If you know you want to play rock, and plan to use an electric guitar when doing it, this is the book for you.

As I state earlier in the introduction, however, rock guitar is a subset of guitar in general, so if you feel you want a more basic approach or just want to expose yourself to more styles than rock, by all means take a look at *Guitar For Dummies.* Because you've purchased a book called *Rock Guitar For Dummies,* I'm not going to make you mess around with songs like "Go Tell Aunt Rhody"; instead, I'm going to let you rock out!

Conventions Used in This Book

I know what you're thinking: rock and roll is supposed to be about rejecting conventions! So, why talk about them now? Actually, I just want to establish some of the assorted terms and practices I use to communicate guitar issues in this book.

Right hand and left hand: I use the terms "right hand" and "left hand" to indicate the picking hand and the fretting hand, respectively. Guitar is one of the few instruments that you can "flip" and play in a reverse manner, where your right hand becomes your fretting hand. But with apologies to the left-handers out there who do flip (and therefore have to perform a translation), I stick to calling the hand that frets, the left one, and the hand that picks, the right hand.

Up and down, higher and lower: Unless otherwise noted, I use "up," "down," "higher," and "lower" to indicate musical pitch, regardless of how the strings or frets are positioned. This sometimes can be confusing to a beginner because when you hold the guitar in a playing position, the lowest-pitched string (the low E) is closest to the ceiling. Also, the angle of the neck tends to make the higher-pitched frets closer to the floor as well. But most people make the transition easily and never think about these directional terms in any way other than with respect to pitch.

"Rock" vs. "Rock and Roll": Some fussy professor-types might distinguish between the terms "rock" and "rock and roll," but I use them interchangeably. It's a "feel thing" (an irrefutable argument you can use to justify virtually any act or decision in rock and roll).

How This Book Is Organized

I have organized the chapters into two distinct categories: information chapters and playing chapters. Information chapters include descriptions of the parts of the guitar and amp, how to hold and tune the instrument, choosing equipment, and caring for the guitar. The playing chapters cover basic techniques, more advanced techniques that make you sound like a rock and roller, and exercises and complete pieces in different musical styles of rock.

I've divided *Rock Guitar For Dummies* into six large-scale parts and each part is further divided into chapters. A chapter is a self-contained unit, allowing you to open to virtually any one of them and start reading without worrying about what came before. At the same time, I organize the book in a linear structure, so reading the chapters in a row provides its own logical satisfaction. And you can always look up a specific issue in the table of contents or the index.

Part 1: So You Wanna Be a Rock-and-Roll Star

In this part, you get exposed to the basic hardware components of rock guitar, how to hold and tune the electric guitar, what that electronic box called an "amp" is all about, and even how to listen to rock guitar. Chapter 1 presents the "hardware," or the physical objects, such as the guitar, amp, effects, and some useful accessories. In Chapter 2 you learn how to hold the guitar, where to place your hands, and how to read the notation. You celebrate the end of the chapter by fingering and strumming an E chord. Chapter 3 looks at the individual components of the amp and how the whole system works to create those Tones of Death.

Part II: Basic Playing Techniques

In Part II, I dig down and explore playing techniques. Chapter 4 shows you how to finger open-position chords, barre chords, and power chords. In Chapter 5, you learn right-hand strumming patterns and fingerstyle techniques. Chapter 6 unveils rock guitar's most coveted technique: lead guitar. In this chapter, you learn to pick single-note leads and play solos over chord progressions. To try out your newly acquired single-note chops, tackle Chapter 7 — a whole chapter on riffs.

Part III: Beyond the Basics: Sounding Like a Rock and Roller

This is the part where you begin to break away from general guitar techniques and focus more on specific rock techniques. Chapter 8 takes you out of the range of open-position chords and into the wild blue yonder of up-the-neck playing. Chapter 9 explores all the different expressive techniques and articulations that help give your playing life, interest, and soul.

Part IV: Mastering Different Rock Styles

Part IV is known as the styles section, where each of the four chapters deals with an important subgenre of rock. Chapter 10 covers the early rock period and includes a look at the styles of Chuck Berry, Bo Diddley, Buddy Holly, the Beatles, and the Rolling Stones. Chapter 11 deals with the classic rock era, which includes everyone from early hard rockers, the Who, to proto-metallers, Led Zeppelin, to Eric Clapton and Jimi Hendrix to the Allman Brothers to U2 to the Eagles. Chapter 12 gets subterranean with a look at the dark side of rock: heavy metal. Here, I run the gamut from early heavy metal bands such as Black Sabbath, Deep Purple, and AC/DC to Metallica and to rap-rockers Korn. If a more sophisticated approach to rock is your thing, check out Chapter 13 on jazz- and progressive rock, where I look at Rush, Steely Dan, Yes, and Pink Floyd.

Part V: Becoming a Gearhead

An essential part in adopting rock and roll culture is knowing about, pining for, and taking care of all the great gear that's out there. Part V has three chapters that deal specifically with handling the hardware. Chapter 14 describes all the different types of guitars, the various amp configurations, and offers tips on shopping around for your dream rig. Chapter 15 is devoted entirely to the gizmos and gadgets used by guitarists, collectively known as effects. In Chapter 16, you discover that guitars and amps are hardy creatures, but that they still need to be properly maintained and stored.

Part VI: The Part of Tens

The Part of Tens is a *For Dummies* trademark that provides cool and useful information in a top-ten format. Chapter 17 lists ten rock guitarists who changed history and should offer some inspiration. For your listening pleasure, I've assembled a top-ten list of great guitar-oriented albums in Chapter 18. And for you "gearheads," Chapter 19 covers ten great rock-and-roll guitars that shake the world. That should whet your appetite for acquiring your own dream rig.

Appendix

The Appendix in *Rock Guitar For Dummies* offer an indispensable reference. It explains how the CD is organized and gives the track listing and titles.

Bonus Web Chapter

For your added pleasure, there is a bonus chapter located on the Web. This extra chapter offers a special section on gigging that arms you with tips on auditioning for a band, forming your own band, and getting that gig you've been dreaming about — whether it's Madison Square Garden or the local Brew 'n' Burger. "The Rock Guitarist's Guide to Gigging" can be accessed at www.dummies.com/extras/Rock_Guitar.

Icons Used in This Book

Scattered throughout the margins of this book you find several types of helpful little icons that flag an important piece of information:

For those who crave even more punishment, you can follow these directives, but you don't need to.

A reference to a well-known song that illustrates the point currently being discussed.

Important info that will come up again and again, so you may want to read this one carefully and tuck it into your memory banks.

Detailed explanations of the trivial and obscure that makes great cocktail party fodder, but that you can skip if you want.

A handy tidbit of info designed to make your life easier and offered at no additional cost.

Serious stuff here that you can't ignore lest you damage something — such as your gear or yourself.

A guide to point you to material that will help clarify what you're listening to on the CD.

Where to Go from Here

If you're anxious to play, you can go ahead and skip Chapters 1 through 3 and get right to the playing chapters. If you've never had a guitar in your hands for longer than a sixteenth note's time, however, go ahead and read the text from the beginning to familiarize yourself with the terrain. If you've played guitar before, know some basic chords, and aren't intimidated by looking at notation when you play, you can skip right to Part III, which presents the techniques you need to master to play the songs. If you're feeling _really_ brave, and think you know most of the techniques already and can recognize their symbols in the notation, skip right to the styles chapters in Part IV. You can always come back and read the text later, after the authorities (whoever they are) have turned off your power or confiscated your gear for creating a rock-and-roll nuisance of yourself. Or as the famous teen-rebel saying goes: "They can lock me in jail for playing rock and roll, but they can't keep my face from breaking out."

Part I
So You Wanna Be a Rock-and-Roll Star

The 5th Wave — By Rich Tennant

"So you're attempting to learn how to play rock guitar, but your wife hates rock music. Go on..."

In this part . . .

It's time to start your engines . . . your rock guitar engines, that is! Chapter 1 gets you revved and in gear by showing you the parts of the electric guitar and the amp, and also discusses how the electric guitar differs from the acoustic guitar (and it's not just the volume!). Moving on to Chapter 2, you get to strap yourself in and sit — or stand, as the case may be — in the driver's seat — because you've got to look cool with the guitar in order to play it! Chapter 2 tells you all you need to know to start playing: how to hold the guitar, how to tune, how to read notation, and how to play your first chord. Part I finishes up with Chapter 3, with an introduction to the guitar's best friend — the amp.

Chapter 1

It's Only Rock Guitar . . . But I Like It

* *

In This Chapter

▶ Hearing the difference between electric guitar and acoustic guitar tone

▶ Discovering the inner-workings of the electric guitar

▶ Knowing the essential components of the electric guitar sound

▶ Getting the gear that goes with your guitar

* *

*R*ock guitar does not have a dignified history in music. It doesn't come from a long lineage of historical development where composers such as Bach, Beethoven, and Brahms wrote lovingly for it, composing concertos and sonatas highlighting its piquant and gentle qualities. It was not played in the great European concert halls or in the parlors of fine households.

Not only was rock guitar unknown to the great composers of the ages, but they couldn't have even conceived of such a thing, even in their worst nightmares. (So imagine what they would have thought of an Ozzy Osbourne concert — a nightmare no matter which century you hail from!) Indeed, even if they could have heard, through some sort of time travel, an electric guitar banging out the riff to "Satisfaction," they would have hardly recognized it as music.

Rock guitar is a modern, late-20th-century invention, a phenomenon of the post-electronic age. It has no memory of a bygone era when youth was respectful of elders, music was a polite pursuit, and musicians gave a rusty E string about social acceptance.

Rock guitar is for people who like their music loud, in your face, electric, and rebellious, and who owe no debt to history. Rock guitar is probably not the wisest choice of instruments to tackle if you want to garner acceptance from the music community.

So, if you want respect, take up the flute. But if you want to set the world on fire, attract throngs of adoring fans, and get back at your parents to boot — pick up an electric guitar and wail, baby, wail, because rock guitar will change your life.

First, though, you gotta learn how to play the thing.

Differentiating Between Rock and Acoustic Guitar . . . It Ain't Just Volume

When you see someone flailing away on rock guitar — on TV, in a film, or at a live concert — be aware that what you're seeing tells only part of the story. Sure, someone playing rock guitar is holding an instrument with six strings, a neck, and a body — qualities that describe the instrument that classical guitarist Andrés Segovia played — but the sound couldn't be more different. That difference in sound is the key to understanding rock guitar. What's important is not the leather, the hair, the onstage theatrics, the posturing, the smoke bombs, or the bloody tongues, but the *sound* coming from that guitar.

It was the sound of the electric guitar, so different from that of its predecessor, the acoustic guitar, and placed in the hands of some early, forward-looking visionaries, that forced a cultural change, a musical modification, and a historical adjustment to the way we experience popular music. Songwriters had to write differently, recording engineers had to record differently, and listeners had to do a major attitude adjustment to get their ears around it. Heck, people even had to learn new dances.

But what makes the sound of an electric guitar so different from an acoustic one? If you didn't think about it, you might say, well, *volume*. Rock guitar is just a whole lot louder than its acoustic counterpart. Although that might be true most of the time, volume alone is not what makes rock guitar unique. True, rock is listened to at high volumes — its message tastes better served up loud — but volume is a by-product, an after-effect, not what makes rock different or what drives it.

To become familiar with the qualities of the electric guitar, try this simple test. Listen to track #66 on the CD that came with this book. As you listen, turn the volume down so that it's quiet, very quiet — quieter than you'd normally listen to music, rock, or otherwise. You'll hear that the guitar sounds, well, just different. In fact, if you have to strain a little bit to make out that what you're hearing is a guitar at all, you'll be aware that the *tone* (the quality, or character of the sound, independent of its pitch and volume), in spite of the low volume, doesn't sound like the guitar that your camp counselor strummed around the campfire when she led you in a rousing chorus of "She'll Be Comin' Around the Mountain" or "Oh Susannah."

To really understand rock guitar, you need to explore some of its qualities *other* than volume. Don't worry, though, the book gets back to volume eventually.

Sound quality, or timbre

When guitarists "electrified" to their acoustic guitars, they originally intended to give the guitar a fighting chance in the volume department. Unsatisfied with the results of placing a microphone in front of the guitar, they sent the guitar's sound to a speaker by placing a magnetic element called a "pickup" under the guitar's strings. (See "Signal" and "Distortion and sustain" later in this chapter for more on pickups.) Players quickly found, however, that, unlike a microphone, a pickup didn't just make the sound louder, it *changed* the tone too. But how? It wasn't that obvious, but it was tangible.

The basic differences between a guitar coming out of a pickup and a guitar playing into a "mike" (slang for microphone) are:

- The sound is smoother and less woody.
- The sound is more electronic, with purer-sounding tones, like that of an organ.
- The sound has a less defined life cycle, or *envelope* — a beginning, middle, and end. These stages, so clear in the sound of a plucked acoustic guitar string, are blurred together in an electric guitar.

Now let's explore how electrifying the instrument affected its sound — to the eventual benefit of rock guitarists.

Signal

When progressive-minded guitarists of the '30s and '40s first put electro-magnetic elements under their strings to "pick up" their vibrations and send them along a wire to an amplifier, they did a lot more than increase the volume — though they didn't know it at the time. They were on their way to creating one of those "happy accidents" so common in art and science (and this was a little of both, really).

Originally, jazz guitarists playing in the big bands of the day were merely seeking a way to cut through all the din of those blaring horns and thundering drums. The mellow guitar, regarded by most other musicians as a mere parlor instrument with dubious stage presence, was no match for the louder brass and percussion instruments. The banjo had a sharp, cutting quality, and was better at projecting on the bandstand, but its tone was falling out of fashion in favor of the more full-bodied, versatile tone of the guitar. Problem was, the guitar just wasn't that loud, so something had to be done.

Slapping on heavier-gauge (thicker) steel strings helped (an improvement over nylon strings), but it still wasn't enough. Placing a microphone in front of the guitar, as was done for vocalists, worked somewhat, but was cumbersome, and the mike picked up the surrounding sound as well as the guitar. Plus, who wanted to bother miking the lowly guitarist way over in the rhythm section when you had some hotshot crooner in the spotlight at center stage?

To avoid these problems, someone got the idea to put a magnetic element just underneath the strings to carry the signal electronically to an amplifier. Because the strings were metal, and, specifically, electrically conductive magnetic metal, the sound of the strings traveled electronically through the "pickup" (so called because it "picked up" the sound of the vibrating string), down the attached wire, into a portable amplifier, and then out of a speaker.

The electric guitar was born, but getting from electrification to rock-and-roll nirvana was still a bit of a journey. It would be some time before guitarists would recognize the monster they had spawned in the unholy union of electricity and acoustic guitar. (Get used to frequent uses of imagery involving evil, wickedness, and other bad stuff; it's all part of rock and roll lore.)

Distortion and sustain

When the six-string Dr. Frankensteins of the '30s and '40s were electrifying their guitars, they weren't envisioning what Jimi Hendrix would do decades later at Woodstock and Monterey. Just like the well-meaning doctor in Mary Shelley's novel, early electronic guitar designers were wholesome and good. These pioneer inventors wanted to reproduce the sound of the acoustic guitar as faithfully as possible. Fortunately for us, they failed miserably. But electronics' loss was music's gain, because even though the electric guitar sound was nothing like the acoustic sound — or the acoustic guitar sound as heard through a microphone — it nonetheless had a very pleasing, and musically useful, quality.

The effort to produce an exact amplified match of the original acoustic guitar failed primarily because it introduced *distortion* (an untrue representation of the sound) into the sound. The louder the sound, or the more the guitar "worked" the electronic circuitry, the more distorted the sound got. As the electronic signal "heated up," the sound became *fuzzier* (where the high frequencies became more muted), and the tone generally *warmed up* (sounding more rounded and less brittle). All this distortion increased the *sustain* (the tendency for the tone to ring indefinitely at the same level), which was noticeable in even the lowest of volumes.

Distortion, normally a bad thing in just about any other electronic endeavor, had a beneficial, musical effect for guitar tone. As the guitar became thought of more and more as a lead instrument, guitarists found they could work the distortion factor to their advantage. A louder guitar wasn't just louder; it had a different, *better* tonal quality than a guitar coming out of the same apparatus, but at a lower volume.

This *timbre* (a fancy musical term for tone, or sound quality), distortion, and increased sustain took the plunkiness out of the guitar's tone, and made it more smoothly melodic — more like the buzzy, reedy qualities of, say, a saxophone or a blues vocalist, which is why so many early rock guitarists cut their musical teeth on the blues. Whereas the guitar had formerly been a rhythm instrument, owing to its clipped sound, rapid decay (the quality of a sound to die away), and strident tone, the "electronic" guitar now had properties more suited to melody-making. The guitar was poised to step out of the background and up to the spotlight itself. All it needed was some brave souls to tame this new sonic monster.

I must note that plenty of acoustic guitarists at that time were playing melody, notably Django Reinhardt. Reinhardt even bent strings (see Chapter 9), something that would become the province of electric guitarists everywhere, but is generally shunned by classic guitarists who deem the technique "unacousticlike."

Oh yes, and volume

Of course, electrifying a guitar did accomplish what it set out to do — make the guitar louder. Although it needed an electronic crutch, in the form of amplification through an external apparatus, this system of pickups, wires, and a portable amplifier (where the guitarist didn't need to rely on the auditorium's sound engineer) gave guitarists the freedom to play in all sorts of styles — melodic, rhythmic, and chordal — and freed them from the "rhythm section ghetto."

An excellent example of an early electric guitarist who realized and exploited the newfound qualities of the electric guitar was jazz guitarist Charlie Christian. It's important to note that even though Christian was not a rock player (rock just didn't exist in the '20s and '30s), he is worshipped by electric guitarists everywhere — from blues to jazz to rock — for being an incredible visionary for realizing the power of the electric guitar's tone.

Some people may claim that Christian was, in part, responsible for inventing the electric guitar pickup, but this is just a myth. However, he certainly did his part to popularize the "pickup configured" electronic guitar, and he is one of its best early practitioners, because he recognized — and exploited through his musical genius — its sustain qualities.

After the guitar could play as loud as the other, more charismatic instruments (such as the trumpet and saxophone), it wasn't long before the guitar would become a featured instrument, both from a personality perspective as well as an instrument for solo exhibitionism.

Listening examples

You can talk all you want about the tone of the electric guitar, but the best way to understand its tonal qualities is to listen to some classic examples. Led Zeppelin's "Stairway to Heaven" is not only a classic song, it's one of the best illustrations of the differences between electric and acoustic guitar.

The song begins with a plaintive vocal by Robert Plant, accompanied by a Renaissance-sounding acoustic guitar. The accompaniment gradually builds, and then at 6:42 guitarist Jimmy Page launches into the solo section with an opening *phrase* (a musically complete passage or thought of any given length) that sums up the essence of the electric guitar in just two short measures. Listen to the first note, which seems to hang in mid air and *sing* — as if powered by its own set of lungs. The rest of the solo is a tour de force of technique, phrasing, and tone, but it's that opening *riff* (a self-contained musical phrase) that grabs you.

Another well-known example is the guitar solo section of the Eagles' "Hotel California," played by Joe Walsh and Don Felder. This solo is given plenty of room to breathe by the accompaniment. The gliding quality you hear at the end of Walsh's first short phrase (the fifth note in the opening sequence) is a *string bend,* where you stretch the string by pushing it out of its normal alignment causing the pitch to rise. Listen to how the note, again, *sings.* This singing quality, broken down to its component attributes, has a smooth sound (timbre); a reedy, fuzzy quality that does not resemble the plucked sound of the acoustic guitar (distortion); and an elongated, non-decaying volume and intensity (sustain).

These examples are both in the melodic vein. Things really get weird when guitarists started abandoning melody altogether and chose to exploit timbre, distortion and sustain for their own purpose. Jimi Hendrix was one of those who took distortion and sustain to the nth degree, but I'll get to him in Chapter 11.

Knowing the Essentials: The Power Trio

All right, the previous section helps you to understand the tonal differences of an electric guitar versus an acoustic one, and that an electric guitar has pickups (or magnetic elements) that carry the sound via an attached wire to a loudspeaker. What else do you need?

A burning question for most aspiring rock guitarists is, "Since I have an electric guitar here, does that mean I also have to have an amp?"

Yes, you do need an amplifier. Just as you can't hear a scream without ears, so, too, can you not hear a guitar without its amplifier and speaker (in guitar terms, an "amplifier" can refer to the amplifier circuitry *and* the speaker, which are often housed in the same box). Electric guitars can have the biggest, most-powerful, nuclear-charged pickups on board, but without an amp, the guitar will make no more noise than if the pickups were absent completely.

Sounds unbelievable, but it's true. No amp, no electric guitar sound. Anytime you see somebody walking around with an electric guitar, you can bet he or she is looking for an amp. Therefore, you must have at least two elements to even be audible on the electric guitar — the guitar itself and the amp. (Technically speaking, you also need a wire, or cord, to attach the electric guitar to the amp.)

Realistically, however, guitarists these days routinely introduce a third element into the signal chain (as the path from the originating guitar pickups to the terminating amp speaker is known): intermediary electronic gizmos known as *effects*. These typically sit between a guitar and an amp, and connect to each other with short cords, via in and out *jacks* (the electronic term for sockets, or something you can insert plugs into). Effects are like a VCR that goes between your cable box and your TV because they pass the signal through, but perform their own magic on the signal.

Following are graphic illustrations of the three essential components in rock guitar playing: the electric guitar, the amplifier, and electronic effects devices.

The electric guitar

The electric guitar is the principal player in the three-part system that comprises the rock guitar sound. And whether it has a natural mahogany finish or is painted Day-Glo green with purple lightning bolts across the body, all electric guitars have common properties. Like a "regular," or acoustic, guitar, an electric guitar has a neck and a body, six strings, and tuning keys on the top of the neck that allow you to tighten or loosen the strings to the desired pitch — the process known as tuning. Unlike the acoustic guitar, however, an electric guitar sports *pickups* (electromagnetic devices that "sense" the strings' vibrations and create a small current), knobs, and switches for controlling the pickups, and possibly other hardware (such as a *bar*, described in the following bulleted list) that acoustic guitars don't have. Figure 1-1 shows the various parts of the electric guitar.

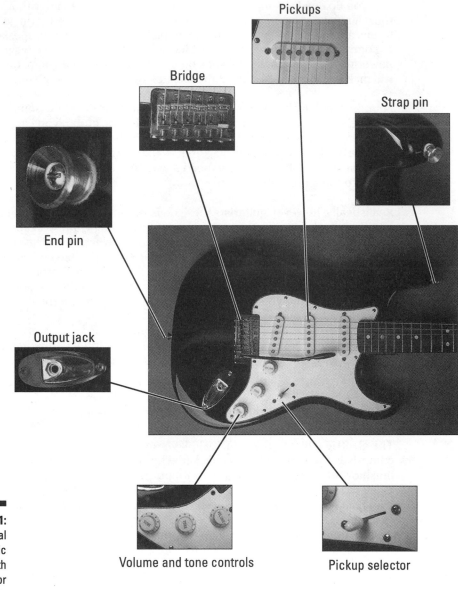

Pickups

Bridge

Strap pin

End pin

Output jack

Figure 1-1:
A typical
electric
guitar with
its major
parts
labeled.

Volume and tone controls

Pickup selector

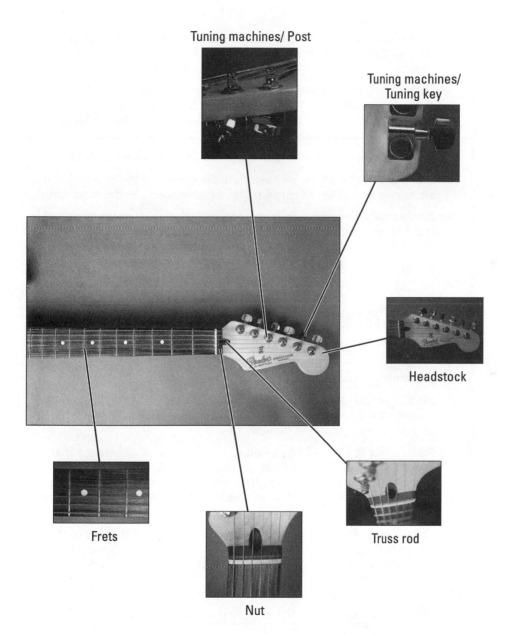

Tuning machines/ Post

Tuning machines/ Tuning key

Headstock

Frets

Nut

Truss rod

The following list tells you the functions of the various parts of the electric guitar.

- **Bar:** A metal rod or arm attached to the bridge that varies the string tension by tilting the bridge back and forth. It is also called the tremolo bar, whammy bar, vibrato bar, and wang bar.

- **Body:** The large, shapely wooden mass that provides an anchor for the neck and bridge. The body can either be solid, hollow, or partially hollow, and houses the bridge assembly and electronics (pickups as well as tone and volume controls).

- **Bridge:** The metal assembly that anchors the strings to the body.

- **End pin:** A metal post screwed into the body, where the rear end of the strap connects. The other end of the strap connects to the strap pin.

- **Fretboard:** A flat, plank-like piece of wood that sits atop the neck and has frets embedded in it. This is where you place your left-hand fingers to produce notes and chords. It is also known as the fingerboard.

- **Fret(s):** 1) Thin metal wires or bars running perpendicular to the strings that shorten the effective vibrating length of a string, enabling it to produce different pitches. 2) A verb describing the action of pressing the strings to the fretboard. 3) A verb describing a guitarist's anxiety, as in, "He frets because he thinks he'll have to replace the frets of his fingerboard so that it frets correctly."

- **Headstock:** The section that holds the tuning machines and provides a place for the manufacturer to display its logo.

- **Neck:** The long, club-like wooden piece that connects the headstock to the body. Some guitarists like to wield their guitars like clubs, and usually do so by holding them by the neck.

- **Nut:** A slotted sliver of stiff nylon or other synthetic substance that stops the strings from vibrating beyond the neck. The strings pass through the slots on their way to the tuners in the headstock. The nut is one of the two points at which the vibrating area of the string ends. (The bridge is the other.)

- **Output jack:** The insertion point, or jack, for the cord that connects the guitar to the amplifier or other electronic device. You will sometimes hear this jack called an "input" because guitarists think of putting a cord "into" the jack. Electronically speaking, however, this is an output jack because it carries signal out of the guitar.

- **Pickup selector:** A switch that determines which pickup or pickups are currently active.

- **Pickups:** Bar-like magnets that create the electrical current that the amplifier converts into musical sound.

✔ **Strap pin:** Metal post where the front, or top, end of the strap connects. The strap pin is screwed into either the guitar's back (as on a Gibson Les Paul) or into the end of one of the "horns" (as on a Fender Stratocaster). The other end of the strap connects to a corresponding pin, the end pin.

✔ **Strings:** The six metal wires that, drawn taut, produce the notes of the guitar. Although not strictly part of the actual guitar (you attach and remove them at will), strings are an integral part of the whole system, and a guitar's entire design and structure revolves around making the strings ring out with passion and musicality (and don't forget volume!).

✔ **Top:** The face of the guitar's body. The top is often a cosmetic or decorative cap that overlays the rest of the body material.

✔ **Truss rod:** An adjustable steel rod that can be rotated using a special wrench and which helps keep the neck straight. You gain access to the rod through a hole in the headstock or at the base of the neck.

✔ **Tuning machines:** Geared mechanisms that raise and lower the tension of the strings, drawing them to different pitches. The string wraps tightly around a **post** that sticks out through the top, or face, of the headstock. The post passes through to the back of the headstock, where gears connect it to a **tuning key.** Tuning machines are also known as tuners, tuning pegs, tuning keys, and tuning gears.

✔ **Volume and tone controls:** Knobs that vary the loudness of the guitar's sound and its bass and treble frequencies.

The amplifier

The amplifier is an all-electronic device with no moving parts (except for its knobs and switches, which control the volume and tone of the incoming signal). You might think that those rather pedestrian-looking, geometrically plain boxes that do nothing but a lot of internal electrical processing are functional and necessary, but not particularly sexy (well, not by electric guitar standards, anyway). Amp lore, however, is every bit as epic and mythological as guitar lore. Entire subcultures (that all, curiously, seem to have an Internet newsgroup devoted to their cause) are devoted to assessing, proselytizing, and otherwise pondering the mysteries and myths of the perfect guitar amplifier. (See Chapter 3 for more details on setting up your amp.)

In any quest for the perfect tone, you must have an amp in the equation, and the history and contributions of such legendary amp manufacturers as Fender, Marshall, and Vox are an inextricable part of the rock and roll gear legacy. Plus, you have to have someplace to set your drink when you go onstage. Figure 1-2 shows the various parts of an electric guitar amplifier.

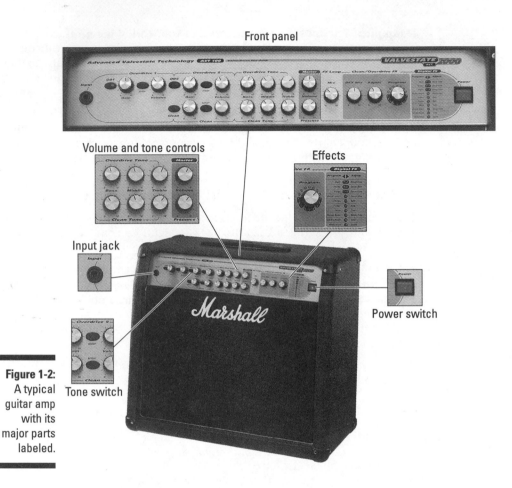

Figure 1-2:
A typical guitar amp with its major parts labeled.

The following list tells you the functions of the various parts of the guitar amplifier.

- **Cabinet:** The box that houses the speaker and electronic components. It is typically made of plywood or pressure-treated wood and encased in a durable protective covering.

- **Effects:** Many modern amps also include onboard digital signal processing, such as reverb, delay, chorus, and flange.

- **Front panel** or **face plate:** The metal plate through which knobs and switches protrude to protect the controls that sit just below the surface.

- **Grille cloth:** The mesh-like fabric, usually made of a synthetic weave, that allows sound to pass through, but keeps foreign, and potentially harmful, objects (such as the toe of a boot) away from sensitive speaker surfaces.

- ✔ **Input jack:** The socket where you put the cord from your electric guitar, or the cord from the output of the last effect in your signal chain.

- ✔ **Power switch:** A switch that turns the amp on and off.

- ✔ **Tone switch:** Two-position, or toggle, switches (not rotary or continuous) that provide additional tonal control.

- ✔ **Volume and tone controls:** Rotary knobs that provide continuous control over the outgoing signal.

Effects

The newest member of the triumvirate of principal players is the group whose members are electronic effects. These self-contained units range in size anywhere from a cigarette pack to a small furnace. The size and range of most effects, though, falls between a bar of soap and a VCR deck. (See Chapter 15 for more details on plugging into effects.) Figure 1-3 shows four of the most common electronic effects used by rock guitarists.

Figure 1-3:
Four common electronic effects used by guitarists (left to right): digital delay, chorus, distortion, wah-wah.

The following list describes the functions of four effects commonly used by guitarists.

- ✔ **Digital delay:** Creates an echo by digitally recording the signal and playing it back at adjustable times after the principal signal has sounded.

- ✔ **Chorus:** Creates a thick, swirly effect by simulating the sound of two or more guitars playing in tandem, but not quite with the exact tuning or timing.

- ✔ **Distortion:** Simulates the sound of an amp that's played too loud to handle a signal cleanly. Distortion devices are used for their convenience, so that the guitarist doesn't have to constantly adjust the amp controls to get a distorted sound.

✔ **Wah-wah:** A foot-pedal rocked by the guitarist's foot, that creates a tonal variation that resembles a horn with a mute, or a human voice saying the phrase "wah wah" (thus the name).

Getting a Grasp on How Electric Guitars Work

Recognizing the different parts of the guitar is important, but knowing what makes an electric guitar work as a whole is essential to differentiate it from, say, a bassoon, accordion, or kazoo. Not that there's anything *wrong* with those instruments, but try doing a windmill (a showy strumming technique where you extend your right arm out and move it in a circular motion, striking the guitar strings once a cycle — Pete Townshend is the windmill's most famous practitioner) with a bassoon and they'll cart you away quicker than your friends can ask the musical question, "Why is the bassoonist having a fit?"

String vibration and pitch

An electric guitar is a string, or stringed, instrument that creates musical sound through a vibrating string. Each string can produce a variety of different notes, but only one at a time. If you want to play two or more notes simultaneously, you must play them on different strings and strike them simultaneously. Because a standard electric guitar has six strings, it can play up to six simultaneous notes, but no more. (Consequently, we guitarists more than make up for this "limitation" by playing extremely *loud*.)

If you tighten a given length of string to a particular tension and then set it in motion (harpists by *plucking*, pianists by *striking*, violinists by *bowing*), the string will vibrate back and forth at a regular rate. This vibration produces a steady tone that we call *pitch*. The pitch remains the same as long as the string vibrates. As the string's vibrations lose power, or intensity, over time, the note gets quieter, but its pitch doesn't change.

Tension vs. length

Two properties determine a string's pitch: tension and length. Therefore, you can change a string's pitch in one of two ways: by changing its tension (which you do when tuning or bending) or by changing its length (which you do when fretting — by changing the length of string allowed to vibrate). You must change pitch to play different notes, whether in a scale, a melody, or a chord progression.

You couldn't do very much with a guitar, however, if the only way to change pitches was to frantically adjust the tension every time you pluck a string. You'd end up looking like the musical equivalent of the circus performer who spins those plates on a stick. So guitarists resort to the other way to change a string's pitch — fretting.

And that's why we have all this fretting about fretting: *Fretting* is the way guitarists change notes on the electric guitar. Without left-hand fretting (see Chapter 2) we could strike the guitar and make a lot of noise, but all the notes would sound the same — worse even than a speech by a boring politician (though I won't name names).

One of the biggest differences between two icons of electric guitar models, the Gibson Les Paul and the Fender Stratocaster, is that their string lengths are different. The Les Paul has a vibrating string length of 24.75"; the Strat (as it's known to its friends) has a vibrating length of 25.5". Not much, maybe, but enough to make a perceptible difference to the hands.

Physics tells us that two different string lengths drawn to produce the same pitch (as they must to be in tune) will have different tensions. The Strat, because it has the longer string length, has slightly higher string tension than does the Les Paul. This creates two key differences in playability for the electric guitarist: tighter, or springier, string response and larger frets in the Strat; and looser, or spongier, string response and smaller frets in the Les Paul.

But before you attempt to draw any conclusions, these descriptions are not value judgments; they do not indicate whether one aspect is good or bad versus the other; and they sure as heck do not carry any endorsement by the author!

These qualities merely describe — hopefully without introducing bias or preference — the physical differences between the feel and playability of the different string tensions. Which one you prefer is just that — your preference. Most professional rock guitarists don't even have an absolute, one-choice-fits-all guitar. Instead, they select guitars based on the type of music they want to play, and will have many different guitars at their disposal to handle a variety of musical styles.

Your hands

Guitar playing requires you to use two hands working together, but performing different actions. This is different than playing, say, the piano or saxophone, where both hands perform the same type of action (striking keys and pressing keys, respectively). Guitar playing has the left hand (see Chapter 4) selecting which notes to sound (by pressing down the strings against frets) and the right hand (see Chapter 5) sounding those notes by striking (or plucking) the strings. And for you lefties, the ones who reverse the strings to play, please understand that I use "left" and "right" for the hand that frets and the hand that picks, respectively. It's not that I'm prejudiced against lefties, it's just that guitar convention dictates using "left" and "right" rather than "fretting" and "picking." Hey, some of my best friends are lefties (though as a right-hander, I've always resented that they're a full stride closer to first base when batting).

At first, this might seem like the musical equivalent of rubbing your stomach and patting your head, but after a while, performing two different actions to produce one sound becomes second nature, and you don't even have to think about it — like walking and chewing gum. And if you can't do *that,* maybe you should think about running for president instead of playing rock guitar.

Pickups and amplification

Vibrating strings produce the different tones on a guitar. You must be able to hear those tones, however, or you face one of those if-a-tree-falls-in-a-forest questions. For an acoustic guitar, hearing it is no problem because it provides its own amplifier in the form of the hollow sound chamber that boosts its sound . . . well, acoustically.

An electric guitar, on the other hand, makes virtually no acoustic sound at all. (Well, a tiny bit, like a buzzing mosquito, but nowhere near enough to fill a stadium or anger your next-door neighbors.) An electric instrument creates its tones entirely through electronic means. The vibrating string is still the source of the sound, but a hollow wood chamber isn't what makes those vibrations audible. Instead, the vibrations disturb, or modulate, the magnetic field that the pickups — wire-wrapped magnets positioned underneath the strings — produce. As the vibrations of the strings modulate the pickup's magnetic field, the pickup produces a tiny electric current.

If you remember from eighth-grade science, wrapping wire around a magnet creates a small current in the wire. If you then take any magnetic substance and disturb the magnetic field around that wire, you create fluctuations in the current itself. A taut steel string vibrating at the rate of 440 times per second creates a current that itself fluctuates 440 times per second. Pass that current through an amplifier and then a speaker and you hear the musical tone A. More specifically, you hear the A above middle C, which is the standard absolute tuning reference in modern music — from the New York Philharmonic to the Rolling Stones to Metallica (although I've heard that Metallica uses a tuning reference of 666 — just kidding, Metallica fans!). For more on tuning, see Chapter 2.

Accessorizing Your Guitar

Even though I've covered the crucial components in the rock guitar arsenal, the accessories don't stop there. You may also want to acquire some other useful, but not essential, components, including various accessories that all serve to make rock guitar playing a little easier. Figure 1-4 shows an assortment of guitar accessories.

In no particular order, following is a list of accessories, and their descriptions, that go with the well-heeled rock guitarist.

Picks

An optional item for acoustic guitarists, a pick is a requirement for playing rock guitar. Sometimes referred to as a *plectrum*, a pick is a small triangular- or teardrop-shaped piece of thin plastic or nylon, about the size of a quarter, that's held between the thumb and index finger of the right, or strumming, hand. When you strum a chord or pluck a note, you use your pick to make contact. You can buy guitar picks (there's no distinction between an electric guitar and acoustic guitar picks) at any music or CD store, in a variety of colors, shapes, and thickness (called gauges). Buy 'em by the bucketful, because you'll lose, break, give away, and squander plenty in your guitar-playing career.

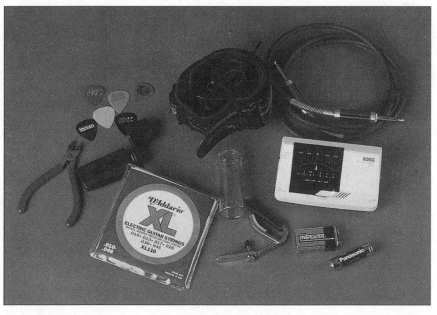

Figure 1-4: A gaggle of guitar gadgetry (clockwise, from top left): picks, strap, cord, electronic tuner, batteries, capo, slide, extra strings, peg winder, wire cutters.

Straps

A strap is also an absolute necessity, but under only one condition: if you plan to play while standing. Straps *can* be used while sitting, but that's a matter of personal preference. (See Chapter 2 for more on how to hold the guitar.) Most people who are interested in playing rock guitar, however, will want to stand for at least some of that time (especially if you plan to perform). A strap is always a good thing to have rolled up and tucked away in your guitar case, even if you do most of your playing sitting down.

Straps come in all materials, from leather to fabric to space-age mesh, so you will certainly be able find one that suits your sense of fashion. You can even have a custom-made strap with your initials or name emblazoned on the side that faces the audience. Looks great for television.

Cords

A cord, sometimes referred to as a "cable," is the technical term for the wire, or lead, that connects electric guitars to amps and other components, so you need at least one. If you use one electronic effects device you'll need two — one to connect the guitar to the effect's input, and one to connect the effect's output to the amp. If you have two effects, you'll need three cables; three effects, four cables, and so on. But whether you use effects or not, carrying an extra cable with you is always a good idea (like straps, cables can be coiled up and unobtrusively stashed in a guitar case). An extra cable is cheap insurance indeed; a bad cable can silence you as quickly as a broken guitar neck or blown speaker.

Tuners

A tuner is a device that helps you to tune your instruments. It won't turn the pegs for you, but its meters tell you when a string is flat or sharp with much more accuracy that your ear can — even if you have perfect pitch. (Chapter 2 deals a whole lot with how to use tuners.) And what's the definition of perfect pitch, you ask? Why, it's when you can toss a banjo into a dumpster without hitting the sides! (I hear you groan.)

Chapter 2

Holding Your Own

*E*lectric guitars are so easy, natural, and inviting to hold, that the moment you strap one on you almost immediately want to jump around and start looking cool — which is precisely what you should do. If you're looking good and feeling cool, you're probably doing something right. Don't you wish that were true of everything in life?

All right, that might be a *bit* hasty, but in the true non-conformist spirit in which it was spawned, rock guitar playing carries with it no right or wrong way for doing anything, let alone adopting a "correct" posture. Perhaps you *could* find a way to hold the guitar upside down, or in such a twisted position that it might cause your hands to cramp, but the point is, you have a wide range of ways to hold the guitar, and all of them are "right." Or at least none of them is patently wrong.

Still, I can give you pointers on how to first hold the guitar until you develop your own personal style. In this chapter, you find out all about holding your guitar in sitting and standing positions and how to hold your hands so that they fall naturally into the playing positions. Plus, you will look like you know what the heck you're doing, and looking the part is halfway to doing the part.

When you get all nice and situated, you need something to do, so I've thrown in a section on tuning and then an explanation of chord diagrams (gasp!) and tablature (shudder!). But don't get alarmed; you don't need to be able to read music (see Appendix A in *Guitar For Dummies* for a guide on how to read music) to understand some simple notational conventions.

Getting a Hold of the Guitar

You can either sit or stand while playing rock guitar, and it won't make a bit of difference to the tone. Most people sit while practicing and stand while performing. (Think about it: When's the last time you saw KISS perform "Detroit Rock City" while slouched in a La-Z-Boy?) You have two reasons to practice standing up, however: you can rehearse your stage moves — such as flying scissor-kicks and splits — (and take a look at yourself in the full-length mirror in the process) and standing can be a nice break for your *derriere* when you've passed your third hour trying to master that Clapton solo.

Seriously, though, sitting or standing makes virtually no difference to your technique, but the sensation *is* slightly different, so you should get used to playing your repertoire in both positions. And when you're *really* good, you can start to play while sitting, rise to a standing position, and kick the door shut with your foot — all without dropping a note.

Sitting position

Here are some basics for playing while sitting: In a comfortable desk or straight chair (not an easy chair or sofa) rest the *waist* of the guitar (the indented part between the upper and lower halves) on your right leg. Sit slightly forward with your feet apart. Place your right forearm on the top edge to balance the guitar, as shown in Figure 2-1. You should be able to take your left hand completely away from the neck and not have the guitar change position. You should not use your left hand to support the guitar neck.

Standing position

To play the guitar while standing, you first need a guitar strap securely fastened to both strap pins. (For the locations of the strap pins, see Chapter 1.) Then stand in a normal, erect way and let the back of the guitar rest against your midsection or hip. Adjust the strap to get the guitar at a height that's comfortable for you. (Sometimes adjusting the strap is easier if you take the guitar off your shoulder first.) The higher you position the guitar, the easier playing it will be. Trouble is, you can look dorky if the guitar is too high. The lower-slung you are, the cooler you look. But playing low is a little more difficult and can strain your left hand. Again, wear the guitar as high as is comfortable.

Figure 2-2 shows a guitarist standing, with hands ready to play. Note that in this example, the guitarist has his guitar at a height comfortable for a beginner, and not a surly, pouting millionaire rock star (who would wear it much lower).

Figure 2-1:
Holding
the guitar
in a typical
sitting
position.

Figure 2-2:
Holding the
guitar in a
typical
standing
position.

When your guitar starts to block your eyesight, then you can think about bringing it down a notch or two.

Just as in embracing a small child or any precious object, your body naturally compensates in going from a sitting to a standing position when holding that object. So just let your arms fall naturally around the guitar — the same standing as when sitting. Strum, move your hands around, stay relaxed, and, oh yes, strike a pose.

If your strap breaks, comes untied, or slips off a pin while you're playing in a standing position, you have very little chance of catching your guitar before it hits the floor (your chances improve the more experience you have with falling guitars). So don't risk serious damage to your guitar by using an old strap with holes that are too large for the pins to hold securely. Pete Townshend (known for destroying his guitar at the end of his shows) created his early stage persona on the principle that guitars don't bounce.

Forming a Left-Hand Position

Here's an exercise that helps illustrate good left-hand positioning: Place a credit card flat on a table, face down, and pick it up with the tips of your left-hand fingers. Hold it at about shoulder level with your bent elbow at your side, and rotate your wrist so that you can see the face of the card. Ignore the card and just look at your hand, and take note of how it feels. Note how the thumb faces the index finger or is between the index and middle fingers. Note how all your knuckles are bent and that a "pocket of air" forms in the area between your palm and curled fingers. Now let the card fall away — back onto the table — but keep your hand relaxed and in the same position. That's how your hand should look when you stick an electric guitar neck in there. In fact, do that now, and take a look at Figure 2-3. Your hand position should look somewhat similar.

Figure 2-3:
The left
hand
looking
relaxed and
poised for
fretting.

Fretting

To fret a note means to press the tip of your finger down on a string, while keeping your knuckles bent. Try to get the fingertip to come down vertically on the string rather than from the side. This position exerts the greatest pressure on the string and also prevents the sides of the finger from touching adjacent strings, which may cause buzzing or *muting* (deadening the string, or preventing it from ringing). Use your thumb from its position underneath the neck to help "squeeze" the fingerboard for a tighter grip.

Building up left-hand strength and facility takes time, and you just have to be patient. Don't try to speed up the process through artificial means. Hand-strengthening devices designed for expediting left-hand endurance are dubious, and at best, marginally effective. The same goes for the home-grown method of squeezing one of those spongy "therapy" balls: okay for strength, but only in that it makes you better at squeezing stuff rather than fretting notes and gripping chords. Nothing helps build your left-hand fretting ability better or faster than simply playing the guitar.

Getting some action

If you've had any experience playing an acoustic, you'll notice immediately that electric necks are both narrower in width (from the 1st string to the 6th) and shallower in depth (from the fingerboard to the back of the neck). Electric guitars also use lighter-gauge strings. You'll notice, too, that they're (not surprisingly) much easier to grip and fret, almost shockingly so. But by far the biggest difference in fretting an electric and fretting an acoustic is the *action*.

A guitar's action is the distance of the strings to the top of the frets. Lower action means easier fretting. If you've found fretting an acoustic to be challenging — if not downright frustrating — fretting an electric is like passing a hot knife through butter. An electric guitar's lower action allows you to use a fairly relaxed left-hand position. Figure 2-4 shows a photo of the left hand fretting a string.

Striking a Right-Hand Position

If you hold an electric guitar as described in the previous section, with your right forearm resting on the top edge, your right hand crosses the strings at about a 60-degree angle — not quite parallel to them and not quite perpendicular. This is the optimum position for striking the strings, whether you're strumming rhythm, picking lead, or fingerpicking arpeggios.

Figure 2-4:
Fretting a string. Note that the finger is not in the middle of the fret, but closer to the fret wire.

As you sweep your arm up and down, your hand should brush lightly over the strings between the bridge and the end of the fingerboard. Figure 2-5 shows the correct sweep of the right hand and arm.

Figure 2-5:
Correct right-hand placement allows you to sweep your arm up and down over the strings between the neck and the bridge.

Playing with a pick

You execute virtually all rock guitar techniques using a pick, whether you're belting out raunchy Rolling Stones riffs or coaxing gentle chords from an Eagles ballad. So get used to it. Buy lots of different shapes and thicknesses and find the one that's comfortable for you. Then buy a whole bunch of picks at that size, because you're going to lose them, lend them, and toss them to adoring fans.

Picking the right one

A pick's *gauge* describes how thick, or stiff, it is. Some pick manufacturers actually measure the thicknesses and stamp these numbers, expressed in millimeters on the pick itself. Other companies just say "Extra Heavy," "Heavy," "Medium," and "Thin." For beginners, thin picks are the easiest to wrangle, because they're more flexible and offer very little resistance when striking the strings. Medium picks are very popular, because they're stiff enough to allow you to really dig in, but flexible enough for light chord strumming. Heavy-gauge picks can seem unwieldy at first, but provide the fastest and most accurate response. Most pros prefer heavy-gauge picks, but there are plenty of exceptions.

You play virtually all *rhythm* (chord-based accompaniment) and *lead* (single-note melodies) using the same pick position: by holding the pick — or plectrum (the old-fashioned term) — between the thumb and index finger. Figure 2-6 shows the correct way to hold a pick with just the tip sticking out sideways from the thumb.

Figure 2-6: Hold the pick firmly, with just the tip sticking out sideways from your thumb.

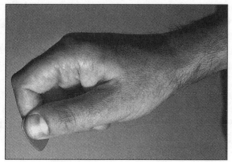

If you're strumming rhythm, use wrist and elbow motion. The more vigorous the strum, the more elbow action you must apply. If you're playing lead, use the more economical wrist motion. Learn to keep your wrist and hand relaxed while maintaining a tight grip on the pick. And plan on dropping your pick a lot for the first few weeks until you get used to playing with it.

When you run out of picks and are desperate — like you have to go onstage in 27 seconds and you have no picks — knowing that a quarter is extra heavy and a matchbook cover is thin is helpful. And any rock guitarist worth her salt has some amusing "war story" about how she was reduced to scouring the broom closet of a club in search of a bleach bottle to cut up for an emergency pick.

Using your fingers

You can use just your fingers to play electric guitar, but for rare and limited uses in rock. The most common application is *fingerpicking arpeggios* — where you play the individual notes of a chord with your right-hand fingertips. When fingerpicking, keep your right-hand wrist fairly stationary but not rigid. Maintain a slight arch in the back of your hand and wrist so that your fingers can approach the strings from a more vertical position.

As a last word on picks, I should mention three notable exceptions in the rock guitar arena who don't use a pick and play with just the tips of their right-hand fingers: Jeff Beck, Lindsey Buckingham (from Fleetwood Mac), and Mark Knopfler (of Dire Straits). These guitarists all approach rock guitar totally differently; all of them wail, yet none uses a pick. Go figure. Chalk another one up to rock guitar's ornery resistance to classification.

Gearing Up to Tune Up: Electric Tuners

Before you can wail on the guitar and not cause people with trained ears to wail back in agony, you need to get your guitar in tune. You can tune a guitar using many methods, including a pitch pipe, a tuning fork, an electronic tuner, a piano or electric keyboard, the fifth-fret method (where one string acts as the fixed point and all others are tuned to it), and even by listening to track #1 on the CD that came with this book, which plays the open strings for you to check your own strings against, using your ear.

Each of these methods is explained in detail in *Guitar For Dummies*. After achieving a certain level of proficiency, however, electric guitarists prefer to tune using one method only: an electronic tuner. After you get the hang of using them, they're the quickest, most accurate, and quietest ways to tune.

What they are

Electronic tuners are small, inexpensive battery-powered devices that you plug into with your guitar cord. (Electronic tuners also come with a built-in mike that you can use with an unplugged acoustic guitar.) When you pluck a string, the signal from the guitar activates sensors inside the tuner that cause the meter to register the pitch of that string. This allows you to use your eyes in addition to, or instead of, your ears to see if you're in tune. If you want to *hear* your guitar, you need to plug a cord into the tuner's output and send that on to your amplifier or to the rest of your effects in the chain. But you don't need to hear the guitar to tune it. Isn't science wonderful? By keeping your tuner on and "inline," you can use it to tune anytime you like. It's always on. Just turn down your amp (but keep your guitar volume knob up) when you want to tune silently, so as not to annoy other bandmates or the audience.

How they work

A tuner senses which pitch you're playing, and tells you, by way of its meter or LEDs (light-emitting diodes), what the closest pitch (A, B♭, B, C, and so forth) is, and whether you're flat or sharp of that. It's a great system, because you can use a tuner not only to *micro* tune (to get pitches in tune that are within a half step), but to *macro* tune, such as when you want to drop your low E string to D (bypassing E♭ along the way), and do it silently and quickly. Figure 2-7 shows a popular pedal version of an electronic tuner.

Figure 2-7:
This Boss TU-2 tuner has a large meter for easy reading of a pitch's flat or sharp status, plus LEDs that show what pitch you're closest to.

If you play with a volume pedal, place your tuner before it in the signal chain. That way, turning down the volume shuts down the signal *after* it has gone through the tuner, allowing you to tune silently. You can always turn down at the amp to achieve the same effect, but sometimes reaching the amp is more cumbersome than stepping on a pedal. In fact, if you have a tuner anywhere in your signal chain (the line-up of your guitar, effects pedals, and amp), it should be in front of (closer to the guitar) any effects.

A tuner can either occupy a permanent berth in your signal chain, or you can just pack it up in your guitar case and carry it with you. Either way, an electronic tuner is the most fundamental electronic device you need to own — more important than any outboard effect. You can play a guitar in tune without effects and still make music, but you can't play out of tune and still make music, no matter what kind of effect you own.

Looking at Music Notation: Not Enough to Hurt

You don't *have to* read music to play rock guitar, but you can benefit from a few simple shorthand aids to help you understand some basic concepts — such as chord construction, chord progressions, and song structure. If you try just a few of these tricks, you'll find you can pick up and remember how certain songs go much more easily.

Reading chord diagrams

Reading a chord diagram is not like reading anything at all. It's more like looking at a picture and interpreting the information — like deciphering which way the rest room is when you're in a foreign country. When you read a chord diagram, you just need to know where to put your fingers — and unlike restrooms, all chords are unisex and can be played legally by both men and women.

Figure 2-8 shows the anatomy of a chord diagram, and the following list defines each of its different elements:

- ✔ **Grid:** The grid of six vertical and five horizontal lines correspond to the strings and frets on the guitar neck, as if you stood the guitar up on the floor and looked straight at it.

- ✔ **Vertical lines:** The left-most vertical line at the far left is the low 6th string; and the right-most line is the high 1st string.

- ✔ **Horizontal lines:** The horizontal lines represent frets. The space between the horizontal lines is referred to as the *fret*. The top line is thicker, because it represents the *nut* of the guitar.

- ✔ **Dots:** The black dots tell you where to place your left-hand fingers.

- ✔ **Numerals:** The numerals directly below each string line indicate *which* left-hand finger you use to fret that note:

  1 = index finger; 2 = middle finger; 3 = ring finger; and 4 = little finger.

- ✔ **Xs and Os:** An *X* above a string means the string is not played. An *O* indicates an open string that is played.

If a chord starts on a fret other than the first fret (which happens a lot in rock guitar because of its reliance on *barre* chords, discussed in detail in Chapter 4), a numeral appears to the right of the diagram, next to the top fret line, to indicate in which fret you actually start.

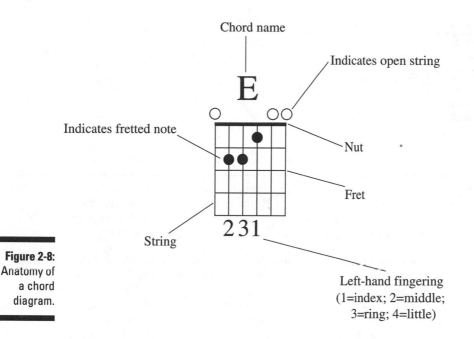

Chord name

Indicates open string

E

Indicates fretted note

Nut

Fret

2 3 1

String

Figure 2-8:
Anatomy of
a chord
diagram.

Left-hand fingering
(1=index; 2=middle;
3=ring; 4=little)

Reading rhythm slashes

Musicians often use just a simple "road map" or "rhythm chart" to convey the basic form of a song, while avoiding the issue of reading (or worse, writing) formal and legitimate music parts. This is a great relief to rock guitarists who avoid reading and writing music like Metallica fans avoid a Barry Manilow concert.

Following are some basic shorthand techniques that will help you navigate the music illustrations in this book:

✔ *Rhythm slashes* are the diagonal marks (/) that simply tell you to play "rhythmically in the style," but not exactly how to play.

✔ The *chord symbol* (letter name with a quality, such as *7* or *m*) determines what you play, and some other indication, like a simple performance note at the beginning of the piece, tells you the style.

For example, if you see the chord symbol E above a staff with four slashes, you know to grab an E chord with your left hand and to strike it four times, or in a manner consistent with the rest of the song. Rhythm notation is not an exact science, because whoever wrote this "chart" (as music on a sheet of paper is called) assumes you know what that style is without writing out the exact notes to play. Figure 2-9 shows a typical bar (or measure) of music using rhythm slashes and a chord symbol.

Figure 2-9:
One bar of
an E chord
with rhythm
slashes.

You can listen to how this sounds in real life by playing Track #5 of the CD that came with this book. Use the track skip button with arrows pointing to the right to play the track a few times so that you begin to associate symbols on a page with sounds from a guitar. In this case, the slashes indicate four pick strokes on the guitar, but in general, slashes don't dictate any particular rhythm, only that you play an E chord for the duration of the bar.

Think of two songs in a similar feel, such as "La Bamba" (by Ritchie Valens, and later covered by Los Lobos) and "Twist and Shout" (first done by the Isley Brothers, then by the Beatles), or "Surfin' U.S.A," and "Fun, Fun, Fun," both by the Beach Boys. The melody and chords are different, but the rhythm guitar parts — as far as the *style* is concerned — are virtually identical. You can play one strumming style to fit both songs. That's what shorthand notaters take advantage of: that rock guitar rhythm parts have only a few basic variations. Another example is the Eagles songs "Lyin' Eyes" and "Peaceful Easy Feeling." To a rhythm guitarist, the strumming style is the same. Similar rhythmic styles among rock songs is one reason musicians who have never played together before — or even met — can get together and "fake" their way through tunes very convincingly.

Reading tablature

Tablature ("tab," for short) is somewhat like a chord diagram in that it shows the frets and strings of the guitar. Tab is more comparable to standard music notation, however, because it tells you how to play music over time. In *Rock Guitar For Dummies,* you always see a tab staff underneath a corresponding standard music staff in every music example, visually aligned with its top half, so you can use whichever one you're comfortable with. The tab shows you the strings and the fret numbers; the music staff shows you the pitches and the rhythms. This way, you have the best of both worlds. No wonder bassoonists (who have developed no known tablature system for themselves) are jealous of guitarists!

You can use both the music and tab staffs simultaneously, or you can elect not to use them at all (relying instead on using the CD to learn the songs by ear). But I'm guessing you'll employ a system using all three. Each has its strengths, and you're not limited to using any one or two, nor do you even have to tell anyone your secret for learning the music in this book. The important thing is that you do get the examples under your fingers and get comfortable with them.

Figure 2-10 shows the anatomy of a tab staff. The horizontal lines represent the strings, as if you faced a guitar that was sitting upright and you rotated it 90 degrees counterclockwise, positioning the high E string on top and the low E string on the bottom. Numerals placed on a line tell you the fret number and string location.

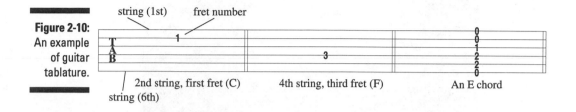

Figure 2-10: An example of guitar tablature.

string (1st)   fret number

2nd string, first fret (C)   4th string, third fret (F)   An E chord

string (6th)

Making Music: How to Play a Chord

A chord is defined as the simultaneous sounding of three or more notes of different-named pitches. On the guitar, you can *strum* (dragging a pick across the strings in a single, quick motion) a chord, *pluck* (with the individual right-hand fingers) it, or even smack the strings with your open right hand or fist. You can't, however, just play *any* group of notes; the notes must form a musically meaningful arrangement. To a guitarist, that means learning chord forms. The following sections show how to play a chord.

Fingering a chord

To play the E chord shown in Figure 2-8, follow these steps:

1. **Place your 1st finger on the 3rd string, 1st fret.**

   Remember, fretting a note means to place your finger between the nut and the first fret, but a little closer to the fret wire.

2. **Place your 2nd finger on the 5th string, 2nd fret.**

   Here, you have to skip over the 4th string.

3. **Put your 3rd finger on the 4th string, 2nd fret.**

   After you've placed your 3rd finger in its proper place, press down firmly on all three fretted fingers, keeping your knuckles rounded, and making sure none of the fretted fingers is covering the open strings — especially the 1st and 2nd strings, which must ring out to help the E chord sound in all its resplendent, six-string glory (see Figure 2-11). Now, quick, read the next section before your fingers fall off!

Figure 2-11:
A photo of
the left hand
fingering an
E chord.
Notice how
the fingers
curve and
the knuckles
bend on an
E chord.

Strumming a chord

Well, now that you've got your left hand all set up, you may as well give your right hand something to do, too. Strum all six strings at once, using a smooth and firm motion, but don't strum too forcefully. Listen to Track 2 and try to match the level of intensity (which is not very intense at all, but relaxed) and evenness. Note, too, that the four strokes are not only smooth and even, they are consistent; that is, one stroke sounds like every other.

When you can strum the E chord with four even strokes, try doubling the number to eight, then to 12.

Chord vs. cord

Don't confuse *chord* and *cord*, either in speech or in print. They both have their place in rock guitar, but are quite different.

Some shared qualities between chord and cord:

✔ They're pronounced the same

✔ You need both to play rock guitar

✔ Both can have unpleasant sonic results if not used correctly

Some differences between chord and cord:

✔ "Chord" has an "h" in it

✔ A *cord* is the wire that connects the guitar to the amp; a *chord* is the simultaneous sounding of three or more notes.

✔ A *vocal cord* is a stringy, wiggly thing in your throat that quivers when you sing; a *vocal chord* is three stringy, wiggly boy-band members singing different notes simultaneously, which makes prepubescent girls quiver.

Buzzes and muffles are the bane of beginning guitarists, and they're especially hard to avoid when playing chords. A muffle results if you don't press down hard enough on the string, or if your fretting finger comes in contact with an adjacent string. Don't worry too much if your strings buzz a little bit; the string buzz issue corrects itself over time without you even doing anything consciously, just like a bad haircut. As your fingers become stronger and more agile, buzzes will gradually "heal" themselves.

Chapter 3

The Other Half: The Guitar Amp

• •

In This Chapter

▶ Setting up your amp

▶ Turning the amp on

▶ Setting up your sound

▶ Getting by without an amp

• •

*W*hen I was a kid, I pined for an eternity (okay, it was one summer) for my first guitar, which hung, unattainable, in the music store window. After several agonizing months of paper routes, odd jobs, and bottle recycling, I finally bought my dream guitar. As the salesman pulled my hard-won treasure from the window, he commented casually, "Yeah, good guitar you're getting here. Whatcha got for an amp?"

An *amp*? I'd never even thought about it! Did I need an amp? Of course I did, but all my energies had gone into buying this guitar. As the meaning of his words flooded over me like a giant tidal wave, I realized I hadn't even considered that I needed something to plug into to be heard. My mom wasn't about to spend one red cent more than she had already contributed to my musical cause, and so she called an electrician friend who ran an appliance repair store across town. To my utter humiliation, we found ourselves in a washing machine fix-it shop buying what looked like a converted toaster oven. It took me six more months to get a *real* amp, which helped me to get up the nerve to play in front of my friends (junior high school kids can be *so* cruel, you know). So take it from one who's been there, don't forget the amp! It does wonders for your guitar sound (not to mention your self esteem).

You may not think that the amp is a very flashy player in the cast of rock guitar characters, especially when it has to share the limelight with its more glamorous counterpart, the electric guitar. But amps are essential to creating a great rock guitar sound and literally contribute one half of the effort. So even though this book is titled *Rock Guitar For Dummies*, it could just as rightfully be called *Rock Guitar and an Amp to Play It Through For Dummies*. Hmm . . . somehow that just doesn't have the same zing.

Next to the electric guitar itself, however, the amp is the single most important piece of gear in your rock and roll arsenal — and the more you understand your amp, the more passionate you become. In this chapter, I let you think "inside the box," separating the amp system into the smaller sections that all amps of various makes and models have in common. I then drill down one level to see how the user (that's you) can manipulate the controls that govern those parts. And don't worry, you don't need a driver's license — or even a learner's permit — to operate one of these babies.

Discovering How Amps Work

Amps are all-electronic devices, and let's face it, that scares some people. Or at least it's intimidating enough that many beginner guitarists have a tougher time relating to an amp than, say, to something you can *play,* such as a guitar.

Just like you can appreciate a sports car's power and performance without knowing the physics of the internal combustion engine; however, so, too, can you enjoy the "internal combustion" of an amp just by taking it for a ride. Like a well-made car, a great amp has a personality, responds to your every movement, and gives you the giddy sense that you're sitting atop something *really* powerful. Knowing just a little bit about what's going on under the hood of your amp increases not only your appreciation, but your pleasure as well.

Following the Signal Chain

An amp has a big job to do, when you think about it. It receives from the guitar a signal that is quite sensitive, having started life as a tiny current produced by skinny vibrating strings and a simple magnet (see Chapter 1 for more details on how the electric guitar produces its signal). The amp must then respect the tiniest nuances of those vibrating strings, because you the player know exactly what you played, and if you don't hear that at the end of the process — coming out of the speakers — the amp has failed in its mission.

The amp, therefore, must shepherd the signal through an electronic journey, all the while preserving its integrity. The amp must then switch gears, applying huge amounts of power to this once-sensitive electrical impulse, to rock stadiums and pulverize screaming fans. That's not an easy task for a box with no moving parts.

A good amp can do all this, plus excite you as a listener and inspire you as a performer in the process. The electronic journey is called the *signal chain.* Technically speaking, the entire signal chain includes at its source the guitar, from whence the signal originates (by you striking the strings), and at its terminus the speaker (which, in a "combo" configuration, is housed in the same box — for more on amp configurations, see Chapter 14), which converts the electrical signal back into acoustic energy — you know, earth-shattering, filling-rattling AC/DC riffs.

In this section, I focus on what happens to the signal after it's inside the amplifier — this sets the stage (so to speak!) for you to better understand how to manipulate the controls and to shape the sound. A guitar signal's journey through the amp goes something like this: An anemic (by electrical standards) signal enters the guitar amp at the preamp stage where sensitive circuitry optimized for handling low levels boosts the signal and sends it through to the section where the amp shapes the tone and adds effects. The signal then goes into the power amp, which applies massive amounts of juice behind it to drive speakers and produce audible — and often *extremely* audible — sound waves we can crowd surf to.

Following is an overview of the four primary sections of the amp, presented in the order that the signal passes through them. Later in the chapter, I discuss the individual components and their controls.

Preamp

Every amplifier, whether it's for a guitar or keyboard — or inside a home stereo receiver — has two stages to actually amplify, or boost, the signal: the preamp and the power amp (see later in this section). In amp systems made for guitars, the preamp takes the puny signal from the guitar (which is, after all, produced by mere magnets), jacks it up so that the power amp can deal with it, and turns it into the screaming tones of death that eventually burst forth from stressed-to-the-brink speakers. The result is the sound that blows back the hair of the audience in the first 10 rows like so many G-forces. (Hey, we can dream, can't we?)

The preamp is the day care center of signal processing, designed to foster and nurture small impulses and guide them in their first baby-steps through amp land. Preamps respond very well to the sensitive but relatively weak messages from the pickups.

The power amp can't do much with an untreated guitar signal, which comes way under its radar, preferring instead to deal with levels that a preamp generates. The power amp takes whatever it sees coming at its input and attempts to churn out an exact copy, but thousands of times bigger (at a strength known as "line level" in electronic terms). A power amp may not be able to do justice to an untreated guitar signal, but it can take a preamp signal, puff it up, and use it to beat the stuffing out of a speaker.

Think of the preamp as a struggling talent agent and the power amp as a big Hollywood movie producer: The preamp polishes the talent of the small-time artist and prepares it for the big screen — er, speaker. The power amp doesn't muck about with the little people, but has the might to take the prepared talent and turn it into box-office dynamite.

The idea of two volume controls is unique to guitar amplification. Normally, household stereo amps don't give users separate access to the preamp and power amp controls. Stereo listeners just want the best *fidelity* (the most accurate signal) possible from their system. But in guitar amps, you can use the relationship of the preamp volume to the power amp volume to actually degrade the fidelity (in the form of distortion, or overdrive) to musical effect, as I discuss later in this chapter.

Tone controls

After coming out of the preamp, the signal then passes through a series of electronic filters, which selectively increase or reduce the level of certain frequencies. Known collectively as the tone controls, these filters make up the *equalization,* or *EQ,* section. Applying EQ is sometimes referred to as "tone shaping."

You sometimes hear the term EQ (pronounced "Ee-Cue") when discussing tonal issues. EQ is short for "equalization" (the bass and treble components of the tone) or "equalizer" (a box or circuit that affects tone). Following are three different uses of the term "EQ" that guitarists often hear:

✔ **As an intangible noun (an entity):** "The overall EQ of your guitar sound makes me feel like I'm chewing aluminum foil. Can't you make it less harsh?"

✔ **As a tangible noun (a device):** "Howdy! I'm your new bass player! Can I borrow your 10-band EQ? I forgot mine."

✔ **As a verb:** "Can you *please* EQ that amp so that it doesn't sound like a chainsaw on a blackboard? Thank you *so* much."

The tone controls on your guitar amp act just like the bass and treble knobs of your stereo: They make your sound *boomier* or *tinnier.* Because these filters don't affect all frequencies equally (which would result in an overall *volume* increase or reduction), but only in specific ranges, we hear the resultant sound as a *tonal* difference. Unlike a stereo receiver, however, a guitar amp has more than just a bass and treble control. Most amps feature at least one in-between knob called, logically enough, the *midrange* (usually abbreviated as *mid*) control. More sophisticated amps even have a *presence* control, which is between the midrange and treble control, and is especially suited to guitar frequencies. Still others have a contour control, and some have two knobs for the midrange that work in tandem — one to select the frequency and another to boost or cut the level of that frequency. But however a specific amp is configured, the controls in the tone shaping section serve to change the bass, midrange, and treble content put out by the preamp.

Don't worry too much about understanding the technical differences between the variously named tone controls. Good tone production involves knowing very little science (at least from the *player's* perspective, anyway), because guitarists — even the best ones — just fiddle with the knobs until they find something they like. Fiddling with knobs is probably not the best way to deliver nuclear power to a city, but it works just fine for guitarists searching for that special tone.

Effects

From the EQ, or tone shaping section, the signal next proceeds to the effects section, which usually consists of at least a reverb control, and may have tremolo, vibrato, or chorus. (These are the same effects that you can find in the outboard variety, in stompboxes or pedals — see Chapter 15 for more detailed descriptions on these sounds.) You can use effects to subtly enhance a sound, give it a certain ambience, warmth, fullness, or just to add a little more "life."

Or not. You can also use effects to make your playing sound completely off the wall, alien, space age, underwater, distorted, tortured, or to give it any other wholly unnatural quality. How you use effects (on your amp and/or elsewhere in the signal chain) is strictly a matter of taste, and depends on the response you want to evoke from your listeners. Ugly, scary, brutal, and just plain rude are all worthy qualities completely at home in rock guitar (especially for punk and heavy metal!), and you often enlist effects (along with sheer overpowering volume) to help you achieve your aesthetic goal. But unless you're going for a *really* wacky sound, you find, as your playing develops, that using effects subtly is best for most musical situations.

Don't confuse an amp's effects section with outboard effects, like stompboxes or pedals, which I describe later in the book. An amp's effects section often performs the same function as its same-named outboard counterparts. Having effects built in to your amp is a great convenience, though outboard effects usually offer a wider variety.

Power amp

The final stop on the signal's electrical journey to the speaker is the power amp — a robust, no-nonsense electrical place where treated but underpowered signals get pumped up into sound-wave warriors. The power amp adds very little color to the sound — at least compared to the three previous stages — because its primary function is to reproduce, as faithfully as possible, the signal it receives from the preamp, tone, and effects sections. You may think, therefore, that the power amp section is comprised of fairly straightforward, unimaginative stuff, which actually isn't the case.

Although its function may be simple to describe, the power amp's processing is a fairly complex and demanding electronic project. In more powerful amps, the power amp section is bigger, heavier, and more expensive to build. And in tube amps, which are objects of lust among amp aficionados, the power amp also adds a bit of color to the sound — something it's ideally not supposed to do (that task being the exclusive domain of the preamp tubes). But at least where tubes are concerned, the result is so musical that guitarists find it pleasing and make an exception — sort of like the famous adage about sausage: If you love it, you don't want to know how it's made.

Taking a Guided Tour of the Amp

The following sections offer a walking tour through each of the amp's individual components. I group the sections here linearly, from start to finish. The exception is the preamp and power amp volume controls, which I tackle simultaneously. I do this because, although the preamp and power amp are at the front and back of the amp's signal chain, respectively, you can best appreciate their functions and how they work together by dealing with them in tandem and in relation to each other — sort of like the bookends that hold up a set of books.

Boxing It In: The Cabinet

The cabinet is a sturdy wooden box that houses the speaker, controls, and electrical guts so that they don't fall all over the floor in a great big mess. The cabinet protects the speaker's surface with a grille cloth stretched taut across its front, serves as an anchor for the *chassis* (which houses the electronics) and the reverb tank (if present), and provides a frame for the *baffle* (the open-holed board that the speaker mounts to). The cabinet is also the acoustic place where the speaker lives and moves, however, and therefore contributes to the overall sound and performance of the amp. It also supports a sweating beverage bottle a *lot* better than the headstock of a guitar. Figure 3-1 shows the cabinet of a typical combo amp.

The cabinet can be open in the back (exposing the amp's interior and offering easy access to the speaker), closed, or sealed (leaving no opening), or "half back," which is like an open-back cab, but with a plank of wood across the opening. Sonically, an open back provides a rounder fuller tone, as sound escapes from both sides of the amp, back and front. A closed-back cab yields a punchier result as all sound is forced through the front of the amp (producing a boost in the bass frequencies in particular), and a half-back cab is a mix of the two sounds, but is closer to the open back in quality.

Figure 3-1:
The cabinet is the wooden box that houses the speaker and electronic components, and provides the acoustic environment for the speaker to operate.

Taking Control: The Control Panel

The control panel is a metal plate that plays host to the amp's knobs, switches, and sockets. Under the knobs and sticking through holes in the control panel are *shanks,* or *spindles,* which rotate, sending messages to the electronic components within the chassis (the metal tray or compartment housing the amp's electronics). The control panel and its knobs are often recessed or angled in such a way to protect them from getting damaged. This helps keep them from getting sheared off as you load your amp into the trunk of a car, and you don't quite clear the back of the trunk. (I *hate* when that happens.) The control panel is where the brains of the operation sit. It is to the signal chain what Houston is to a NASA space shuttle. Figure 3-2 shows a control panel of a typical combo amp.

Channel inputs

Channel inputs are the sockets, or jacks, where you insert your guitar cord for access to a particular channel. A channel is an individual path through the amp's signal-processing sections. Many amps have two channels optimized for producing different sounds. Typically, one channel favors setting up a "clean" sound, the other a high-volume, distorted sound. One input often serves two channels, allowing you to switch between channels instantly, without having to re-plug (see the section on channel switching later in the chapter). Some multi-channel, multi-input amps even accept two instruments simultaneously — great for keeping handy two different types of guitars that you must switch between quickly, such as a 12-string and a six-string, or an acoustic-electric and a regular electric. You can switch between channels instantly, via a footswitch to give your guitar a new sound.

Figure 3-2: The control panel groups together and supports the jacks, switches, and knobs of an amp.

Preamp and power amp controls

The preamp takes a signal and boosts it so that it can survive the journey through the tone shaping and effects sections and wind up intact for the G-forces it's subjected to in the power amp section. The power amp determines the actual human-hearing volume coming out of the speaker. Guitarists control the output of each of these stages with separate level, or volume, knobs. Figure 3-3 shows the volume controls of the preamp and power amp.

Gain/drive

Gain and *drive* are synonymous terms that simply describe the volume controls for the preamp. The higher you turn *any* preamp volume control, the more distortion you introduce into the signal. Preamp volume distorts in musically pleasing ways, however, and rock guitarists use that as part of their tone quality and sustain. (See Chapter 1 for more detailed descriptions of the electric guitar's sustain and tone quality.)

Figure 3-3:
The tale
of two
volumes:
preamp and
power amp,
channel and
master.

Volume/master volume

The power amp volume control determines the overall or absolute loudness of the amp. In amps containing more than one channel, the term *master volume* distinguishes the power amp control from the channels' preamp controls. If you run the master volume high (on high numbers, such as 6, 7, 8, 9, and 10), the sound coming out of the amp is loud. If you run the master volume low (1, 2, and 3), the amp is soft. This is important to remember when balancing the preamp channel volume with the power amp master volume (see the section on setting the controls later in this chapter).

Boost switch

Often an amp has a switch that activates a boost circuit, which just jacks up the power amp's volume by a fixed level. A boost switch can be very handy because it keeps your basic sound intact, retaining the specific tone and effects settings, and applies a volume increase. This way, a guitarist can have two versions of a carefully crafted sound: loud and really loud.

Tone controls

In the tone shaping stage of an amp, various electronic filters add or subtract frequencies, giving the guitarist tonal control over the sound apart from what the volume and effects controls provide. Most of the tone controls are intuitively named and produce expected results. For example, when you turn up the treble you brighten the tone. Figure 3-4 shows the tone shaping section of an amp's control panel.

Bass

The bass control determines how low or boomy the sound is. Turning up the bass provides more "girth," turning down the bass reduces "rumble."

Middle or midrange

For a fuller or warmer sound, guitarists reach for the midrange control. Conversely, to sharpen a sound, or to accentuate high highs and low lows, guitarists will cut, or "dial out," midrange frequencies. Heavy metal bands such as Pantera and Metallica often cut, or "scoop," their midrange frequencies.

Treble

The highest of the tone controls, the treble can restore luster to a signal that's become dull from passing through too many effects pedals. If a signal is too harsh sounding, cutting back the treble makes it mellower.

Presence

Technically, this is a high-mid control that sonically resides somewhere between the mids and the treble. "Presence" is sort of a misnomer because applying it doesn't really bring the sound any "closer to the listener;" it just adds a "gloss" or "sheen." Presence can really sweeten up a signal, but too much of it can fatigue the ears and create a saccharine sound.

Bright switch

The bright switch is a two-position *toggle* (a switch that alternates between two states) that selects between the normal sound and a brighter sound. Most rock guitarists who have amps with bright switches keep them on all the time. For that occasional jazzy passage, however, you may want to flick this one to the "normal" position.

TIP

Don't think that just because you adjust one control that you're affecting only one range of notes. For example, turning down the treble doesn't affect just the high notes; it affects the entire high frequency content of the signal. So even if you play only low notes, turning down the treble will affect the high end of those low notes, inhibiting their ability to "sparkle." Be aware that although the controls have the most noticeable effect over the frequency ranges they're named for, they influence the total tonal quality of the entire signal.

Amp effects

Although most tone shaping sections on amps are fairly standardized, amp manufacturers differ widely with respect to what effects they include. Following are some fairly universal effects found on many guitar amps.

Reverb

Reverb is short for "reverberation" and is a basic staple guitar effect, one that is heard on virtually every recorded example of rock guitar music. Older amplifiers actually use metal springs (secured in a box or "tank" bolted to the inside of the cabinet) that will jiggle and make a crashing sound if you shake the amp. Newer amps deliver reverb through the less-costly technology of microchips and digital circuitry, but the intent is the same: to simulate the sound of a guitar played in different acoustical settings, from a small room to a concert stage to a giant cavern or cathedral. A single knob controls the intensity of the effect. Figure 3-5 shows the reverb control knob on an amp.

Tremolo

Tremolo is regular, rapid wavering of a signal's volume. Old Fender amps used two controls, *speed* (the rate of the fluctuations) and *intensity* (to determine the distance between the loud and soft portions of the sound). At lower settings, the sound has a slight quiver. With the intensity cranked, it sounds like you're playing through an electric fan. These days, newer amps include tremolo only if they're going for that vintage vibe.

You sometimes hear amp tremolo described as "vibrato," but this is a misnomer. *Vibrato* is the rapid fluctuation of *pitch*, tremolo the rapid fluctuation of *volume*. Fender has an entire series of amps with the prefix "Vibro" to describe amps sporting a feature that is actually tremolo. Rock guitar is full of misnomers, but that's just part of its rebellious charm.

Chorus

Chorus simulates the sound of many guitars playing at once, creating an overall fuller sound that's slightly swirly. Turning up the speed yields a warbling effect; increasing the intensity produces lush, whooshy sounds. Figure 3-6 shows the chorus controls of an amp made famous by its classic onboard chorus: the Roland JC-120.

Figure 3-5:
The control for amp reverb is usually limited to one knob: the volume or intensity of the effect.

Figure 3-6:
The two controls that modify the chorus effect on the Roland JC-120 are *speed* and *depth*.

Making a Graceful Exit

Other than pumping the signal out through a speaker, an amp can output a signal through other points. Knowing these different output destinations helps in understanding how the amp contributes to the quality of the sound, rather than just acting as a "guitar megaphone." Alternate outputs allow for options like sending your guitar signal to a P.A. (sound system), headphones, and mixing boards for recording. An amp's output jacks are typically found on the back panel.

Speaker out

The main *speaker out* is an output jack that connects the amp's power amp to its internal speaker (if it's a combo) or to the main cab (if the amp is in a separate housing from the speaker). Some amps offer additional speaker outs for hooking up additional cabs. Ninety-nine times out of 100, you want your amp sound coming out through the speaker, because this is how electric guitars are heard — realized through a speaker. This is different than, say, a piano, flute, or even *acoustic* guitar where we can experience them live, without the benefit of a speaker. It's only on *recordings* where we must enlist the aid of a speaker. But an electric guitar knows no audio reality — live *or* recorded — without a speaker. Even if a direct out is used (as described later in this section), a speaker simulator is thrown in to simulate the sound of the signal coming through a speaker.

Headphone out

In the post-Walkman era, everyone understands the importance of listening to music through headphones. Many amp makers realize this too, and so provide a headphone output for speaker-less listening. By listening to your guitar through headphones, you can wail away to your heart's content (and experience thundering levels of distortion via an overdriven preamp) and still not disturb the person next to you watching TV. Headphone outputs are great for practicing late at night or in close proximity to other humans.

Direct out

You sometimes want the signal to not go into the power amp and through the speaker but to some other destination, such as a mixing board (for recording directly onto tape or hard disk) or even to another amp. You can't successfully plug a guitar directly into a mixer channel, because you need the treatment that the amp's preamp, tone shaping, and possibly effects sections provide. But an amp's power amp and speaker exist only to make the sound audible in the room, which is not necessarily what you want when sending a direct-out signal. You want to route the signal to a mixer or recording deck where you can then *monitor* (listen to the resultant sound) from the mixer or deck's headphone jack or speakers.

Effects loop

You can insert an outboard effect device (such as a rack-mount multi-effects processor, described in Chapter 17) between the preamp and the power amp sections of the amp, which is the optimal place for many effects, like delay, chorus, and flange, that just sound better placed between the preamp and the power amp, rather than before the preamp, which is the situation when using pedals. If you desire an effect not provided by your amp's built-in circuitry, but that you have in an external box, you use the effects loop to "patch" it in. The effects loop consists of two jacks, an output and an input. With an extra guitar cord you plug the output (sometimes called "send") of the amp into the input of the external effects box. You then take another cord and plug the output of the effects box back into the amp, at the input (sometimes called the "return") jack. The amp has provided a "loop" for you to route the signal out and back in, allowing you to enhance it along the way. Figure 3-7 shows the diagram for plugging in an external device via the effects loop.

Figure 3-7:
With an effects loop, you can route your signal out of the amp for external processing and then send it back in.

Power amp in

You may have occasion to use your amp just for its power amp capabilities only — to make an external sound source (such as a CD player) audible by means of the amp's speaker. In this case, the sound comes to the power amp from a source other than the amp's onboard preamp. For those situations, you take the output of the external device and insert it into the *power amp in* jack. Doing this skips all the circuitry before the power amp stage (preamp, tone shaping, and effects sections), which the CD player doesn't need or want.

Use the power amp in jack to patch in a CD player (although you may have to tweak the tone controls to get a decent sound). This allows you to perform two common and useful tasks:

- ✔ Play recorded music in close proximity to your guitar-playing activities, instead of over the stereo speakers — wherever they are.

- ✔ Play recorded music through your amp on a gig during the break. (This is great if the venue has no "house system" of its own, or if you want to control what the audience hears — such as your newly minted demo!)

Various other "holes"

I've tackled the important jacks that appear on most amps, but you may discover amp models that have additional jacks. A footswitch jack allows you to plug in a pedal that you can operate with your foot, for instantaneous and hands-free control. Typical footswitch jacks include channel switching, effects on/off, and, on digital amps (covered in Chapter 15), preset advance (where you can "step through" different setups you've created and stored in the amp's memory). High-quality amps often include several places where you can "tap" (gain access to) the signal: after the preamp, after the power amp but at non-speaker-level (for additional processing), and speaker level (which can only be connected to a speaker, lest you risk damaging the amplifier's circuitry). Some amps offer additional inputs, too, like an "aux in" which allows you to plug in, say, a CD player, so you can practice along with your favorite CD.

Sounding Out: The Speaker

The speaker's function is pretty obvious to anyone who's grown up around stereos, radios, and TVs: It magically converts that mystical stuff called electricity into acoustic sound waves that we can hear with our ears and feel in our bodies (if it's loud enough).

For all the advancements in electronics, speakers today look and operate pretty much the same as they did half a century ago. Electricity passes through a cylindrical metal coil at the speaker's center, surrounded by a doughnut-shaped magnet. This causes the coil to vibrate inside a magnetic field. The speaker's cone of paper-like material exaggerates and amplifies this movement, creating audible sound. If this process sounds familiar it should: It's essentially the way a pickup works — but in reverse. (See Chapter 1 for more on the pickup's workings.)

Speakers are delicate by design, because they must react to the minute electrical fluctuations in the coil. Guitar amp speakers are called *woofers* (as opposed to their higher-pitched brethren, *tweeters*), and are suited for cranking out the midrange-rich frequencies of electric guitars. The majority of guitar speakers measure 12 inches in diameter, though 10 inches is quite popular too. Figure 3-8 shows a typical guitar speaker.

Plugging In and Turning On

Because an amplifier plugs into the wall, and because it's capable of delivering signals both electrical and acoustic in high doses, you must follow some simple but vital rules for operating an amp. Do not skip this section!

Figure 3-8: A 12" speaker (measured by its diameter), built especially for a guitar amp.

Safety first

First and foremost, a guitar amplifier is a high-voltage, electricity-driven device, such as any TV, stereo, radio, or appliance in your kitchen. Following are some "never" directives to keep you and those near you safe and injury free.

- ✔ **Never stick your hands inside the amp** to check connections, to find loose or rattling parts, or to otherwise poke around. Even when you unplug the amp its components store electricity for several minutes afterwards.

- ✔ **Never operate an amp with water anywhere in the vicinity,** either on your body or in an open container. Mixing water with a plugged-in amp — even if it's not turned on — can be lethal. Treat the cord to the wall socket with respect and care. Always turn off the power switch when the amp is not in use for an extended period of time, and always turn off the power switch before unplugging the amp.

- ✔ **Never operate an amp in the rain or near a sprinkler or garden hose** (which may happen if you play in a garage, back yard, or patio). Have fun with your music, but always treat electricity with grave seriousness.

The six-step program

Following is a quick-start chart of six steps for plugging your guitar in and turning it on in the right order. Doing this protects your speakers from sonic assaults and rude pops and preserves your eardrums from unexpected, irritating — and potentially damaging — sonic blasts.

To turn on an amp:

1. **Turn all amp volume controls off or to their minimum position.**

2. **Plug one end of the guitar cord into the guitar, the other end into the amp.**

3. **Turn the amp's power switch on.**

4. **Turn the volume knob(s) of your guitar all the way up.**

5. **Turn up the amp's master volume to about four or five, or up to about half way.**

6. **Slowly turn the preamp or channel volume knob up and check for the presence of audible signal by strumming your guitar.**

Here's how you reverse the process to ensure a safe and pop-free shutdown routine.

To shut off an amp:

1. **Turn off the guitar's volume knob(s).** Do this as a courtesy so unintended sound won't escape from the ringing open strings as you reach over to the amp's controls.

2. **Turn down the amp's master volume controls.**

3. **Optional: Turn down the channel or preamp volume control(s).** (Do this as a courtesy to the next player — even if that's you — so he or she can make his own preamp adjustments. Conversely, you can *keep the preamp volume level where it is* to recall easily your sound upon restart.)

4. **Turn off the power switch.**

5. **Optional: If you're leaving the amp unattended for a long period of time, or you can't predict who will be in the room with the amp when you're not there, unplug the amp from the wall socket.**

6. **Unplug the cord from the amp.** Unplug the cord from the guitar.

Additional hints:

✔ Never unplug a guitar cord — from either the guitar or the amp — without first turning down all the way the master volume knob.

Sudden loud noises in the form of "pops" from inopportunely connected or disconnected cords can damage the speaker (and at the very least are amateurish and annoying).

✔ Never move an amp any significant distance without turning down the volume and shutting off the power. This is important to consider when you're attached to a long extension cord.

✔ When plugging different guitars into one amp in rapid succession (such as when you're auditioning a bunch of guitars), turn down only the master volume control. This shuts off the signal from reaching the speaker. Note the volume knob's position before you bring it down so that you can restore it to the same place after you have safely unplugged and plugged the guitar cord.

Getting a Sound

When you have an understanding of the amp's different sections and the controls that govern them, use them to set up your own sound. You can't make any mistakes when creating a sound, so experiment until you find something you like — something that's not too loud or too soft, too muddy or too shrill. Then go from there.

First decide what kind of sound you want. Something clean and crisp, say, for chords? Or something raunchy and snarly for low-note Led Zeppelin–type *riffs* (self-contained single-note phrases). Always have a vision in your mind's eye — make that ear — of what you're seeking, rather than blindly spinning controls hoping to stumble on something you like.

Setting the controls

Start with your tone controls in the 12:00 position, or at "5," so that they're "flat" (adding no boost or cut). That will help you hear your basic guitar sound in the amp's most neutral setting. Turn off all effects too, so that you hear the pure guitar signal through the circuitry. Then decide whether you want a sound that's *clean* or *distorted*. Figure 3-9 shows an amp with its controls in the neutral position.

Clean

The term *clean* in guitar parlance simply means distortion-free and is not necessarily better or worse than an overdriven, or heavily distorted, sound. You can obtain a clean sound by running the power amp volume (or master volume) high and the channel, or preamp, volume relatively low. If you want the sound louder, turn up the master volume, not the channel volume. If you want the sound grittier, turn up the channel volume, and back off the master volume accordingly to compensate for the increase in gain from the preamp. The net result is a sound that produces about the same in overall loudness, but has a more fuzzy, overdriven quality.

Distorted

If you're trying to get a distorted sound from an older amp that has no separate volume controls for the channel and the master (sometimes referred to as "non-master-volume" models), you have but one choice: crank that sucker until the sound starts to break up. In the process, hope that the neighbors don't call the police. If your amp has two volume controls, though, your options are a little more versatile. Set up the master volume to about half way, and bring up the channel volume to a comfortable listening level (whatever that is, depending on your environment). To create a distorted sound using the two volume controls in conjunction with each other, turn up the channel volume and compensate for the increased volume by turning down the master volume. By turning down the master as you turn up the channel, your overall loudness should remain fairly constant. But as the preamp works harder and harder, it will begin to distort — even though the volume doesn't change. The twin-volume approach to distortion is a beautiful thing for guitarists, because it means you can achieve overdriven preamp distortion at low volumes. Figure 3-10 shows two setups, one clean, and the other overdriven. In both settings the overall volume — or absolute loudness — is about the same. Only the distortion content changes.

Figure 3-9:
When starting to build a sound from scratch, place the controls in a neutral position with the volume reduced, the effects off, and the tone controls "flat."

Don't get too caught up in all the semantics and synonyms for distortion. Technically, distortion is the result of any signal that gets overdriven.

Channel switching

Most modern amps that allow you to create sounds on separate channels also allow you to switch between them by means of a front-panel switch. This enables you to set up two channels independently and switch between them instantly, and at will. Typically, you assign two contrasting sounds for these channels, such as clean and distorted, or variations on those qualities (perhaps "ultra-sheen" and "super-stun").

Careful crafting of two independent clean and distorted sounds may produce righteous tones on their own, but they aren't much use to a guitarist who in the same song wants a clean sound on the verses (to, say, accompany a singer), and mondo-distortion for the Big Guitar Solo (and rock guitarists should *insist* every song include at least one of these). In a single-channel amp, reconfiguring the controls for real-time use between song sections is a practical impossibility, and in multiple channels, even throwing a front-panel switch requires the guitarist to take one hand off the instrument and reach for the amp. And hey, who has that kind of time?

The footswitch is an inexpensive (about $20, if not already included with the amp), "stompable" device that sits on the floor and plugs in the back of your amp. Its sole purpose in life is to alternate between two states — 1 and 2, A and B, on and off, and so on. A footswitch allows the guitarist to play with both hands on the guitar the entire time, and when the moment comes to switch seamlessly from dutiful backup drudge to distortion-diva superstar, she can step surreptitiously on a pedal and have her sound magically and instantly launch into hyperspace.

Figure 3-10:
These two
setups yield
about the
same
overall
loudness.
The first
setup,
however,
produces a
clean, or
undistorted,
sound, while
the second
produces
a heavily
distorted, or
overdriven,
sound.

A footswitch has other uses besides hands-free channel switching. You can use a footswitch to turn your effects on and off. Or you can try to step on two footswitches at once, to turn on the effects *and* to change channels. This sometimes poses a problem because you have to twist your foot sideways so that your toe and heel can simultaneously press two switches at once. Miscalculation of this move may leave audience members wondering, "Why did that knock-kneed guitarist suddenly fall over just before the guitar solo?"

Making Do If You Don't Have an Amp

Certainly a guitar amp is an important thing to have. But sometimes you simply have to choose between getting a really good guitar now and waiting for an amp, or spending the same money for two pieces — and comprising on the quality of both.

For those who have faced this cosmic struggle, know that you have alternate means of amplification available to you that won't cost nearly as much as a quality amplifier. You may even have the technology right now and not even realize it. (Cue mysterious organ music.)

Plugging into a home stereo or boom box

You can get away without buying an amp at all, if you plug your electric guitar into the auxiliary input of your home stereo. All you need is a special, inexpensive adapter. You can readily purchase these devices at electronic or music stores for less than $3. (Just tell the salesperson what you want to do, and he can supply the correct unit.) The adapter is just a metal or plastic-coated plug that has a female quarter-inch jack on one end and a male RCA (sometimes called *phono*) plug on the other. Many boom boxes have inputs as well, but use a 1/8" connection, so for one of these you need a female quarter-inch jack on one end and a male 1/8" stereo plug on the other. Make sure, if you buy your adapter at a place other than a music store, that the adapter's female end is mono; that's the end you plug your guitar cord into.

Before you go plugging anything in to a stereo or boom box, make sure that the volume control on the receiver is all the way down. This precaution prevents any sudden pop or surge in the system, which can potentially damage the speakers.

Because you plug into, say, the left input of your receiver, you hear music only out of the left speaker. This is normal. Some higher-end receivers enable you to set the *output mode* (the stereo configuration) of the source signal. If you see a bunch of settings such as L, R, L+R, and so on one, set that knob to L (which routes the left channel to both speakers). The resultant sound is not stereo, but it sounds fuller and more widely dispersed than if your guitar comes out of only one speaker. And hey, it's better than a converted toaster oven any day!

Figure 3-11 shows how to plug into the back of your receiver. Plug one end of the guitar cord into your guitar and the other end into the adapter. Check to see that the receiver's volume is down. Plug the adapter into the left auxiliary input in the back of your receiver. On the receiver's front panel, select "Aux 1" or whatever is the corresponding name of the input into which you plugged your guitar. (It may be called "Tape 1" or some other name — check the input itself or your owner's manual if in doubt.) Turn your guitar's volume up full. Then slowly turn up the receiver's volume knob until you hear sound at a comfortable listening level. You can adjust the receiver's tone controls to better shape your sound as well.

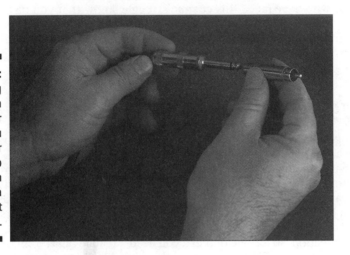

Figure 3-11:
Plugging into an adapter allows you to use your home stereo or boom box for a makeshift amp.

Headphone amps

Because of the miniaturization of all things electronic, you can now get full-sounding, authentic guitar sounds from a unit the size of a disposable camera — as long as you listen to it through headphones (meaning that it has no speaker or power amp of its own). These strap-on wonders come with belt clips and are battery powered for untethered practicing (great for walking into the bathroom and standing in front of the mirror to check your stage moves). And virtually all headphone amps offer a full menu of distortion, EQ, reverb, and a whole host of other digital effects, many of them simultaneously. So a headphone amp can usually double as a multi-effects processor, which is quite cool. Headphone amps also provide numerous *presets* — sounds pre-programmed, or set up, by the manufacturer, plus full stereo sound (especially effective over headphones). Headphone amps are great for playing in a moving vehicle, at the beach, in a hotel room, or in the airport lounge, and they can even output the signal to tape or disk, suitable for recording. The cost starts from about $200 (the Korg Pandora, Scholz Rockman, Ibanez Rock 'n' Play, and Zoom 9000 series are just some makes and models), and are well worth the price if portability, privacy, and authentic tone are important for your practice routine. Figure 3-12 shows a headphone amp for guitar.

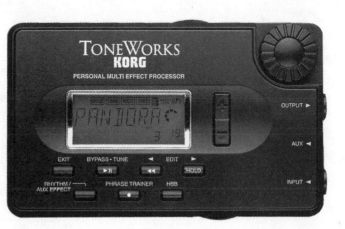

Figure 3-12:
The Korg Pandora PX-3, a multi-effects processor that features several types of distortion, EQ, effects, a metronome, and many other features — all in a unit about the size of a deck of cards.

Demystifying the Gizmology

Amp functions and their controls may seem daunting at first, but if you just remember to break them down to their basic sections, you have a much better time of dealing with them. Especially when you shop for an amp, and are faced with a myriad of choices, remember that the rows of dials, knobs and switches all have common purposes among models. Occasionally, you see something unique to that manufacturer or model, but if you come prepared in the basics, you should have an easier time recognizing what that feature is and to what section it belongs.

Above all, don't let the number of knobs intimidate or impress you. The important thing about an amp is how it sounds — and more specifically, how it sounds to you when you play your guitar through it. Some of the best amps in the world have very few knobs and look rather low tech.

So make sure you check out an amp the way you would a guitar — by listening to it as well as playing through it, and developing a rapport and feel for the vibe it produces.

Part II
Basic Playing Techniques

The 5th Wave   By Rich Tennant

"Okay- I'll front the band. But I want someone other than Dopey on lead guitar."

In this part . . .

In Part II, you get down to the nitty-gritty and put those fingers to work! Chapter 4 is all about left-hand chords: open-position, barre, movable, and power. And, so that your right hand doesn't feel left out, Chapter 5 is devoted to strumming and to some fancy fingerpicking. Check it out and impress your friends! Next, Chapter 6 takes you to that hallowed ground of lead guitar. Here you find out how to play single notes, melodies, riffs, and the almighty Guitar Solo (the crowd goes "oooh"). Chapter 7 gets you grooving on riffs. Now, you're really playing!

Chapter 4

What the Left Hand Is Doing: Chords

. . . .

In This Chapter
▶ Trying your hand at open-position chords
▶ Jump-starting with power chords
▶ Mastering barre chords

. . . .

*W*hen rock guitarists play, chords are what they play most of the time. You may have a vision of your favorite guitar hero up on stage wailing away on a single-note lead passage, but the rest of the time, when he's singing or when someone else is singing or when someone else is the featured soloist, he's playing chords. And although the best guitarists are known for their lead playing, between these fleeting moments of immortal glory those guys are churning out chords.

Chords are the workday week of the playing rock guitarist. Leads arc Saturday night. And in rock and roll, just as in life, you have to work all week to earn your Saturday night. (I know, rock guitar guitarists aren't supposed to have day jobs, but you get the point.)

Because chord playing constitutes what you do the majority of your rock-guitar-playing life, in this chapter I show you some essential chords to master. But don't take the comparisons of chord playing and working all week too literally. If playing rock guitar chords is any kind of *work*, put me down for a double shift!

You Gotta Have Chords

Chords are built in the left hand and realized as sound by strums from the right hand. In Chapter 2, I present an E chord to enable your left hand to turn the strings into a meaningful arrangement so that when you strum them it makes at least enough sense for you to check your tuning.

But you don't create music on the guitar by strumming something once and letting it sit there ringing indefinitely. Music has to move, and rock music has to move mightily. The two ways to do that are to strum cool rhythms and to play awesome-sounding chords.

Because this chapter focuses on chords and your left hand, don't worry about what your right hand is supposed to do. For now, you can execute the figures and rhythm charts in this chapter by playing one strum (that is, one downward stroke across the strings) per slash. Things get fancier in Chapter 5, but playing one strum per slash allows you to concentrate on your left-hand chord work.

Of course you don't *have* to play the figures using only the one-stroke-per-beat approach. If the spirit moves you — and the musical feel allows — try throwing in some in-between, up-and-down strums to get your music moving a bit. Just don't let any right-hand fanciness get in the way of the business of switching chords.

If you listen to the CD you hear all the figures in this chapter played as simple *downstrokes* — strums where your right hand drags the pick down toward the floor across all the playable strings in the chord. The CD is there to help you hear what you are supposed to sound like, and frees you up to concentrate on learning chords, chords, and more chords.

Fingering or "grabbing" chords is the hardest thing beginning guitarists encounter — much harder than anything the right hand has to do. In this section I tackle some chords, and then I focus on ways to get them memorized and under your fingers quickly. I'll make it easy on you, too, by showing some chord changes that require little more than sliding one chord form around on the neck.

Facility is strength combined with speed and accuracy. Playing chords on an electric guitar is fairly undemanding, from a strength perspective (unlike acoustic guitar, where developing your left-hand strength is a major struggle). So that leaves you to concentrate on speed and accuracy in shifting. You get there eventually, but you have to remember to push yourself.

Playing Open-position Chords

Open-position chords, so named because they involve unfretted strings, are allowed to ring open, along with the fretted notes. Open-position chords have a "jangly," pleasing quality and are sometimes called "cowboy chords" — probably because you can play simple, plaintive, spur-janglin', chip-kickin' songs with them.

Figure 4-1 is a chart of 24 chords that comprise just about all the useful chords you use for rock guitar in open position. If you've never tried your hand (pun intended!) at open-position chords before, refer to *Guitar For Dummies*. There you'll find in-depth lessons on how to form and play these fundamental chords. Whether or not you can grab them with ease already, there's no need to get bogged down. I'm going to rope you into rock guitar playing whether you're a bona fide cowboy or not.

You don't need to memorize this chart because it's duplicated on the yellow perforated Cheat Sheet located at the front of your *Rock Guitar For Dummies* book. You can detach this chart and keep it close at hand at all times — taped to a wall, propped up on a music stand, or sitting on a table top next to any sheet music you work on.

Remember, an "X" over a string means that it is *not* played or sounded; an "O" indicates an open string that *is* sounded when strumming. (Chapter 2 explains chord diagrams in detail.) Note that alternate fingerings appear below the primary ones.

Putting Power Chords into Play

Now it's time to put the cowpokes out to pasture. While open-position chords are not uncommon in rock guitar, players tend to favor their fast-moving, hard-hitting counterparts: *power chords*. Power chords are even easier to finger than open-position chords and they provide a simple means for moving beyond those first three frets. They represent rock guitar playing in all its raw and rugged glory, and once you understand how to use the 6th and 5th strings to name them, placing them on the neck is as easy as A-B-C♯.

A *power chord* is a two- or three-note chord that contains only the root and 5th degree of the chord. A two-note power chord contains the root on the bottom and the fifth degree on top. A three-note power chord is built (from the bottom up) as root, 5th, root, so it has a root at the bottom, the 5th on top of that, and then the root again, one octave higher than the chord's lowest note. So an open-position A power chord would be either one of the two examples presented in Figure 4-2.

Missing from power chords is the all-important 3rd degree (in the traditional sense, a chord is defined as three or more different notes, so a power chord is something of an exception). The 3rd of a chord is what determines whether the chord is major or minor. The flat 3rd (one-and-a-half steps from the root) makes the chord minor. The major 3rd (two whole steps from the root) makes the chord major. In either chord, though, the root and the 5th don't change. So take away the 3rd and you have a chord that is neither major nor minor: it can function as either, without being "wrong." This ambiguity is precisely what makes power chords so versatile to rock guitarists.

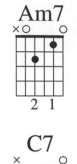

Figure 4-1:
A chart
showing
24 open-
position
chords
and their
fingerings.

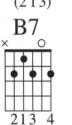  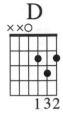

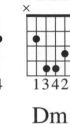

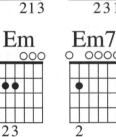 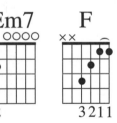  

 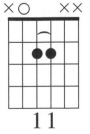

Figure 4-2:
Two ways
to play an
A power
chord.

Power chords have another desirable quality, other than their stark construction and open sound: They sound great when played with distortion. This is because distortion imbues tones with *harmonics*, or different high-pitched notes in varying degrees of intensity, that make a sound much more harmonically rich than a non-distorted sound. (Don't confuse the term "harmonics" in this sense with the bell-like tones discussed in Chapter 9.) Heavy distortion doesn't sound as good on full major or minor chords, because the harmonics of those closely spaced intervals (the root, 3rd, and 5th) clash in the upper registers, making the sound brittle and strident. But with just the root and 5th, the upper harmonics get close enough to dance together beautifully without stepping on each other's toes.

Moving power chords

Unlike their open-position brethren, power chords do not incorporate open strings and are therefore *moveable chords*. Any chord that you can move from one position on the neck to another without rearranging your fingers is a moveable chord. Because they're moveable, not to mention minimal, you can switch from any power chord to another without twisting your fingers up like so much linguini. If you can count up to 12 and spell up to the letter G, you can find every power chord. Welcome to Easy Street.

Power chords take their name from the root note, as all chords do. In a G power chord, G is the root. Because power chords incorporate only the root and the 5th, they are often referred to as "5" chords. When you see a chord written "G5," it's a G power chord.

The power chord shown in Figure 4-3 has its root on the 6th string. Because the note on the 6th string at the 5th fret is A, it's an A power chord (A5). Move the whole chord up a step (two frets) and it becomes B5. Likewise, move it down a step and it's G5. Move it down one more step and it becomes — any guesses? — F5.

The 5th-string based power chord looks almost exactly the same except it's shifted over a set of strings. Figure 4-4 is a 5th-string-based power chord played at the 1st fret.

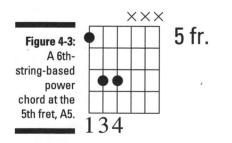

Figure 4-3:
A 6th-string-based power chord at the 5th fret, A5.

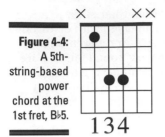

Figure 4-4:
A 5th-string-based power chord at the 1st fret, B♭5.

Like the 6th-string based power chords, 5th-string based chords can be moved around with ease. Move the B♭5 up a step (two frets) to get C5, up another step to D5, and so on.

Pulling the power together

Position is the term used to describe where a chord is placed on the neck. A chord's position is named for the fret where you plant your first finger. It doesn't matter which string you're on, just which fret. The 5th-string-based B♭5 is in first position. The first power chord you played — the 6th-string based A5 at the 5th fret — is in 5th position. Are you with me, people? I thought so.

Before you jump onstage with Aerosmith, try mixing up 6th- and 5th-string based power chords. Since power chords have so few notes and always assume the same shape, it's a breeze to move them around the neck. Figure 4-5 is a typical power-chord progression.

This example appears as track #2 on the CD that came with this book. The white type inside the black box indicates on what number track the performance of the written music appears (see Appendix B for more on how the CD is structured). You don't have to keep up with the performance you hear on the CD track when trying to finger and strum these chords. Just try switching the chords *in time* — that is, after every four beats.

Figure 4-5:
Mixing 6th- and 5th-string-based power chords in a single progression.

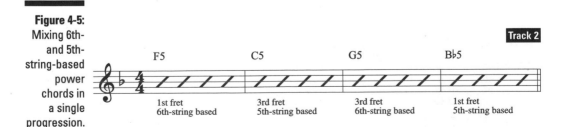

Track 2

F5   C5   G5   B♭5

1st fret   3rd fret   3rd fret   1st fret
6th-string based   5th-string based   6th-string based   5th-string based

Much like you need the individual words to form the sentences that describe thoughts and ideas, so too must you have individual chords that can be later arranged into longer musical segments, called *chord progressions.* Chord progressions form the structure, or harmonic framework, for songs.

Getting Behind the Barre

So now you're slinging power chords all over the neck, and you're thinking that all you need to be a rock god is a pair of leather pants and some friends who don't smell so good. Well, pull your Lear jet back into the hangar for a minute. While countless songs have been written using only the chord forms we've already covered — open-position and power chords — your musical vocabulary is about to expand a thousandfold. It's time to saddle up to the barre chords.

The term *barre chord* strikes fear into the hearts of beginning guitarists everywhere. Technically, a barre chord is just a chord where your left-hand 1st (index) finger lies flat across the strings, forming a "bar," with the rest of the chord made up by other fingers. Nevertheless, the term usually carries with it connotations of medieval torture practices.

Beginners have trouble with barre chords, because they seem to require an inordinate amount of strength — strength that you may think is better applied to a stuck lid on a pickle jar, not having fun playing the guitar. Although strength is certainly involved, you don't need quite so much of it after you become good at playing barre chords. Playing barre chords is like riding a bicycle: It's really tough at first, but then it becomes second nature. The difference is that barre chords hurt more when you're on them than when you fall off. Don't worry. It'll feel better when it stops hurting.

In rock, barre chords separate the men from the boys, the women from the girls, and those who rule from them that drool. A thorough lesson on barre chords can be found in *Guitar For Dummies.* But because they are the meat 'n potatoes of rock guitar, we're going to dig in here as well.

Getting a grip on barre chords

Memorize the Barre Chord Creed for the most important aspects to learning and mastering barre chords: A day without orange juice is like a day without sunshine. Oh, wait, that's not it. Here are the tips to keep in mind:

✓ **Press firmly.** You don't need to embed the strings permanently into your flesh, but apply strong, even pressure with your 1st finger. Rotate the finger slightly onto its side — the side away from the 2nd finger.

✔ **Thumb it.** Keep your thumb placed directly in the center of the neck's back. This is where the strength comes from. You'll know you're doing it right when the heel of your hand gets sore. Isn't this the greatest?

✔ **Keep your arms in.** Don't let your elbow stick out at your side like a chicken wing. Pull your elbow into your side, and keep your left shoulder relaxed and down.

✔ **Be fat-free.** Make tiny adjustments so that the fleshy parts of your fingers aren't touching adjacent strings, causing them to muffle. Keep your knuckles rounded and try to press straight down on the strings, rather than from the side. Also make sure that a string isn't running directly under the crease in the knuckle between your first and second finger joints.

Barre is the Spanish word for *bar*, and guitarists use this spelling because a lot of guitar notation uses Spanish terms (the same way other terms in music, such as *piano* for "soft," *fortissimo* for "very loud," and *scuza plisa tu pasa di pasta* for "the band is hungry" are in Italian), and because *barre* distinguishes itself from *bar*, the metal arm on the bridge of some guitars.

Playing E-based barre chords

Barre chords are formed as open-position-based chords with an added barre (your 1st finger) placed over the top. Again, an in-depth, step-by-step procedure for creating these and other barre chords is offered in *Guitar For Dummies*, but I'll address the key points here.

The first step is to finger an open-position E form (see Chapter 2 for a detailed explanation, if you're a bit rusty). But instead of using your first three fingers, fret the chord with your 2nd, 3rd, and 4th fingers. This leaves your 1st finger free to barre.

Right now, the nut — that slotted bar between the headstock and the fretboard — is acting like a barre. You're going to move the whole chord up and take over the nut's job with your first finger.

1. **Slide all the fretted notes up (away from the headstock) exactly one fret.**

2. **Lay your index finger down in the first fret, across all six strings, parallel to the nut.**

3. **Minding the Barre Chord Creed, apply pressure and strum away.**

Congratulations. You are now playing an F barre chord (see Figure 4-6). And, in a manner of speaking, you are now the nut.

F

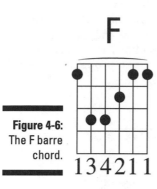

Figure 4-6:
The F barre
chord.

134211

Unless you're the type weakened only by kryptonite, you will have trouble getting the F chord to sound good and feel comfortable. In the beginning, playing an F chord will strain your hand, muffle the strings, and cause you to holler at various inanimate objects. This is normal.

Barre chords are harder to play in the first few frets, where the nut offers resistance, and way up the neck, where the action is higher and the frets are narrower. Once you can form the F chord immediately, without agonizing through the steps shown above, try moving your F chord to the 5th fret (where, by the way, it becomes an A chord). It should be easier to press the strings down here than at the 1st fret.

Moving the E-form barre chord around the neck

All barre chords are moveable chords — that's the beauty of 'em. Now that you've formed a barre chord (and can play it so that the strings, when strummed, ring through clearly), you're ready to move this sucker.

You've already had a glimpse of the thinking involved because you've moved power chords around the neck. (And some brave souls followed the advice in the last section to move the F chord up to the 5th fret.) Apply what you know about moving power chords to barre chords. The only difference is that you're moving *more* notes per chord.

To identify which chords you're playing on the neck as you move around, take the 6th-string shortcut. Because the lowest string of the guitar is called E, you can use the name of the notes on the 6th string to tell you where to play a given E-based form, just as we did with power chords. For example, the 5th fret of the E string is A, so the chord formed at the 5th fret using an E form is A. This shortcut enables guitarists to place chords on the fretboard by using the lowest note of the chord as the guide. The barre chord I've been calling "E-form" can also be called a 6th-string based chord. Unless something heavy has fallen on your head in the last few minutes, you probably remember 6th-string based chords from power chords, too.

Other E forms: Minor, dominant 7, minor 7, and 7sus

So far, we've built and moved only the E-major barre shape. As you know from open-position chords, there are chordal varieties other than major. Chords that are given simple letter names (E, B♭, D) are majors — all others are qualified (E minor, B♭ minor7, D7sus).

Here's where your hard labor on that first barre pays off. Having successfully wrangled the E-major barre-chord form, you can easily start adding other chord qualities. All of these forms can be played with small, easy changes to the E-major barre. And all of them correspond directly with open-position E chords you already know. You are about to be so very happy.

To make things even easier for yourself, try these new forms at the 3rd fret, where it starts getting more reasonable to finger chords *sans* buzz and rattle.

Using the 6th-string shortcut, you know that an E barre form played at the 3rd fret is a G chord. So if you play these forms in 3rd position, they'll all be G chords of one type or another. But pay attention to the shapes, which you'll move around, rather than the chords' letter names.

To change a G major into a G minor, lift your 2nd (middle) finger. Let the newly exposed note — 3rd string, 3rd fret — ring out with the rest of the barred notes. Yeah, that's all there is to it! Figure 4-7 shows a 3rd-position G minor barre chord.

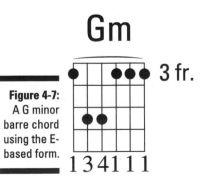

Figure 4-7: A G minor barre chord using the E-based form.

To change an G major into an G7 (also known as G dominant7), lift the 4th finger, as shown in Figure 4-8.

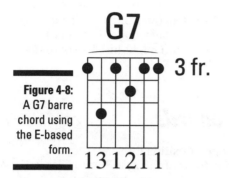

Figure 4-8:
A G7 barre chord using the E-based form.

To change an G major into an Gm7 (G minor7), lift the 2nd and 4th fingers, as shown in Figure 4-9.

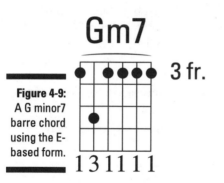

Figure 4-9:
A G minor7 barre chord using the E-based form.

To change an G major into an G7sus (where the 3rd degree is suspended, or raised a half step, to the 4th degree), lift the 2nd finger and move the 4th finger over to the 3rd string.

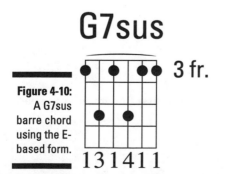

Figure 4-10:
A G7sus barre chord using the E-based form.

You've just learned four new chord forms — which, because they're applicable anywhere from 1st to 12th position, give you 48 new chords. Holy harmony. Go write a song, already.

Create your own exercise by moving these forms all over the neck. Then switch between forms as you move them around: Play a major chord in 1st position, a minor in 3rd, and a dominant7 in 8th. You might just trip onto the next "Freebird." We could use a new "Freebird."

Playing A-based barre chords

Just as the family of E-based barres have open-position E forms (they are simply open-position shapes with a barre in front of them), A-based barres have open-position A forms. To form these chords, apply the same logic used to get from an open-position E major chord to a 1st position F major barre. No need to reinvent the wheel — save your creativity for your playing or your excuses for practicing at 2 a.m.

To create an A-based barre chord (see Figure 4-11), grab a plain ol' open A major (check the Cheat Sheet if you need a refresher), but use fingers 2, 3, and 4, instead of 1, 2, and 3, and then follow these steps:

1. **Slide all the fretted notes up exactly one fret.**

2. **Lay your index finger down in the first fret, across the top five strings, parallel to the nut.**

3. **Minding the Barre Chord Creed, apply pressure and strum away.**

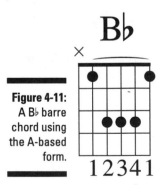

Figure 4-11:
A B♭ barre chord using the A-based form.

For A-based barre chords, the barre is shorter: Your first finger needs to span only the top five strings.

You don't have to barre all six strings for the A-based barre because its root is on the 5th string: it's a 5th-string based form. If your index finger does lay across the 6th string (which can be hard to avoid), be careful not to strum the 6th string with your right hand. You might want to let your index finger lay limply on that bottom string, which will help mute the sound if you strum it accidentally. Be careful, because the results can be horrific once you start moving the A-based barre chord around the neck. An open low E string against a 6th-fret E♭ major chord? Ick.

The hard part about this chord is pulling up the 3rd-finger knuckle so that the barred 1st string can sound. Because most guitarists find that to be too much trouble, they just end up playing the inner four strings (2 through 5) on the A major form. When they do this, they no longer have to make a barre out of the 1st finger — just the 3rd finger — which makes this a pretty easy chord to play. Try Figure 4-12, compare it with your success on the previous fingering, and choose which form works best for you.

Figure 4-12: The alternative way to finger an A-form barre chord.

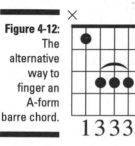

Astute players who are not yet blinded by pain may have spotted something familiar in the bottom strings of the A and E barre forms: power chords. All three lower strings of the A major and E major barres contain the same notes as their power-chord counterparts. Also, you might recall that power chords do not carry a chord's 3rd degree; in keeping, the bottom three strings of the A minor and E minor barre shapes are identical not only to their power-chord counterparts but to their major brethren. Wow. Full circle, dude.

Moving the A-form barre chord

Because you can play a B♭ chord as a barre chord, you can now play all 12 A-based major barre chords (the entire chromatic scale). All A-based chords are moveable and get their name from the 5th string (just as the open A chord does, and similar to how the E-chord form derives its name).

Figure 4-13 uses all A-based major barre chords. Say the names of the chords aloud as you play them at their corresponding frets. Trust me, all this naming is good for you. Listen to and play along with the CD to check your work. Don't worry about matching the strumming pattern you hear on the CD; just strum along at your own pace and switch between chords after every bar.

Figure 4-13:
A progression using A-based major barre chords.

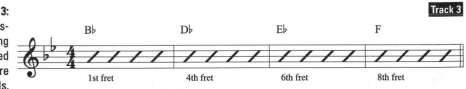

`Track 3`

A forms: Minor, dominant 7, minor 7, 7sus, and major 7

Everything you already know about moving chords around the neck carries over to these other barre-chord forms. Playing the minor, 7, or minor 7 versions is no more physically demanding than playing the major barre forms, it's just a matter of learning the fingering.

You can follow the numbered list in the section "Playing A-based barre chords" for creating the other versions of these A-based forms, or you can just try to form them after placing your 1st-finger barre over the appropriate fret and forming the chords from your remaining three fingers.

Figure 4-14 is a chart of five chord forms in A. The possible chord forms extend beyond these five, but these are the key chords for playing most rock music.

You can find barre forms that directly correspond with open-position chords. For example, the 5th-string based D minor played in 5th position has all the same notes (though some in different octaves) as the open-position D minor. Look over the Cheat Sheet chart for chords you can re-create in barre form, and listen for the similarities as you play them.

The number of chords you now can play up and down the neck is just plain incalculable (a fancy word for "too dang many"). You are a veritable font of chord knowledge. Dip into the fountain and enjoy this progression, which alternates between E- (6th-string) and A-based (5th-string) forms as the chords descend the neck. The changes in Figure 4-15 fit Bob Dylan's "Lay Lady Lay."

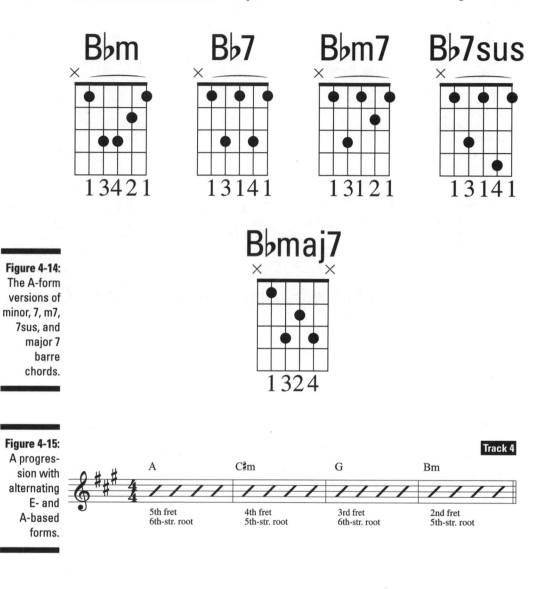

Figure 4-14:
The A-form versions of minor, 7, m7, 7sus, and major 7 barre chords.

Figure 4-15:
A progression with alternating E- and A-based forms.

Chapter 5

The Right Stuff: Right-Hand Rhythm Guitar Techniques

In This Chapter

▶ Strumming with your right hand

▶ Using your palm to mute and accent

▶ Exploring different rhythm feels

The right hand marshals the chords and notes you form in the left hand into the synchronized sounds you actually hear. The right hand is the engine that drives rhythm guitar, the fabric of the rock and roll rhythm section that weaves together the bass and drums and provides the underpinning for the singer, lead guitar, or other melodic instruments.

Whether it's playing in a steady eighth-note groove, a funky 16 feel, or a hard-swinging shuffle, the rhythm guitar and the right-hand strumming that propels it forge the chords and riffs you learn into a moving musical experience.

So in this chapter I show you all the ways you can strum the guitar to make the rhythm fit a bunch of different styles and feels. These variations help keep your music vital-sounding, and help you to develop your skills as a rhythm guitarist — one who provides the backing and the foundation to support the melody, and who can act as the glue between the other rhythm instruments such as the bass and drums.

Strumming Along

Strumming is defined as dragging a pick (or the fingers) across the strings of the guitar. In Chapter 4, you drag the pick in a downward motion (toward the floor) to sound the chords formed by the left hand, but don't try to do anything except sound the chords. In doing even that, however, you create rhythm.

If you "pick-drag" in regular, even strokes, one per beat, adhering to a tempo (musical rate), you're strumming the guitar in rhythm. And that's music, whether you mean it to be or not. More specifically, you're strumming a quarter-note rhythm, which is fine for songs such as the Beatles' "Let It Be," and other ballads. For the record, strumming an E chord in quarter notes looks like the notation in Figure 5-1. Note that I use rhythm slashes to show that you should play the entire chord, as opposed to note *heads* (which indicate only a single pitch).

Figure 5-1:
Playing an
E chord in
one bar of
four quarter
notes.

Track 5

The hardest part of learning rhythm guitar is realizing — and then maintaining — all the repetition involved. It's not what people expect when they pick up the guitar and want to learn a smorgasbord of cool licks and great riffs. But being able to play *in time* with unerring precision and rock-steady consistency is an essential skill and a hallmark of solid musicianship. Most rhythm playing in rock guitar involves a one- or two-bar pattern that gets repeated over and over, varying only where there are accent points that the band plays in unison.

After you learn to play consistently, you can then deviate from the established pattern you lay down and work on your own variations, as long as they're tasteful, appropriate, and not too numerous. Like a rock and roll rebel once said, "You have to know the rules before you can break them."

Downstrokes

A *downstroke* (indicated by the symbol ⊓ is the motion of dragging the pick toward the floor in a downward motion, brushing across multiple strings on the guitar in the process. Because you execute a downstroke quickly (even on slow songs) the separate strings are sounded virtually simultaneously. If you play three or more notes this way, you produce a chord.

Strumming in eighth-note downstrokes

To get out of the somewhat plodding rhythm of a quarter-note-only strumming pattern, you turn to eighth notes. As the math implies, an eighth note is one half the value of a quarter note, but in musical terms that equates to twice as fast, or more precisely, twice as frequently.

So instead of playing one strum per beat, you now play two strums per beat. This means you must move your hand twice as fast, striking the strings two times per beat, instead of once per beat as you did to produce quarter notes. At moderate and slower tempos, you can do this easily. For faster tempos you use alternating upstrokes and downstrokes (explained in the section on combining downstrokes and upstrokes later in this chapter). For playing the progression in Figure 5-1, however, simply using repeated downstrokes is easiest.

Figure 5-2 uses eighth notes for the first three beats of each bar and a quarter note for the last beat of each bar. The quarter note allows you a little more time to switch chords between the end of each bar and the beginning of the new bar. Isn't that humane?

Figure 5-2:
An eighth-note progression using right-hand down-strokes.

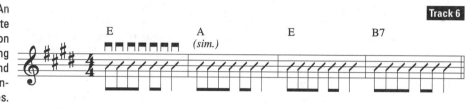

Track 6

The term *sim.* in the music notation tells you to continue in a similar fashion. It's typically used for articulation directions, such as down- and upstrokes.

Reading eighth-note notation

Notice that instead of the previously used slashes, you now resort to slashes with *stems* (the vertical lines coming down from the note head) and *beams* (the thicker horizontal lines that connect the stems). Quarter notes have single stems attached to them; eighth notes have stems with beams connecting them to each other. An eighth note by itself, or separated by a rest, will have a flag instead of a beam: ♪

Even though this newly introduced notation denotes specific rhythmic values (quarter notes, eighth notes), the note heads are still elongated and angled — not the same kind of smaller, rounded note heads used to indicate individual pitches. The symbols used in this chapter are still rhythm slashes that tell you *how* (in what rhythm) to play, but not exactly *what* (the individual pitches) to play. Your left-hand chord position determines the pitches. I discuss individual pitches and notation in Chapter 6.

Upstrokes

An upstroke (indicated by the symbol ⋁) is just what it sounds like: the opposite of a downstroke. Instead of dragging your pick down toward the floor, as you would in a downstroke, you start from a position below the strings and drag your pick upward across the strings. Doing this comfortably may seem a little less natural than playing a downstroke. One reason for this is that you're going against gravity. Also, some beginners have a hard time holding on to their pick or preventing it from getting stuck in the strings. With practice, however, you can flow with the ups as easily as you can with the downs.

You use upstrokes for the upbeats (offbeats) in eighth-note playing as the strokes in between the quarter-note beats.

When you start playing, don't worry about hitting all the strings in an upstroke. For example, when playing an E chord with an upstroke, you needn't strum the strings all the way through to the sixth string. Generally, in an upstroke, hitting just the top three or four strings is good enough. You may notice that your right hand naturally arcs away from the strings by that point, to an area above the center of the guitar. This is fine.

Upstrokes do not get equal time with their downwardly mobile counterparts. You typically use upstrokes only *in conjunction* with downstrokes. Whereas you can use downstrokes by themselves just fine — for entire songs, even — very rarely do you use upstrokes in isolation or without surrounding them on either side with downstrokes. (Some situations, such as the "Reggae rhythm" presented in Figure 5-21, do call for just upstrokes.)

So you should first tackle upstrokes in their most natural habitat: in an eighth-note rhythm figure where they provide the in-between notes, or *offbeats*, to the on-the-beat downstrokes.

Combining downstrokes and upstrokes

The easiest way to perform an upstroke smoothly is in its reciprocal response to a downstroke. Play Figure 5-3 with a relaxed, free-swinging up-and-down arm motion, working to get equal emphasis on each stroke, and being aware that your downstrokes will naturally include more (and lower) string-strikes than your upstrokes. The time signature is 4/4, which means the measures contain four beats, and each quarter note receives one beat.

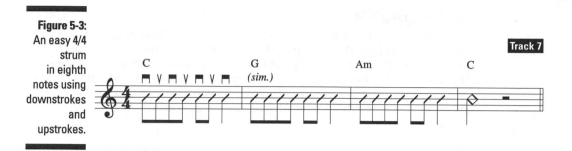

Figure 5-3:
An easy 4/4 strum in eighth notes using downstrokes and upstrokes.

At this easygoing tempo, you can probably play Figure 5-3 with all downstrokes. If you try that, however, you discover that it introduces a tenser, more-frantic motion in your own strumming motion, which is not in character with the song's mellow feel. Frantic motion can be a very good thing in rock, though. Figure 5-14, for example, shows you how an all-downstroke approach on a faster song is more appropriate than the easy back and forth of alternating downstrokes and upstrokes.

Whether an eighth-note pattern takes an all-downstroke approach versus a downstroke-upstroke approach is determined more by the feel, rather than the speed. (Although, it is physically easier to play eighth notes with alternating strokes.)

Playing a combination figure

Quarter notes and eighth notes make up much of medium-tempo-based music, so Figure 5-4 shows how a progression might use a mixture of quarters and eighths to help convey different rhythmic intensity levels in a song.

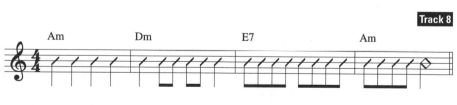

Figure 5-4:
Strumming in quarter notes and eighth notes to convey different levels of intensity.

Be aware that you not only have to control the strums in your down and up picking, but which strings you strike in each chord as well. Don't forget that you play only the top four strings in a D chord and only the top five in a C chord.

Strumming in 16ths

Sixteenth notes come twice as fast as eighth notes, or four to the beat. That can seem pretty twitchy, so 16th notes are almost always played with alternating downstrokes and upstrokes. Some punk and metal bands play fast 16th-note-based songs with all downstrokes, but their songs are usually about pain and masochism, so it's understandable, given the circumstances. The acoustic guitar part in the Who's "Pinball Wizard" is a classic example of 16th-note strumming.

I start off with a progression played at a medium tempo, using a common 16th-note figure. Figure 5-5 is based on an R&B progression and uses a repeated 16th-note scheme. I leave true *syncopation* (rhythms employing dots and ties) out of the picture until later in the chapter.

If the rhythmic notation seems like it's getting a little dense, don't worry too much about understanding the notation thoroughly or being able to play it at sight. What's important is to learn the figure, memorize it, and to play it correctly and with confidence. Listening to the CD repeatedly to learn this figure is okay, too. (Just don't tell your fourth-grade piano teacher I told you it was okay to memorize the recorded sound and not to read the music!)

Track 9

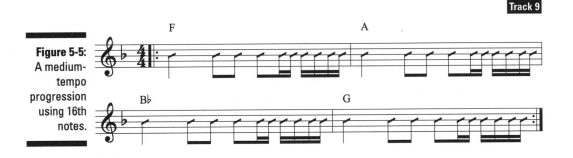

Figure 5-5:
A medium-tempo progression using 16th notes.

Reading 16th-note notation

Sixteenth notes are indicated with two beams connecting their stems (or if they're by themselves, two *flags* ♬).

Getting a shuffle feel

An important rhythm feel used extensively in rock is the *shuffle*. A shuffle is a lilting eighth-note sound where the beat is divided into two unbalanced halves, a long note followed by a short. Think of the riffs to such songs as Elvis Presley's "Hound Dog," the Beach Boys' "California Girls," Fleetwood Mac's "Don't Stop Thinking About Tomorrow," and the Grateful Dead's "Truckin'." These are all based on a shuffle feel.

The shuffle is formed from triplets, where the beat is first subdivided into three equal parts. Then the first two notes are held together.

Rather than thinking about it too much, try this simple exercise, which can help you hear the difference between straight eighth notes (equally spaced) and triplet eighth notes (the first held twice as long as the second):

1. **Tap your foot in a steady beat and say the following line, matching the bold syllables to your foot taps:**

   Twink-le **twink**-le **lit**-tle star.

   That's the sound of normal, equally spaced, straight eighth notes.

2. **Now in the same tempo (that is, keeping your foot tap constant), try saying this line, based in triplets:**

   Fol-low the **yel**-low brick **road**.

   That's the sound of triplets. In both cases you should keep your foot tap at exactly the same tempo and change only how you subdivide the beat internally.

3. **Create shuffle eighth notes by sounding only the first and third notes of the triplet.** You do this by sustaining the first note through the second or by leaving out that second note entirely. The new sound is a limping, uneven division that goes *l-o-n-g-short, l-o-n-g-short, l-o-n-g-short,* and so forth.

   A good way to remember the sound of triplet eighth notes (the basis of a shuffle feel) is the song "When Johnny Comes Marching Home Again." If you tap your foot or snap your fingers on the beat and then try saying the lyrics in rhythm, you get:

   When **John**-ny comes **march**-ing **home** a-**gain**, hur-**rah**

   The bold type represents the beat, where the syllables coincide with your foot tap or finger snap. The phrase "Johnny comes" is in triplets, because each syllable falls on one note of the three in between two beats. The rest of the phrase, "marching home again, hurrah" divides each beat into two-syllable pairs, the first syllable longer than the second. This is the sound of eighth notes in a shuffle feel.

Figure 5-6 is a shuffle feel that uses downstrokes and upstrokes. To reward you for saying "twinkle, twinkle little star" out loud while you tapped your foot, I'm going to give you three new bonus chords that are easy to play and will give your shuffle progression a real lift.

Actually, the chords aren't so much new as they are a one-finger variation of chords you already play. These new "chords" are easily executed by moving one and only one finger, while keeping the others anchored. It's the first step to getting both hands moving on the guitar, a really exciting accomplishment that makes you feel like a real guitar player. Have fun with this one!

The upstrokes still come at the in-between points — within the beats — but because of the unequal rhythm, it may take you a little time to adjust.

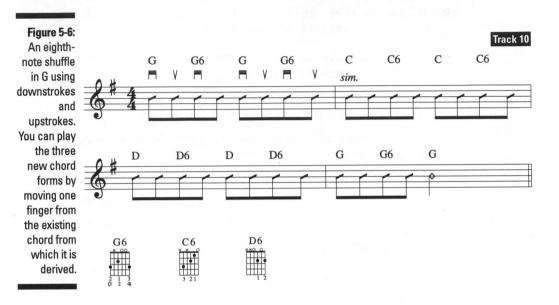

Figure 5-6: An eighth-note shuffle in G using downstrokes and upstrokes. You can play the three new chord forms by moving one finger from the existing chord from which it is derived.

Mixing Single Notes and Strums

Rhythm guitar includes many more approaches than just simultaneously strumming the multiple strings of a chord. A piano player doesn't plunk down all her fingers at once every time she plays an accompaniment part, and guitarists shouldn't have to strike all the strings every time they bring their pick down.

In fact, speaking of pianists, guitarists borrow a technique from their keyboard-plunking counterparts, who separate the left and right hands to play bass notes and chords, respectively. When guitarists separate out the components of a chord, they don't use separate hands, but combine both aspects in their right hand. Playing bass notes with chords is called a *pick-strum* pattern.

The pick-strum

Separating the bass and treble so that they play independently in time is a great way to provide rhythmic variety and introduce different chordal textures. Guitarists can even set up an interplay of the different parts — a bass and treble complementarity or counterpoint.

Dividing up a band's songs by straight eighths or shuffle feel

If you've never thought of songs by your favorite band as being in a straight-eighth feel or a shuffle feel, it's fun to go down their hits and see in which category their individual songs belong. Here's how some of the Beach Boys' and the Beatles' hits break down:

The Beach Boys

Straight Eighth	Shuffle
Surfin' USA	Good Vibrations
Surfin' Safari	Barbara Ann
Kokomo	California Girls
I Get Around	Wouldn't It Be Nice
Fun, Fun, Fun	Help Me Rhonda

The Beatles

Straight Eighth	Shuffle
Hard Day's Night	Can't Buy Me Love
I Want to Hold You Hand	Love Me Do
I Saw Her Standing There	Revolution
Yesterday	Got to Get You into My Life
Twist and Shout	Penny Lane

Boom-chick

The simplest accompaniment pattern is known by the way it sounds: *boom-chick*. The boom-chick pattern is very efficient because you don't have to play all the notes of the chord at once. Typically you play the bass note on the *boom*, and the all the notes in the chord except the bass note on the *chick* — but you get sonic credit for playing twice.

Figure 5-7 shows a boom-chick, or bass-chord pattern in a bouncy country-rock progression.

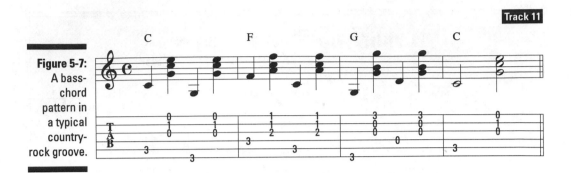

Figure 5-7:
A bass-
chord
pattern in
a typical
country-
rock groove.

Track 11

The symbol *C* immediately to the right of the treble clef of Figure 5-7 is a shorthand way to indicate 4/4 time. The examples in this book use *4/4* to indicate music in 4/4 time, but many examples of printed sheet music use *C* to indicate *common*, or 4/4, time.

Separating the bass notes from the treble chord forms is also useful for creating a more dynamic and interesting rhythm sound in a straight-ahead rock groove, like Figure 5-8, which is in a funky, Led Zeppelin-type of feel.

Figure 5-8:
The bass-
note-and-
chord
treatment
provides
a more
varied and
interesting
treatment of
chords than
does a
straight
strum.

Track 12

Moving bass line

An important musical device available to you after you separate the bass from the chord is the moving bass line. Examples of songs with moving bass lines include Neil Young's "Southern Man," Led Zeppelin's "Babe, I'm Gonna Leave You," the Grateful Dead's "Friend of the Devil," and the Nitty Gritty Dirt Band's "Mr. Bojangles." A moving bass line can employ the boom-chick pattern.

Figure 5-9 shows a descending bass line, made even more effective by isolating the bass line from the chords. Although this is left-hand movement within a chord form, similar to the shuffle figure in Figure 5-6, you can think of this as new chord forms entirely, if that's conceptually easier for you.

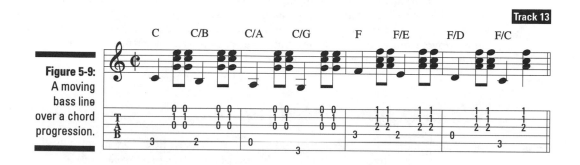

Track 13

Figure 5-9: A moving bass line over a chord progression.

When a chord symbol features two letters separated by a forward slash, it indicates the chord and the bass note over which that chord sounds. For example, C/G is a C chord with a G in the bass. In this case, the bass note is a chord member (the notes of a C chord are C, E, and G), but it doesn't always have to be that way. In the chord progression C-C/B-C/A, the bass notes B and A are not part of the chord but help to provide motion to another chord.

Disrupting Your Sound: Syncopated Strumming

After you develop a feel for strumming in different combinations of eighths, quarters, and 16ths, you can increase the rhythmic variation to these various groupings by applying syncopation. *Syncopation* is the disruption or alteration of the expected sounding of notes. In rock and roll right-hand rhythm playing, you do that by staggering your strum and mixing up your up- and downstrokes to strike different parts of the beats. By doing so, you let the vehicles of syncopation — dots and ties — steer your rhythmic strumming to a more driving and interesting course.

Syncopated notation: Dots and ties

A dot attached to a note increases its rhythmic value by half its original value. A dot attached to a half note (two beats) makes it three beats long. A dotted quarter note is one and a half beats long, or, a quarter note plus an eighth note.

A tie is a curved line that connects two notes of the same pitch. The value of the note is the combined values of the two notes together, and only the first note is sounded.

Figure 5-10 shows some common syncopation figures employing dots and ties. The top part of the table deals with dots and shows note values, their new value with a dot and the equivalent expressed in ties, and a typical figure using a dot with that note value. The bottom part of the table deals with ties and shows note values, their new value when tied to another note, and a typical figure using a tie with that note value.

Playing syncopated figures

So much for the music theory behind syncopation. Now how do you actually play syncopated figures? Try jumping in and playing two progressions, one using eighth notes and one using 16th notes, that employ common syncopation patterns found in rock.

Figure 5-11 shows a useful syncopation scheme for an easy 4/4 rhythm at a moderate tempo. Pay close attention to the downstroke (⊓) and upstroke (∨) indications. Because the normal flow of down- and upstrokes is interrupted in syncopation, it's important to remember which stroke direction to play a note to avoid getting your strums out of synch.

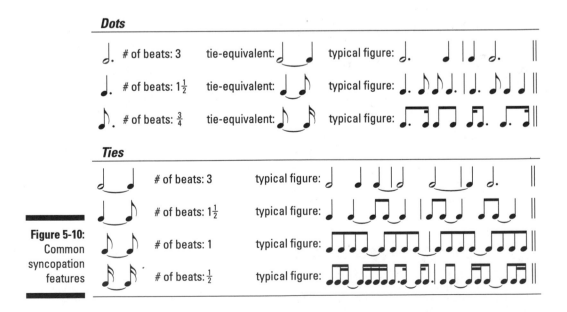

Figure 5-10:
Common syncopation features

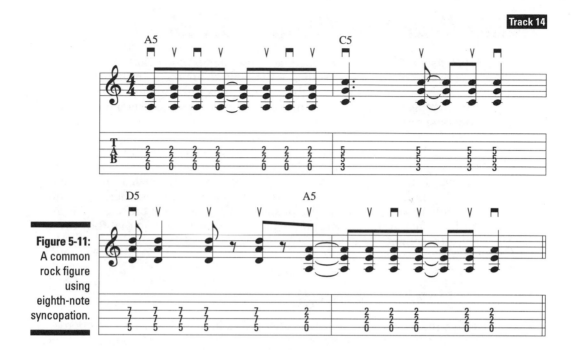

Figure 5-11:
A common
rock figure
using
eighth-note
syncopation.

Figure 5-12, which uses eighth- as well as 16th-note syncopation, is not particularly difficult to play after you can hear the sound in your head. If it helps, listen to Figure 5-12 on the CD first to get the rhythm memorized in your head before attempting to play it on the guitar.

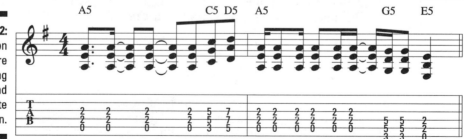

Figure 5-12:
A common
rock figure
using
eighth- and
16th-note
syncopation.

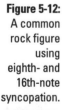

If you're having trouble playing the figures exactly, or you can't quite anticipate where the next strike comes after the dot or tie, try simply saying the rhythm of the figure on the syllable *dah* while tapping your foot or snapping your fingers. The best way to learn a figure is to internalize it and then — and only then — worry about getting your hands to execute what's in your head.

Giving Your Left Hand a Break

If you listen closely to rhythm guitar in rock songs, you hear that strummed figures are not one wall of sound — that minute breaks occur in between the strums. These breaks prevent the chord strums from running into each other and creating sonic mush. The little gaps in sound keep a strumming figure sounding crisp and controlled.

To form these breaks, or slight sonic pauses, you need to stop the strings from ringing momentarily. And I'm talking very *small* moments here — much smaller than those pauses on a greeting card commercial when the daughter realizes she's just like her mother as they sip cocoa and look out the window. Controlling the right hand's gas pedal with the left hand's brake pedal is a useful technique for cutting off the ring-out of the strings so that they don't all run together.

Left-hand muting

To get the left-hand to mute the in-between sound between any two chords, just relax the fretting fingers enough to release pressure on the fretted strings. These strings will instantly deaden, or muffle, cutting off sound. What's more, if you keep your right-hand going along in the same strumming pattern, you produce a satisfying *thunk* sound as the right hand hits all these deadened strings. This percussive element, intermixed among the ringing notes creates an ideal rock rhythm sound: part percussive, part syncopated, and all the while driving. If you relax the left hand even further so that it goes limp across all six strings, then no strings will sound, not just the ones the left hand fingers cover. Also, allowing your left-hand to do the muting means you can keep your right hand going, uninterrupted, in alternating down- and upstrokes. The notation indicates a left-hand mute with an *X* note head.

Implying syncopation

Figure 5-13 is technically a straight-ahead down-and-up eighth-note strum in the right hand. But because you employ left-hand muting, the sound seems to cut off in the just the right places, creating an almost syncopated sound. Your right hand isn't performing true syncopation, because it's playing straight through. It's just that some of the notes don't come through audibly. More than creating a syncopated sound, however, left-hand muting provides the guitarist with another means for controlling the strings' sound.

Left-hand muting is one of those rhythm techniques that guitarists just seem to develop naturally, almost as if it weren't a technique you *had* to learn because you'd invent it anyway, so obvious and useful is its benefit. And like riding a bicycle, left-hand muting is more difficult to execute slowly. So don't analyze it too much as you're learning; just strum and mute in the context of a medium-tempo groove. Your hands will magically synch up and you won't even have to think about it.

Although left-hand muting belongs to the hand not named in this chapter, its impetus is drawn from the right hand motion. Plus, performing a left-hand mute is impossible without another hand to turn it into sound.

Figure 5-13:
A straight-eighth-note strum employing left-hand muting to simulate syncopation.

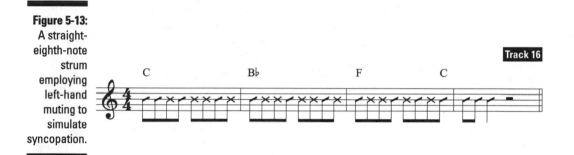

Track 16

Suppressing the Right Hand

You can also mute with your *right* hand (using the heel of the palm), but this produces a different effect than I discuss in the preceding section on left-hand muting. In right-hand muting you still hear the sound of the fretted string, but in a muted and subdued way. You don't use right-hand muting to stop the sound completely, as you do in a left-hand mute; you just want to suppress the string from ringing freely. Like left-hand muting, right-hand muting keeps your tone from experiencing runaway ring-out, but additionally it provides an almost murky, smoldering sound to the notes, which can be quite useful for dramatic effect. You sometimes hear this technique referred to as *chugging*.

Right-hand muting

You perform a right-hand mute by anchoring the heel of your right hand on the strings just above the bridge. Don't place your hand too far forward or you'll completely deaden the strings. Do it just enough so that the strings are dampened (*damping* is a musical term which means to externally stop a string from ringing) slightly, but still ring through. Keep it there through the duration of the strum.

If a *palm mute* (as right-hand muting is known) de-emphasizes a string strike, then its evil twin, the *accent*, draws attention to a string strike. An accent is easy to execute: Just strike the string or strings harder than usual, and lift your right hand palm from the strings as you do, to allow the strings to ring free. The result is that the accented strum stands out above all the rest. An accent is indicated with a > just above or below the note head.

Palm mutes are much easier to perform if only one or two of the strings are struck, due to the restricted movement of the right hand caused by anchoring it to the strings' surface above the bridge. Figure 5-14 is a rhythm figure where you strike only the lowest note of the chord on the palm mutes, and the upper strings on the accents. Play this progression using all downstrokes to add intensity.

Figure 5-14:
A rhythm figure with palm mutes and accents. Strike only the lowest note of the chord when a *P.M.* (palm mute) appears.

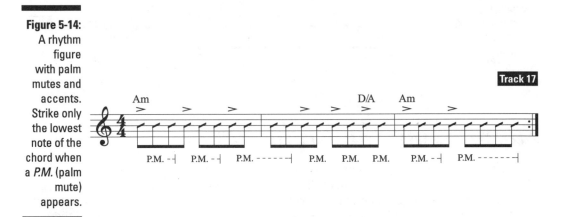

The interplay between the palm muted notes and the accented chords creates a sound that makes it seem like two instruments playing.

Breaking Out of the Chord Box: Left-hand Movement within a Right-hand Strum

In this chapter I deal mostly with right-hand movement using static left-hand chord forms. When you begin to move the left-hand in conjunction with the right, you uncover an exciting new dimension in rhythm guitar: left-hand movement simultaneous with right-hand rhythm. (It's what I flirted with in Figure 5-6, but I'm now going to explore it fully.) This "liberating of the left hand" is also the first step in playing single-note riffs and leads on the guitar, which I get to in Chapter 6.

Figure 5-15 features a classic left-hand figure that fits either a straight-eighth-note groove or a shuffle feel (although it's placed here in a straight-eighth setting). The changing notes in this example are the 5th degrees of each chord, which move momentarily to the 6th degree. So in an A chord, the E moves to F♯; in a D chord the A moves to B; and in an E chord the B moves to C♯.

This pattern is known by various names, but I refer to it as the "5-6 move." (Clever, eh?) You can find it in songs by Chuck Berry, the Beatles, ZZ Top, and plenty of blues-rock tunes. The 5-6 move fits over any I-IV-V progression, but I've put it here in the key of A.

Note that to more easily accommodate the 5-6 move, I've supplied alternate chords and fingering to satisfy the A, D, and E chords. In each case the chords use only three strings, all adjacent to each other.

And even though it's in steady eighth notes, this progression should be played using all right-hand downstrokes. If you can throw in some palm muting (as is done on the CD), so much the better!

Track 18

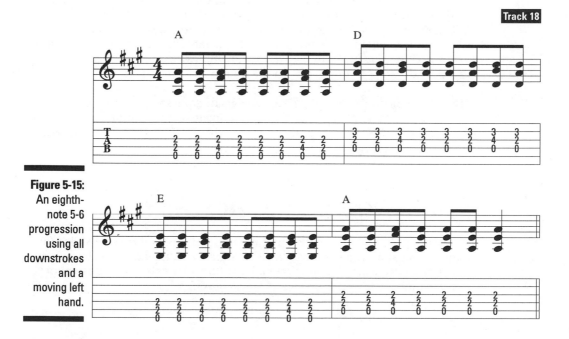

Figure 5-15:
An eighth-note 5-6 progression using all downstrokes and a moving left hand.

Giving Your Fingers Some Style

Although more than 99 percent of all rock playing is played with a pick, occasions for *fingerstyle* do pop up from time to time. Fingerstyle, as the name implies, means that you pluck the strings with the right-hand fingertips. For these times you can put the pick down, stick it between your teeth, or tuck it in your palm, whichever allows you to grab it the fastest after the fingerstyle passage is over.

Fingerstyle is especially suited to playing *arpeggios,* or chords played one note at a time in a given pattern. Fingerstyle is a much more facile way to play different strings in rapid succession, as you must do for arpeggiated passages. Generally speaking, the thumb plays the bass strings and the fingers play the upper three strings. Think of the opening figure to Kansas's "Dust in the Wind," Fleetwood Mac's "Landslide," or Simon and Garfunkel's "The Boxer," and imagine trying to play those patterns with your pick hopping frantically around the strings.

Position your right hand just above the strings, so your fingers can dangle freely but in reach of the individual strings. In Figure 5-16, the thumb plays the downstem notes and the right-hand fingers play the upper notes. (For you classical guitar aficionados out there: The standard way to notate the right-hand fingers is with the letters *p*, *i*, *m*, and *a,* for the Spanish words for the thumb, index, middle and ring fingers.) In the example here, you don't need to be that careful about which fingers play which strings, so I don't indicate any left-hand fingerings. But a good way to approach Figure 5-16 is to use the index finger to play the 3rd string, the middle finger to play the 2nd string, and the ring finger to play the 1st string. Work for an even attack in the fingers and a smooth flow between the thumb and the fingers.

Of course, you don't *have* to play an arpeggiated passage fingerstyle, if it's slow and there's relatively little string skipping involved. But for longer passages, or if the tempo is fairly rapid and the string skipping is relentless, work out the passage as a fingerstyle exercise.

Getting Into Rhythm Styles

To close out this chapter and your study of the right-hand rhythm styles (and some left-hand movement that I sneaked in here), this section tackles some song-length exercises that illustrate many of the characteristics, both chordal and rhythmic, of standard grooves or feels in rock music.

Figure 5-16: Fingerstyle arpeggios played with the right-hand thumb, index, middle, and ring fingers.

On your CD, you can hear that these exercises are more "produced" than the other exercises in this chapter. They are fleshed out with bass, drums, keyboard "pads" (sustained chords), and some melodic figures to help you memorize the sequences — and to have more fun playing them! Work to learn the patterns exactly as written, but then feel free to try your own rhythmic variations. And did I mention to have fun?

Rhythm section players often talk to each other in terms of feel, and standard terms have developed to describe some of the more common rhythmic accompaniment styles.

Table 5-1 provides a list of different feels by their popular name, what time signature they're in, what their characteristics are, and some classic tunes that illustrate that feel.

Table 5-1	Classic Songs in a Variety of Grooves		
Name	**Time Signature**	**Characteristic**	**Tunes**
Straight-four	4/4	Easy, laid-back feel	Tom Petty: "Won't Back Down," Eagles: "New Kid in Town," The Beatles: "Hard Day's Night"
Heavy back-beat	4/4	Like straight-four, but with a heavier back-beat (accent on beats 2 and 4)	Bachman Turner Overdrive: "Taking Care of Business," Bob Seger: "Old Time Rock and Roll," Spencer Davis/Blues Brothers: "Gimme Some Lovin'"
Two-beat	¢, 2/2, or 2/4	jumping boom-chick	Creedence Clearwater Revival: "Bad Moon Rising," The Beatles: "I Feel Fine," Pure Prairie League: "Amie"
16-feel	4/4	Funky or busy accompaniment	James Brown: "I Feel Good," Sam and Dave/Blues Brothers: "Soul Man," Aerosmith: "Walk This Way"
Metal gallop	4/4	Driving 16th-note sound like a horse's gallop	Metallica: "Blackened," Led Zeppelin: "The Immigrant Song"
Shuffle	4/4	Limping, lilting eighth notes; swing feel	Fleetwod Mac: "Don't Stop," ZZ Top: "La Grange" and "Tush," The Beatles: "Can't Buy Me Love" and "Revolution"

Name	Time Signature	Characteristic	Tunes
Three-feel	3/4, 6/8, 12/8	Meter felt in groups of three	The Eagles: "Take It to the Limit," The Beatles: "Norwegian Wood" (6/8) and "You've Got to Hide Your Love Away" (6/8)
Reggae/ska	4/4	Laid back with syncopation	Eric Clapton: "I Shot the Sheriff," Bob Marley: "No Woman, No Cry," Johnny Nash: "Stir It Up"

Straight-four feel

Figure 5-17 is an easy, laid-back straight-eighth-note groove in 4/4. It's perfect for songs in the style of the Eagles, Tom Petty, and soft-rock ballads or medium-tempo songs. When you get the rhythm down, try varying the speed of your strum by making the quarter-note strums a little slower and more drawn out than the eighth-note strums. This will give your strings a nice *k-e-r-r-r-a-n-g* sound.

`Track 20`

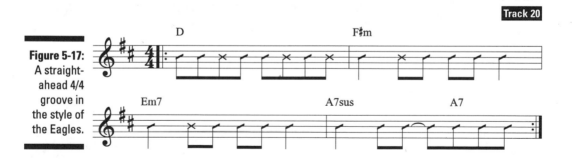

Figure 5-17: A straight-ahead 4/4 groove in the style of the Eagles.

Two-beat feel

Figure 5-18 is in a cut-time, or two-beat, feel using a boom-chick or pick-strum pattern. *Cut time* refers to the time signature, where a vertical line "cuts" the

C, the shorthand symbol for 4/4, in half. A two-beat feel features a heavy bass on the first and third beats, and chord fills on beats two and four. I throw in bass runs (single bass notes that connect chords together) for some extra left-hand movement.

16-feel

The "16" in the title refers to 16th notes. In a 16-feel groove, the unit of subdivision is the 16th note, and its spirited activity here creates a funky feel (see Figure 5-19). You can play many songs in a 16-feel with the pick-strum approach, where individual bass notes are pitted against chordal figures in a low-high dialog.

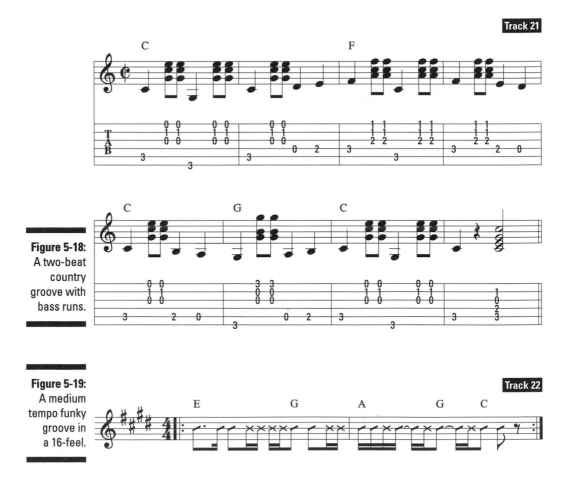

Figure 5-18: A two-beat country groove with bass runs.

Figure 5-19: A medium tempo funky groove in a 16-feel.

Track 21

Track 22

Heavy metal gallop

Heavy metal is an entire subculture in rock music, but it can claim as its own one unique accompaniment figure: the gallop, which is composed of an eighth note followed by two 16ths, repeated over and over. Figure 5-20 shows a two-bar gallop figure using up- and downstrokes. The palm mutes and accents make this passage sound almost ominous — a desired quality in heavy metal rhythm playing.

Figure 5-20:
A heavy metal gallop using eighths and 16ths.

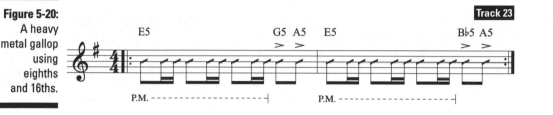

Reggae rhythm

Reggae is a wonderfully laid-back rhythm style that features sparse chordal jabs from the guitar delivered on the offbeat. Reggae can exist either in a straight-eighth or shuffle feel, but I put it here in a medium-slow shuffle, in Figure 5-21. Pay particular attention to the upstroke indications — several of them occur in a row, resulting from the successive offbeat strums.

Figure 5-21:
A typical Reggae backup pattern highlighting the offbeats. Note the successive upstrokes.

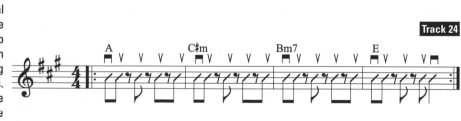

Three feel

A song in a three feel is pretty easy to spot — it's counted in groups of three (not the usual two and four), and you can do the waltz to it. If you played hooky from ballroom dancing lessons as a kid and don't know how to waltz, you can usually hear a strong beat one, followed by the weaker beats two and three. The Eagles' "Take It to the Limit" is in 3/4, and the Beatles' "Norwegian Wood" is in 6/8. Technically, a song in 6/8 is felt in two, because it's separated into two halves each receiving three eighth notes. But in the unfussy world of rock rhythm, anytime a guitarist has to strum in three — whether it's in 3/4 or whether it's in 6/8 or 12/8 (as in some doo-wop-type songs), he just calls it a "three feel." So "Norwegian Wood" and "House of the Rising Sun," which are in 6/8, and "You Really Got a Hold on Me" and "Nights in White Satin,' which are in 12/8, can be described as "three feel" songs. You can either strum in groups of three or go *boom-chick-chick*, depending on the tempo (it's sometimes easier on faster tempos to go *boom-chick-chick*).

Figure 5-22 is written in 3/4, and features a descending bass line, which is fairly common in songs in three.

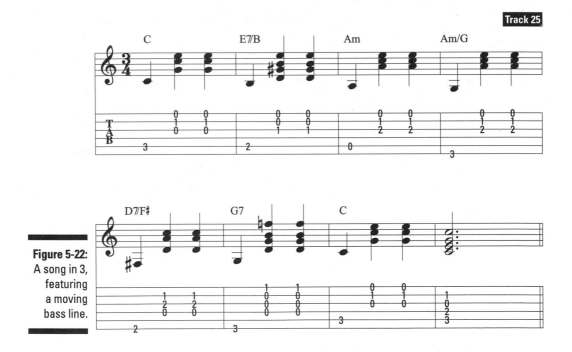

Track 25

Figure 5-22:
A song in 3, featuring a moving bass line.

Chapter 6

The Leading Edge: Introduction to Lead Rock Guitar

● ●

In This Chapter

▶ Learning scales, arpeggios, and lead patterns

▶ Reading notation

▶ Practicing riffs

▶ Improvising good solos

● ●

*L*ead guitar is the most spectacular and dazzling feature of rock guitar playing. Lead guitar can embody emotions that run the gamut from mournful and soulful to screaming, frenzied abandon — sometimes in the same solo. Whereas riffs are grounded, composed, and can manifest their power through their unflinching solidity, lead is beckoned by the music to launch into divinely inspired flights of fancy, to be forever soaring.

The greatest lead guitarists, from Eric Clapton and Jimi Hendrix to Eddie Van Halen and Steve Vai, have all been able to soar, but they have also all been disciplined masters of their instruments. They have resolved the ultimate artistic paradox: total freedom through total control.

As you begin developing the basic technique for playing lead, never forget that your playing possesses the potential for evoking enormous emotional power. And kick over a few amplifiers while you're at it too!

Left-hand movement and precise single-string picking are the focus in this chapter. I also tell you just what makes it worth all this effort.

Taking the Lead

You must play many before you can play one, grasshopper.

This saying of unknown but vaguely Eastern origin certainly applies to rock guitar playing, because you need to learn to play chords (note groupings of at least three notes) before you can learn single-notes — the stuff of leads.

Actually, you don't *have* to learn chords before lead, but in rock guitar it's a good idea, at least from a technical standpoint, because when playing rhythm you don't have to be as precise with your right-hand motions. Most beginning guitarists find striking multiple strings easier than plucking individual ones.

Now, however, the time has come to venture into the world of single-note playing, where you pick only one string at a time, and which string you play is critical. Single-note playing also involves a lot more movement from the left hand.

Single-note playing provides a variety of musical devices. Four of the most important ones for playing rock include:

- **Melody:** A major component of single-note playing on the guitar is melody. Melody can be the composed tune of the song played instrumentally, or it can be an improvised break or solo, using the melody as the point of departure.

- **Arpeggio:** An arpeggio is playing a chord one note at a time, so, by definition, it's a single-note technique. You can use arpeggios as an accompaniment figure (as you did in the fingerstyle example in Chapter 5) or as lead material, as many hard rock and heavy metal guitarists, such as Eddie Van Halen and Randy Rhoads have done. Lead guitarists burn up many a measure just by playing arpeggios in their lead breaks, and the results can be thrilling.

- **Riff:** A riff is a self-contained musical phrase, usually composed of single notes and used as a structural component of a song or song section. A riff straddles the line between melody and rhythm guitar, because it contains elements of both. A riff is typically repeated multiple times and serves as a backing figure for a song section.

Think of the signature riffs to the Beatles' "Day Tripper" and "Birthday," the Rolling Stones' "Satisfaction," Aerosmith's "Walk This Way," Cream's "Sunshine of Your Love," Led Zeppelin's "Whole Lotta Love" and "Black Dog," Ozzy Osbourne's "Crazy Train," and Bon Jovi's "You Give Love a Bad Name." These are all songs based on highly identifiable and memorable riffs.

Riffs aren't always composed of just single notes. Deep Purple's "Smoke on the Water" and Black Sabbath's "Iron Man" are actually composed of multiple-sounding notes moving in unison. And two or more guitars can play riffs in harmony too. The Allman Bros. and the Eagles are famous for this.

✔ **Free improvisation:** This isn't a recognized technical term, but a descriptive phrase of any lead material not necessarily derived from the melody. Free improvisation doesn't even have to be melodic in nature. Wide interval skips, percussive playing, effects used as music, and melodic note sequences (such as patterns of fast repeated notes, or even one note) can all contribute to an exciting lead guitar solo or passage.

The terms *lead, melody, single line, riff, solo,* and *improv* are all types of single-note playing and are often used interchangeably. The phrase "single-note playing" is a little cumbersome, so you can refer to any playing that is not rhythm playing as lead playing, even if it's to indicate playing a riff.

Strictly speaking, lead playing is the *featured* guitar, which is usually playing a single-note-based line. But it doesn't always have to be playing only single notes; it could be playing *double-stops,* which are two notes played together. Also, the designation *lead guitar* helps to distinguish that guitar from the other guitar(s) in the band playing rhythm guitar.

Sometimes the featured guitar can consist of a strummed chordal figure. The guitar break in Buddy Holly's "Peggy Sue" and the opening riff to the Who's "Pinball Wizard" are two standout examples of the rhythm guitar taking a featured role.

Holding the Pick

You don't need to hold the pick any differently for lead playing than you do for rhythm playing. Have the tip of the pick extending perpendicularly from the side of your thumb, and bring your hand close to the individual string you want to play. Refer to Figure 2-6 to see the recommended way to hold a pick.

You may find yourself gripping the pick a little more firmly, especially when you dig in to play loudly or aggressively. This is fine. In time, the pick becomes almost like a natural extension of one of your fingers.

Attacking the Problem

The sounding or striking of a note, in musical terms, is called an *attack*. It doesn't necessarily mean you have to do it aggressively, it's just a term that differentiates the beginning of the note from the sustain part (the part that rings, after the percussive sound).

To attack an individual string, position the pick so that it touches or is slightly above the string's upper side (the side toward the ceiling) and bring it through with a quick, smooth motion. Use just enough force to clear the string, but not enough to sound the next string down.

The yin and yang of rhythm and lead

If a band has two guitarists, a logical division of duties is to have one guitarist play rhythm and the other play lead. Often, the better guitarist will be the lead guitarist. Sometimes, however, dividing the duties this way is not necessarily for reasons of musical talent, but because the rhythm guitarist is the principal songwriter (as in the case of Tom Petty and Metallica). And in many bands with two guitarists, the divisions of lead and rhythm are not clearly defined, as in the case of Lynyrd Skynyrd, the Allman Bros., and Judas Priest. In the following list, however, the duties between lead and rhythm are clearly separated.

Group	Rhythm	Lead
Beatles	John Lennon	George Harrison
The Rolling Stones	Keith Richards	Brian Jones/ Mick Taylor/ Ron Wood
The Kinks	Ray Davies	Dave Davies
Grateful Dead	Bob Weir	Jerry Garcia
AC/DC	Malcolm Young	Angus Young
Creedence Clearwater Revival	Tom Fogerty	John Fogerty
Aerosmith	Brad Whitford	Joe Perry
Kiss	Paul Stanley	Ace Frehley
Tom Petty	Tom Petty	Mike Campbell
The Cars	Ric Ocasek	Elliot Easton
The Clash	Joe Strummer	Mick Jones
Def Leppard	Steve Clark	Phil Collen
Bruce Springsteen	Bruce Springsteen	Nils Lofgren
Metallica	James Hetfield	Kirk Hammett
Guns N' Roses	Izzy Stradlin	Slash

This motion is known as a downstroke, which is just like the downstroke I discuss in Chapter 5, except that here you strike only one string. To play an upstroke, simply reverse the motion.

Striking the Downs and Ups of Lead Playing

Striking a string with a downward motion (toward the floor) is called a *downstroke* and is indicated by the symbol ⊓. Striking the string by bringing the hand up is called an *upstroke* and is indicated by the symbol ∨. In rock guitar, rhythm guitarists tend to favor downstrokes. Downstrokes are more forceful and are generally used to accentuate notes to play even, deliberate rhythms. Alternating downstrokes and upstrokes is called *alternate picking* (covered later in this chapter) and is essential for playing lead guitar.

Playing Single Notes

Playing chords involves a lot of arm and wrist movement. Single-note playing requires much less arm movement, because most of the energy comes from the wrist. You may be tempted to anchor the heel of the right hand on the bridge, which is okay, as long as you don't unintentionally dampen the strings in the process.

As you move from playing notes on the lower strings to notes on the higher strings, your right-hand heel will naturally want to adjust itself and slide along the bridge. Of course, you don't *have* to anchor your hand on the strings at all, either; you can just let your hand float roughly in the area above the bridge.

Even when you play loud and aggressively, your right-hand movements should remain fairly controlled and contained. When you see your favorite rock stars on stage flailing away, arms wildly windmilling in circular motions of large diameters, that's rhythm playing, not single note playing.

I start you out with some easy exercises for learning to play single notes on the guitar. Then I move to things that actually sound cool and are fun to play.

Single-note technique

Using all downstrokes, play the music in Figure 6-1. These are six passages, each on separate strings that require you to play three different notes. All the melodies are in quarter notes, which means the notes come one per beat (or one per foot tap if you're tapping along in tempo).

The trick here is to play single notes on individual strings accurately, without accidentally hitting the wrong string. You don't have to play any fancy rhythms or down- and upstroke combinations, you just have to hit the desired string cleanly. Obviously, it's harder to do that on the interior strings (2nd, 3rd, 4th, 5th) than on exterior ones (1st, 6th).

TIP Try playing the music by yourself (without the aid of the CD), counting (and tapping) out a bar of tempo before you begin to play. After you think you've mastered the exercise and can play it without stopping or making a mistake, try playing it along with the CD.

TIP Each exercise is written in a different feel (as evidenced by the CD recording), but don't let that throw you. As long as you count out the quarter notes with the count-off on the CD (heard as the percussive click of the struck hi-hat cymbals, as a drummer would do when counting off a song) and focus on playing smooth, one-note-per-foot-tap notes, you should do fine.

Track 26, 0:00

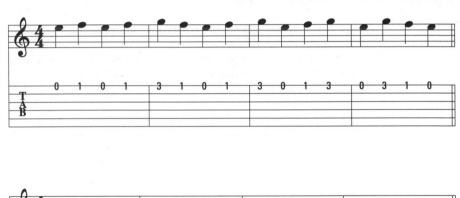

Figure 6-1:
Quarter-note melodies on each of the guitar's six strings in open position.

The next exercise is a bit harder, because it requires you to switch strings as you play. When you play the examples in Figure 6-2 try to go between the strings smoothly, without breaking the rhythm, and without varying your dynamics (the intensity of your pick attack) as you switch strings.

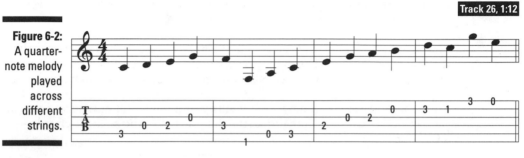

Track 26, 1:12

Figure 6-2:
A quarter-note melody played across different strings.

As a guitarist, you not only have to focus on keeping the rhythm steady between bars, but also when switching strings.

Alternate picking in downstrokes and upstrokes

Now I double the pace by introducing eighth notes into your playing. Keep in mind that in rhythm playing, you can often play eighth notes by just speeding up your downstroke picking. But in lead playing, you must always play eighth notes using the technique called *alternate picking*.

Alternate picking requires you to follow a simple rule: Downbeat notes are played with downstrokes; upbeat notes are played with upstrokes. Sounds mundanely simple, but in practice, maintaining this strict alternating pattern while crossing — and even skipping — strings can be difficult. Still, alternate picking works, even when it seems illogical, or at least inefficient, and virtually every guitarist on the planet who plays with any facility uses alternate picking.

Playing melodies across strings

The alternate-picking technique doesn't care whether you have to cross strings or not. In an eighth-note melody, the alternate-picking technique requires that the downbeat notes take downstrokes and the upbeat notes (the ones that fall in between the beats) take upstrokes.

Scales

By definition, a scale proceeds in stepwise motion. Scales are the dreaded instruments of musical torture wielded by Dickensian disciplinarians (like your fourth-grade piano teacher), but they do serve a purpose. They are a great way to warm up your fingers within a recognizable structure and they reveal available notes on the fingerboard within a key.

Plus, playing scales provides a familiar-sounding melody ("do re mi fa sol la ti do") that yields a certain satisfaction upon correct execution — at least until you've done them two or three billion times and you can't stand it anymore.

But for now, try an ascending, contiguously sequenced set of natural notes in the key of C beginning on the root (the first degree of the scale or chord) — a C major scale.

Playing in the majors

Figure 6-3 is a one-octave C major scale in eighth notes. Note that the pick-stroke indications are given for the first two beats, and then the term *sim.* (which is short for *simile*, or "in the same fashion") tells you to continue on in the same way.

Left-hand fingerings are also provided in the standard music notation staff. The idea is not that you sight read all this stuff — the notes, the right- and left-hand indications, and so forth — but that you learn this passage and play it whenever you feel like warming up, playing a C scale. Or you can just play the scale when inspiration waits in the wing space of your mind, mute and mocking, and you can't think of anything else musically cohesive to play.

Track 27, 0:00

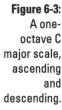

Figure 6-3:
A one-octave C major scale, ascending and descending.

Now for another scale that's musically about the same, but in a different key, and somewhat harder to play. Figure 6-4, a two-octave G major scale, ascending and descending. What makes it harder is the left-hand fingering: You use all your left-hand fingers for this scale, in a four-fret span.

Track 27, 0:14

Figure 6-4: A two-octave G major scale, ascending and descending.

Keep your left hand fairly stationary above the strings, and let your fingers stretch and reach for their correspondingly numbered fret (the 1st, or index, finger plays the 1st fret; the 2nd, or middle, finger, plays the 2nd fret; and so forth). As your hand becomes more agile, your finger span will widen and you will be able to reach the frets comfortably while keeping your left hand almost perfectly stationary.

A minor adjustment

Because I backed you into scales by way of stepwise motion, I feel I should give equal time to the major scale's gloomier cousin, the minor scale.

Actually the "family" analogy isn't that far off because minor scales are related to major scales. Every major scale has a corresponding minor scale, the *relative minor,* which you can play in its entirety using the same key signature. In any major key, the natural minor scale (so called because you can play it naturally, with no altering of the major-scale notes) begins at the 6th degree.

So in the key of C, the 6th degree would be A (remember the musical alphabet only goes up to G). Figure 6-5 is a one-octave minor scale, in eighth notes, starting on the open 5th string, A.

Skips

Skips are melodic movements of non-contiguous letter names, such as A, C, E, G, B. Skips can be of any interval and don't have to follow the notes of a chord. So all arpeggios are skips, but not all skips are arpeggios. Figure 6-6 shows an Am7 arpeggio. The notes of the chord are played one after the other: A-C-E-G.

Combining steps and skips

Most melodies are composed of a mix of stepwise motion and skips, and sometimes melodies can include an arpeggio (such as in the army bugle calls "Taps" and "Reveille"). Scales are a series of notes organized by key, where you play the notes in order, ascending and/or descending. Arpeggios can be skips in any order, but are limited to the notes of the chord.

Starting at the Bottom: Low-Note Melodies

For some reason, all traditional guitar method books start with the guitar's top strings and work their way down to the low strings. But in the true rebellious spirit of both rock and roll and the *For Dummies* series, I start at the bottom.

The reason why I start at the bottom is not just pure rebelliousness, either (although it certainly is fun to be contrary for its own sake!): It's because the impetus for so many of the world's greatest melodies, riffs, and rock rhythm figures have low-born origins (from a guitar perspective, anyway). Think of all the classic riffs already mentioned in this chapter — "Smoke on the Water," "Iron Man," "Day Tripper" — and how many of them are low-note riffs.

So in that spirit, try Figure 6-7, which is a low-note melody, in the style of a classic-rock riff. Note how it almost revels in its own subterranean girth. Spinal Tap would be proud.

Figure 6-8 is another melody, more nimble than the one in Figure 6-7. This figure moves in steady eighth notes and features some unexpected changes in direction. It also contains a series of melodic skips, which in this case is an arpeggio because it outlines the notes of an A minor chord.

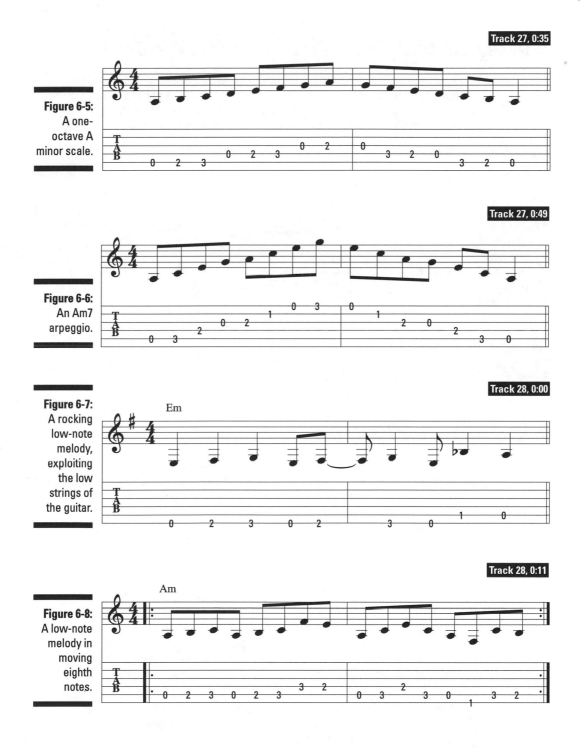

Figure 6-5:
A one-octave A minor scale.

Track 27, 0:35

Figure 6-6:
An Am7 arpeggio.

Track 27, 0:49

Figure 6-7:
A rocking low-note melody, exploiting the low strings of the guitar.

Track 28, 0:00

Figure 6-8:
A low-note melody in moving eighth notes.

Track 28, 0:11

Going to the Top: High-Note Melodies

Lead playing typically exploits the upper registers of the guitar, where melodic material is most naturally situated. Before you get really high up on the neck, play the melodic example in Figure 6-9, to hear the ability of the guitar's upper registers to cut through the rhythm section's din.

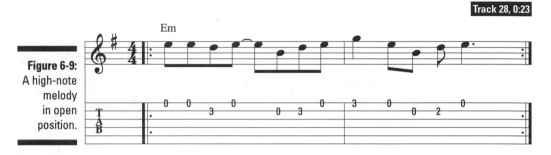

Track 28, 0:23

Figure 6-9: A high-note melody in open position.

If your guitar sounds twangy instead of smooth and creamy, try increasing the distortion factor of your sound. See Chapter 3 for information on how to dial up a more distorted sound if necessary.

Playing in Position

So far you've played all of your melodies and exercises in the lower regions of the neck, between the 1st and 4th frets. This is where it's easiest to place the notes that you see written on paper onto frets of the guitar neck.

But the guitar has many more frets on the neck than just the first four. Playing in the lowest regions of the neck is where you play most of your low-note riffs, a lot of chords, and some lead work, but the bulk of your lead playing takes place in the upper regions of the neck for two reasons:

✔ The higher on the neck you are, the higher the notes you can hit. The guitar is sort of a low instrument, because the notes you read on the treble clef actually sound an octave lower. For this reason, it's a good idea to get as far up the neck as possible if you want to distinguish yourself melodically, above the low end rumble of basses, drums, and, of course, other guitars playing rhythm in the lower range.

✔ The strings are more flexible and easily manipulated by the left hand, which means you have better expressive opportunities for bends, vibrato, hammer-ons, pull-offs, slides and other expressive devices (all of which I cover in Chapter 9).

Open position

Playing in open position is where you've spent your time thus far, but by *design*. When you have complete command of the entire neck and you can play anywhere you can find the note, playing in open position will be a *choice*. In other words, you play in open position only because you want to, because it suits your musical purpose.

Rock guitar uses both open position and the upper positions (the positions' names are defined by where the left-hand index finger falls) for the different musical colorings they offer. By contrast, jazz guitar tends to avoid open position completely, and folk guitar use open position exclusively. But rock uses both, and so you need to understand the strengths offered by both open position and the upper positions.

Remember the G scale of Figure 6-4? That's an open position G scale because it utilizes the open strings of the guitar. Now it's time to explore playing the same exact notes in the same exact rhythm another way.

Moveable, or closed, position

Playing in a *moveable position* allows you to take a passage of music and play it anywhere on the neck. If you play a melody on all fretted strings (incorporating no open strings), it doesn't matter if you play it at the first fret or the 15th. The notes will preserve the same melodic relationship. It's sort of like swimming: After you learn the technique of keeping yourself afloat and moving, it doesn't matter if the water is five feet or five miles deep — except if you're in five-mile deep water, it's probably a lot colder.

A moveable position is sometimes called *closed position,* because it involves no open strings. After you play anything on all-fretted strings, you have created a great opportunity to slide it anywhere on the neck and have it play exactly the same — except of course that you're apt to find yourself in another key. This has equally profound implications for chords, as I discuss in Chapter 4 when I cover moveable chords and barre chords.

The best part is the ability to move closed-position melodies around — instantly transposing their key — which is something that no piano player, trumpet player, or flute player can do easily, and they will be eternally jealous of you.

To demonstrate a moveable position, first take your two-octave G major scale and play exactly the same pitches, but place them on all fretted strings. Figure 6-10 is, then, a two-octave G major scale in 2nd position. It's 2nd position because the lowest fret played defines the position's name, and here it's the 2nd fret.

Track 29

Figure 6-10: A two-octave G major scale in 2nd position.

After you master Figure 6-11, try sliding your hand up and down the neck, playing the scale in different positions. By doing this you will *transpose* your G major scale into other keys.

Getting in Tune with Lower Register Riffs

I tackled the topic of riffs in the example on low-note melodies earlier in the chapter, but now you should take a look at them in earnest — not because they help illustrate alternate picking or string-crossing strings, but for their own sake. Finally, you're making music to make music!

The best thing about the lower register of the guitar is its powerful bass notes. You simply have no better arsenal for grinding out earth-shattering, filling-rattling, brain-splattering tones than the lower register of the guitar, and so this is where 99 percent of all the greatest riffs are written.

Start off with a classic riff in quarter notes, called, variously, boogie-woogie, boogie, or walking bass. Figure 6-11 is a classic boogie figure using only the notes of the chord, plus one, the sixth degree, in a fixed pattern for each chord. But notice that its repetition is its strength. Your ears want to hear the same pattern for each of the chords, so infectious is the sound!

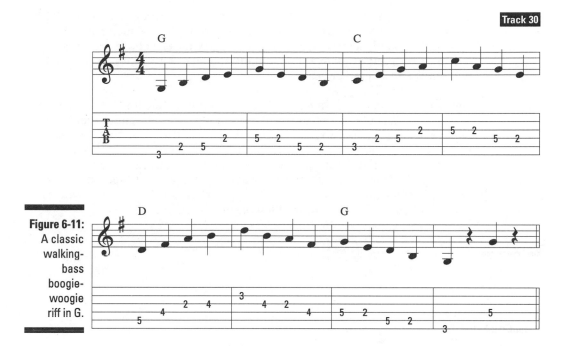

Figure 6-11:
A classic walking-bass boogie-woogie riff in G.

Making It Easy: The Pentatonic Scale

The major and minor scales may be music-education stalwarts, but as melodic material they sound, well, academic when used over chord progressions. Rock guitarists have a much better scale to supply them with melodic fodder: the pentatonic scale.

The pentatonic scale is not the only scale available for playing rock lead, but it is the most widely used and easiest to learn. The beauty of this scale is that it sounds great over every chord change in a key, and you can begin to make music with it almost immediately.

As its name implies, the *pentatonic scale* contains five notes, which is two notes shy of the normal seven-note major and minor scales. This creates a more open and less linear sound than either the major or minor scale. The pentatonic scale is also more ambiguous, but this is a good thing, because it means that it's harder to play "bad" notes — notes that, although they're within the key, may not fit well against any given chord in the progression. The pentatonic scale uses just the most universal note choices.

I cannot stress enough the importance of the pentatonic scale. It is to the rock guitarist what anesthesia, the printing press, and the cordless screwdriver are to modern civilization — an indispensable entity without which life would be much more difficult.

The first scale you learn is the A minor pentatonic. A minor pentatonic can be used as a lead scale over chord progressions in A minor, C major, and A blues ("blues" can imply a specific, six-note scale, as well as a chord progression). It also works pretty well over A major and C blues. Not bad for a scale that's two notes shy of a major scale.

Figure 6-12 is a neck diagram outlining a pentatonic scale form in 5th position. The neck is positioned as if you are facing an upright guitar that is laid on its side, to your left. So it looks like tablature in the sense that the first string is on top, but it's a schematic of the actual neck instead of the tab staff. On track #31 on the CD, it's played from top (the 1st string, 8th fret) to bottom (6th string, 5th fret) in quarter notes. Try playing it, and don't worry about playing along in rhythm with the CD; the track is just there so you can make sure you're in the right position hitting the right notes.

Figure 6-12:
A neck diagram showing the pentatonic scale in 5th position.

Track 31

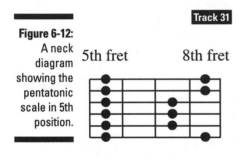

5th fret   8th fret

In the neck diagram, just like in a tab staff, the 1st string is the top line. Also, this is not a chord, but all the available notes for the pentatonic scale. The left-hand index finger plays all the notes that occur at the fifth fret; the ring finger plays all the seventh-fret notes; and the little finger plays all the eighth-fret notes. In this particular scale pattern, the middle finger doesn't play at all.

Playing the Pentatonic Scale: Three Ways to Solo

In this section you learn to play one pentatonic scale pattern in three different musical contexts:

- A progression in a major key
- A progression in a minor key
- A blues progression

You can use just one pattern to satisfy all three musical settings. This is an unbelievable stroke of luck for beginning guitarists, and you can apply a shortcut, a quick mental calculation, that allows you to instantly wail away in a major-key song, a minor-key song, or a blues song — simply by performing what is essentially a musical parlor trick. This is a great quick-fix solution to get you playing decent-sounding music virtually instantly.

As you get more into the music, however, you may want to know why these notes are working the way they do. But until then, let's jam!

Place your index finger on the 5th fret, 1st string. Relax your hand so that your other fingers naturally drape over the neck, hovering above the 6th, 7th, and 8th frets. You are now in 5th position ready to play.

Work to play each note singly, from top to bottom, so that you get your fingers used to playing the frets and switching strings. Don't worry about playing downstrokes and upstrokes until you're comfortable moving your left-hand fingers up and down the strings, like a spider walking across her web.

Now try Figure 6-13, which is a descending scale in C pentatonic major in eighth notes, beginning with your left-hand little finger on the 1st string, 8th fret.

Track 32, 0:00

Figure 6-13:
A
descending
eighth-
note C
pentatonic
major scale.

This particular pentatonic pattern allows you to keep your left hand stationary; all the fingers can reach their respective fret easily without stretching or requiring left-hand movement.

Now that you've played the scale, try it in a musical context. This is where you witness the magic that transpires when you play the same notes over different feels in different keys. Let the games begin!

Pentatonics over a Major key

Figure 6-14 is a C major progression in a medium-tempo 4/4 groove. The written solo is a mix of quarter notes and eighth notes comprised of notes from the C major pentatonic scale, moving up and down the neck. The left channel of your CD has the rhythm instruments, and the right features the lead guitar. As soon as you get the idea about how the lead sounds, dial it out (I won't be offended) and try to play the melody against the recorded rhythm sound by yourself. Then check your work by dialing back in the right channel and see how close you got.

Track 32, 0:11

Figure 6-14:
Solo in C major over a medium-tempo 4/4.

Pentatonics over a minor key

And now, as Monty Python once said, for something completely different. Or is it? In Figure 6-15, the feel changes (to a heavy back-beat 4/4), the key changes (to A minor), but you still play the same notes. Notice the strikingly different results.

Pentatonics over a blues progression

And now, incredibly, a different groove again that will work with the same scale you played for the progression in Figures 6-18 and 6-19. Figure 6-16 is an up-tempo blues shuffle in A. Note that the eighth notes in this example swing — that is, they are to be played in a long-short scheme. Make it cry.

Track 32, 0:35

Figure 6-15:
An A minor
solo over
a heavy
backbeat
4/4.

In the next section, you don't have to master any music at all. You get to make up your own.

Improvising Leads

In rock, jazz, and blues, improvisation plays a great role. In fact, being a good improviser is much more important than being a good technician. It's much more important to create honest, credible, and inspired music through improvisation than it is to play with technical accuracy and perfection.

The best musicians in the world are the best improvisers, but they are not necessarily the best practitioners of the instrument. About the only thing that competes with the ability to improvise a good solo is the ability to write a song.

And so I devote the last exercise in this chapter to improvising — where you take a collection of notes and turn it into music. To do this, use the 5th-position pentatonic scale you learned earlier in this chapter to play over. Figure 6-17 is a slow, gutbucket blues shuffle in A. Don't forget to swing those eighth notes and remember the blues credo: You don't have to feel bad to play the blues . . . but it helps.

A Final Note

Improvising is, at the same time, one of the easiest things to do (just find your notes and go) and one of the hardest (try to make up a meaningful melody on the spot). The more note choices you have, the more vocabulary you'll be able to pull from to express your message.

The pentatonic scale is a great way to start making music immediately, but plenty of other scales exist to help you in your music making. And you still have to listen to other guitarists for ideas. Go outside any scale you use to get unusual notes, and learn passages of classic solos on recordings to see what makes them tick. Above all, you must develop you own sense of phrasing and your own voice.

Figure 6-16:
An A blues solo over an up-tempo shuffle.

I present the tools to accomplish all those tasks in Parts III and IV, so for now practice to get your fingers working smoothly through the notes up and down the neck. Try to surprise yourself by changing direction, skipping strings, and even repeating notes for dramatic effect. Some of the highest musical moments of your improvising career will be the results of something completely unintentional — a happy accident. But to have such "musical mishaps," you must put yourself in harm's way. Be bold, be daring, take chances, improvise!

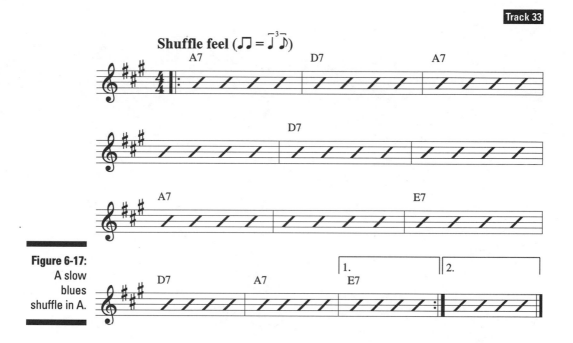

Track 33

Figure 6-17:
A slow
blues
shuffle in A.

Chapter 7

Groovin' on Riffs

*R*iffs are often the most memorable component of a rock and roll song and can form the perfect bridge between a chord progression and a melodic lead phrase. Although technically a short, self-contained musical phrase, a riff is much, much more than that. A riff sticks in your head long after you forget the lyrics — and even the melody — and at a noisy party, it is the riff that makes a song instantly recognizable when you can't quite make out the rest of the music. In many cases, the riff is the backbone of the song, its *raison d'être* (a fancy French term for mojo), and the rhythm, melody, and chords are all derived from the riff.

Chapter 6 covers the mechanics of single-note playing and allows you to play riffs as a way of illustrating just one of many single-note techniques in rock guitar. In this chapter, you venture deep into riff territory to see where rock and roll *lives* and discover why riffs themselves are such a vital and inextricable component of rock and roll. Hey, where do you think the phrase "a riff-roarin' good time" came from?

This chapter also covers two other rock staples, the *power chord* and the *double-stop*. Power chords are actually easier to play than the open-position chords covered in Chapter 4, and a *whole* lot easier than the dreaded barre chords also discussed in Chapter 4. (Oh, barre chords are not *that* bad, really — at least for us electric guitarists.)

Then, just when you think having any more fun in this chapter couldn't possibly be legal, I show you how to combine riffs, power chords, and double-stops into full-blown, fully realized *rhythm figures*. Rhythm figures embody the total approach to rhythm guitar. Virtually any strumming or single-note technique you can come up with can be pressed into rhythm-guitar service and incorporated into a rhythm figure. And although lead guitar might be the brain surgery of the rock world — the glamorous specialty skill that garners a lot of prime-time glory with its dramatic life-saving techniques — rhythm guitar is the daily exercise and good living that keeps you healthy and prospering for 95 percent of your medical, er, musical, lives.

Getting Your Groove On: Basic Riffs

I start off with riffs that exploit the lower register of the guitar. Make sure that you strike only one string at a time, but that your pick strokes carry the same confidence and power that they had when playing chords. Even if the riffs sound familiar, make sure you execute the rhythms and articulations precisely as written; don't let your ears allow you to gloss over the tricky parts.

Half- and whole-note riffs

A riff doesn't have to be flashy to be memorable. Figure 7-1, in the style of the band Black Sabbath, uses only half notes and whole notes to create an eerie, menacing effect.

Track 34, 0:00

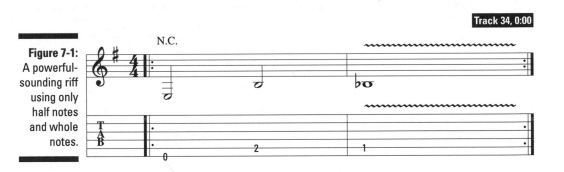

Figure 7-1: A powerful-sounding riff using only half notes and whole notes.

You can give fretted notes with long values (half notes and whole notes) more life by applying left-hand vibrato to them. Gently pull and release the string (causing it to bend slightly) very rapidly, causing the note to waver. Vibrato helps give slower notes more intensity. A wavy line placed above the note (⌇⌇) tells you to apply vibrato.

Eighth- and quarter-note riffs

Other than slow riffs created from half notes and whole notes, the simplest riffs to play are formed from the straightforward, non-syncopated rhythmic units of quarter notes and eighth notes. Figures 7-2 and 7-3 are riffs that mix quarter notes and eighth notes. Be sure to observe the pick-stroke indications for downstrokes and upstrokes (⊓ and V, respectively).

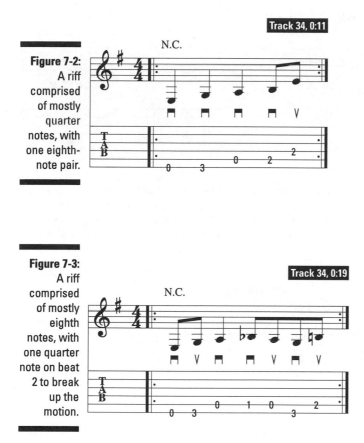

Figure 7-2: A riff comprised of mostly quarter notes, with one eighth-note pair.

Figure 7-3: A riff comprised of mostly eighth notes, with one quarter note on beat 2 to break up the motion.

Track 34, 0:11

Track 34, 0:19

Note the presence of F♯ in the key signature of Figures 7-2 and 7-3. This means that all Fs are sharped and that the key is either G major or E minor. So even though these two riffs don't contain any Fs, the key signature tells us that the examples are in E minor, which we know because the riffs gravitate to and around the root note, E.

Now try the boogie riff in Figure 7-4 (an expansion of the boogie riffs presented in Chapter 6), which is comprised of mostly quarter notes, but with a couple of shuffle eighth notes thrown in to give the groove an extra kick. The tempo is fairly bright here, so watch that you execute the long-short rhythm of the shuffle eighth notes correctly.

Track 34, 0:27

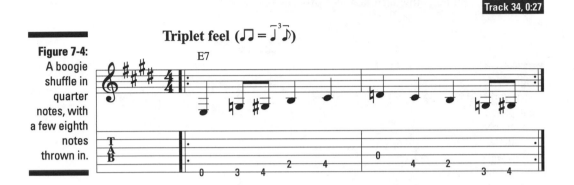

Figure 7-4:
A boogie shuffle in quarter notes, with a few eighth notes thrown in.

Riffs that consist of all eighth notes create a sense of continuous motion and can really help propel a song along. Figure 7-5 is in all eighth notes, and notice how easily the end of the measure leads into the beginning of the second measure, creating a seamless sound. Note too the presence of the B♭ and D♯ — two chromatic, or "out of key," notes in E minor.

Track 34, 0:37

Figure 7-5:
A steady-eighth-note riff in E minor, with two chromatic notes, B♭ and D♯.

While Figure 7-5 is a simple one-bar riff that repeats over and over, Figure 7-6 is a longer steady-eighth-note phrase that goes for two measures before repeating.

Track 34, 0:45

Figure 7-6:
A two-bar riff in steady eighth notes.

Because riffs are short and self-contained, they can be easily looped, or repeated back to back with no break. All the riffs presented in this chapter can be played seamlessly, and you are encouraged to play multiple repetitions until you execute the notes flawlessly — both from a technical standpoint (no missed or *fluffed* notes, no buzzing) as well as a rhythmic one. Pay particular attention when *rounding the corner* (going from the end of the riff back to the beginning). The barrier preventing a smooth transition can be more psychological than technical.

It's one thing to maintain a steady, consistent delivery for two bars. It's quite another to stay solid over bars upon bars or minutes upon minutes of playing the same riff within a groove. So repeat the riffs in this chapter in a loop fashion; that is, play them numerous times until you're sure you've got the long-term as well as the short-term consistency considerations under control. Or at least repeat the riffs until you can't stand it anymore. Either way, it's good training for playing with any band claiming the Allman Bros., the Grateful Dead, or Phish as an influence.

16th-note riffs

A 16th-note riff doesn't have to be fast or syncopated (for more on syncopation, see Chapter 5) just because it contains 16th notes. Figure 7-7 is a riff that builds up speed by going first through quarter notes, then eighth notes, then 16ths. Does this riff sound familiar?

Many hard rock and heavy metal riffs are based in 16th notes, including the infamous "gallop" pattern, discussed in Chapter 6. Figure 7-8 is a gallop riff that takes you on a wild ride. Buckle up — or should that be saddle up?

Track 34, 0:57

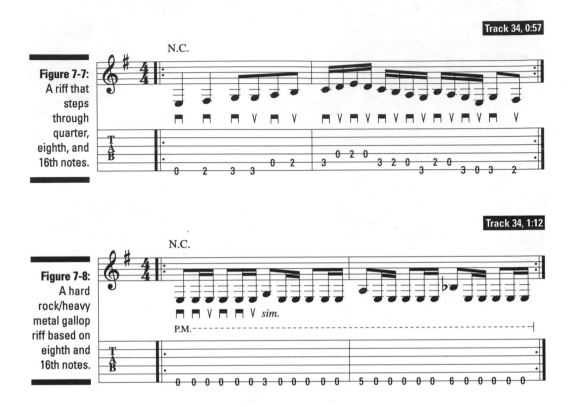

Figure 7-7: A riff that steps through quarter, eighth, and 16th notes.

Track 34, 1:12

Figure 7-8: A hard rock/heavy metal gallop riff based on eighth and 16th notes.

Then again, sometimes a riff written in 16th notes is just plain doggone fast, such as the hard-rock groove in Figure 7-9. Be sure to observe the alternate-picking indications in this example.

Track 34, 1:23

Figure 7-9: A fast 16th-note-based riff in a hard-rock style.

Eighth-note syncopation

Technically, playing a syncopated riff is no harder than playing a non-syncopated riff; it's just trickier to read in printed music. The more experience you have with syncopation, the more you can learn to recognize typical syncopation patterns. So you don't have to count your brains out with every dot and tie that appears, you can use your memory to help you. Syncopation is not intentionally designed to trip you up (although it may seem like that at first); it's there to put a kick into the music. Learn a few patterns and combinations, and you'll start to recognize them when they reappear. Memorizing a vocabulary of pre-existing syncopation patterns helps so that you don't have to reinvent the wheel every time you encounter a syncopated rhythm.

A great example of eighth-note syncopation occurs in the first line of the Beatles song "Eleanor Rigby." If you tap your hand or foot in time and sing, or say in rhythm, the words "Eleanor Rigby picks up the rice in the church where a wedding has been," you notice that the words "Rigby," "rice," "church," "wedding," and "been" all fall on the offbeat.

Figure 7-10 is a steady eighth-note figure where only the last eighth note in the bar is syncopated — here, through the use of a tie that binds it to the first note of the next measure. This particular syncopation device is called an *anticipation,* because it anticipates the downbeat, or first — and strongest — beat, of the measure. In fact, an anticipation is such a common and cool-sounding syncopation device that often players will introduce it, even when it's not written into the music. It's one of the those rock and roll situations where something can be justified simply because "it's a feel thing."

Figure 7-10:
An eighth-note riff with beat 1 anticipated, or tied over from beat four-and-a-half.

Track 34, 1:33

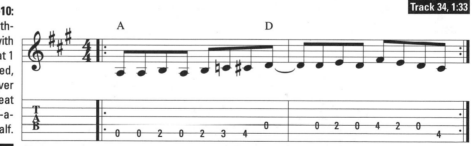

Now, double your syncopation efforts and put anticipations before beat 3 (the beginning of the second half of the bar) as well as beat 1, in Figure 7-11.

Figure 7-11:
An eighth-note riff with anticipations on beats 1 and 3.

Track 34, 1:46

Finally, Figure 7-12 is an ultra-syncopated figure where none of the notes in bar 2 fall on the beat; they all fall in between. The band Deep Purple wrote the riff to their classic hit, "Smoke on the Water," using a similar syncopation scheme.

Figure 7-12:
A highly syncopated eighth-note riff.

Track 34, 1:58

The melody to the Beatles' "Eleanor Rigby" is highly syncopated. In the same scheme as used in Figure 7-11, beats 1 and 3 are anticipated throughout the verse section.

Playing Two Notes Can be Better than One: Double-Stops

Stuck in a categorical netherworld between single notes (see Chapter 6) and power chords (see Chapter 5) is the two-note phenomenon known as the double-stop. A *double-stop* is simply two notes played simultaneously — on adjacent strings or separated by one to four (the maximum) strings in-between. The term comes from violin lingo, where a finger pressing a string to the fingerboard — remember the violin has no frets — is called a *stop*,

probably because the finger "stops" the open string at that particular location. So two stopped strings constitute a double-stop. Then again, if the
string were *truly* stopped it wouldn't be able to make a sound, now, would it? I
know, it doesn't make a whole lot of sense, but then neither do many violinists I've met over the years. I can say this because:

✔ I'm joking.

✔ I'm married to a violinist.

✔ She's not in the room as I write this.

Because it is obviously not a single note, and because a chord requires at
least three notes, the double-stop wanders between the two camps like some
musical double agent — sometimes masquerading as a chord, sometimes
exhibiting single-note properties. As such, it's a tremendously useful tool in
rhythm guitar playing. Because of its facile properties, you can use it for lead
playing, too, which I discuss in Chapter 6.

Right now, though, you employ double-stops in a rhythm context. A two-note
power chord is technically a double-stop, because it's two strings played
together. But conceptually, guitarists don't really think of power chords as
double-stops. Figure 7-13 is more of a true double-stop, especially in its usage
here. Note how its movement — between the fretted and open strings — is
much easier to execute and less clunky than, say, switching between two
chords (such as A and G) in the same tempo. Yet the double-stop movement
still retains a chord-like sound and feel.

Track 35, 0:00

Figure 7-13:
A moving
double-stop
figure, used
as a chordal
device.

Note that you've crept up, register-wise on the guitar. You're now not playing
just low notes, but have moved to the midrange of open position.

Figure 7-14 is a chord progression based on A, D, and E minor, but the ascending double-stop movement lends a nice melodic, quasi-single-line feel to the
passage. In this case, the double-stops are not on adjacent strings, as in

Figure 7-11. Here, they have a string separating them (the open 3rd string, G), so you have to "pinch" the 2nd and 4th strings with your right-hand middle finger, or, if you want to employ a little fingerstyle action, the middle or index finger and thumb.

Track 35, 0:10

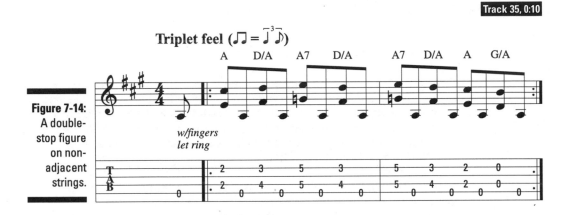

Figure 7-14: A double-stop figure on non-adjacent strings.

If you accidentally let the middle string (the open G) ring while playing Figure 7-14, you notice it doesn't sound half bad. So try playing the open G string intentionally, either by plucking all three strings, or by strumming the three interior strings (4th, 3rd, and 2nd) with your pick. The unchanging bass note (the open A string) sounded against changing ones (in this case the ascending double-stops) is called a *pedal tone*, or just a *pedal*, in music. Usually a pedal is the bass note, less often it's the highest note, but sometimes it's in the middle.

Combining Single-Note Riffs and Chords

While lead guitar is a studied craft with an established orthodoxy (that is, you can buy books on the subject), rhythm guitar is a universe without any rules. No one can say for sure what makes up a good rhythm guitar part, but you can sure know one when you hear it. The best rhythm players in rock — such as Pete Townshend, Eddie Van Halen, and Keith Richards, just to name a few — all play in a style that's hard to label or analyze. (I'd like to see someone try to notate the famous Pete Townshend "windmill.") But part of that indefinable magic comes from the fact that these guitarists don't limit themselves to just chords when playing rhythm guitar. They mix a healthy dose of single notes into their playing.

Although he was known for his fiery leads and stage antics (such as playing with his teeth and lighting his guitar on fire), Jimi Hendrix was a superb rhythm player. In his ballads, notably "Little Wing" and "The Wind Cries Mary," Hendrix plays lovely Curtis-Mayfield-inspired R&B chords that sound like a cross between gospel, country, and piano figures. Hendrix also played his share of double-stops, too.

Figure 7-15 is a hard rock progression that mixes power chords, open position chords, and single notes into one cohesive part. Note how it builds up dramatic power by starting slow and becoming increasingly active.

Track 36

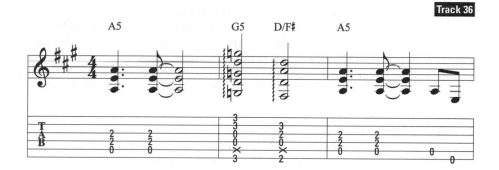

Figure 7-15: A hard rock progression mixing chords and single notes.

The squiggly vertical lines in bar 2 of Figure 7-15 tell you to draw the pick across the string in a quick arpeggio, creating a kerrrang sound. Experiment to see just how long you can drag out the strums without losing the sense of the rhythm.

Discovering Your Own Style

Don't be discouraged if you can't make the riffs you see written in the notation sound exactly like the version you hear on the CD. As long as you can play the correct pitches in the specified rhythm, you're doing fine. You have to find your own style. That's why Mozart wrote a piano sonata one way, but there are as many interpretations for that written piece as there are musicians playing it. The same is true for rhythm guitar. Each guitarist will play a 12-bar blues, or a power-chord sequence, or a double-stop figure in a slightly different way. But as long as that individual guitarist believes in what he or she is doing, each rendition will be unique, honest, and heartfelt.

The most important thing when tackling these — or any — rhythm figures is to develop a natural feel for them. A natural, comfortable, and confident delivery in rhythm guitar playing is vitally important — more important than even in lead playing. So repeat these exercises till you know them cold, till you own them, and then relax and play them like it ain't no thang.

Part III
Beyond the Basics: Sounding Like a Rock and Roller

The 5th Wave   By Rich Tennant

"First you play a G7 demolished chord followed by a fragmented 9th chord, then a perverted 32nd chord ending with a mangled 11th chord with a recovering 3rd."

In this part . . .

Anxious to take on that rock star persona? Well, grab your spandex, plaid, or greasepaint and come break out the big guns. Chapter 8 leaves behind the regular ol' open-position playing and travels up the neck to expose you to some honest-to-goodness rock playing power. And to help make your message heard, Chapter 9 blazes the path to rock-and-roll righteousness, or at least gives you the techniques you need to develop your own playing style.

Chapter 8

Playing Up the Neck

• •

In This Chapter

▶ Playing up the neck

▶ Learning lead scale patterns

▶ Playing in position

▶ Shifting positions

• •

*T*o sound like a true rock and roller and to share the stratospheric heights frequented by the legions of wailing guitar heroes, you must learn to play up the neck. I take you up the neck in Chapter 6 when I cover the pentatonic scale, but in this chapter, I not only let you play up the neck, I show you how to *think* up the neck.

Playing up the neck requires both a theoretical approach and a technical adjustment. In fact, it's probably a little harder on the brain (at least at first) to figure out what to play than it is for the fingers to fall in line. Those smart-alecky digits, which acclimate very quickly, just prove the old saying, "the flesh is willing but the spirit is weak." Or something like that.

Rock players play up the neck a lot — a whole lot. Many rock players play way, way up the neck, higher than any folk-based music would dare venture, and beyond the range of many jazz players. In many folk-based and singer-songwriter-type songs, you often don't have to play beyond open position at all. Or if you do, it's just to grab the occasional oddball, up-the-neck chord.

In rock, however, playing up the neck is essential, especially for lead playing. Playing up the neck not only gives you access to the higher-pitched and more brilliant-sounding notes, but also allows you to play the same notes many different ways. Barre chords (see Chapter 4) also allow you to use chords of the same name but which appear in different parts of the neck (all of them "up" from open position). When you add barre-chords you then have a complete picture of what it's like to play using the entire neck of the guitar. And to suddenly glimpse what it's like to have a command of the entire fretboard is a very exciting and empowering feeling.

Beyond Open Position: Going Up the Neck

You are now leaving the relatively safe haven of open position for the great unknown — that vast uncharted sea of wire and wood they call (cue dramatic music) . . . the upper frets! It's time to unbolt those training wheels, cut the apron strings, loose the surly bonds of earthbound music, and fly high. You're going up the neck into the wild blue yonder.

Playing up the neck opens up a whole new world of possibilities for playing rock guitar music. If you know only one way to play an A chord — or to play a riff one way when you hear an A chord — then all your music will have a certain sameness about it.

But if you have the entire neck at your disposal, are able to play A chords in several different places, can form lead lines in four or five places, and have opinions and associations on what effect you'll produce when you choose one over the other, then you're tapping the true potential of the possibilities the guitar neck has to offer.

 When playing up the neck, you really need to keep an eye on what your left hand is doing, unlike playing chords and riffs in open position where you really don't need to keep an eye on your left hand. So get used to keeping your head cocked to the left (if you're right-handed) and really looking at — and learning the locations of — those fret markers (the dots or other decorative inlays on the side of the neck and sunk into the fingerboard). They will be your signposts in your up-the-neck journeys.

Choking up on the neck

The best way to get moving up the neck is to start out with an exercise that doesn't introduce any new or intimidating techniques, either chordal or melodic. I'm just going to get your left hand moving around the neck a little. So I start with some known chord forms that you can move up and down to good musical effect over an open-D-string pedal (see the explanation of *pedal* in Chapter 7).

Figure 8-1 is a rhythm figure that pits an open D string against some chord forms that move up and down the neck. Notice that forms themselves are the familiar D, Dm, Dm7, and D7 shapes. But they move around the frets, rather than staying in one place, as they do when they're just doing "D" duty in open position. Be sure you observe carefully the fret-number indications in the diagrams.

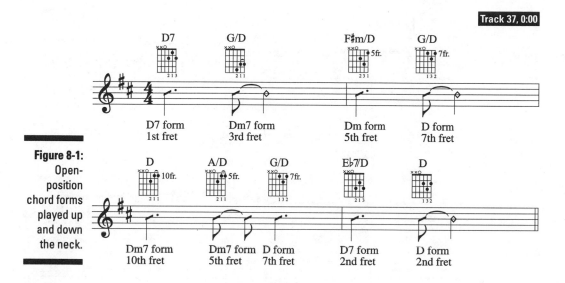

Figure 8-1: Open-position chord forms played up and down the neck.

Conveniently, you can refer to these forms by their open-position shapes: D, Dm, Dm7, and D7. But these forms don't necessarily *sound* like those chords, because they've been moved or transposed. When they're moved out of their original, open position, they now produce a different-sounding chord. When discussing chord forms, be aware of the difference between a D *shape* versus a D *chord*. A D shape played at the 7th position actually sounds like a G chord — because it *is* a G chord. As I discuss in Chapter 4, on barre chords, you can play many different forms to create a given chord, so chords are named by their absolute sound — their *musical* result — not the shape used to create them.

Playing double-stops on the move

Now move to the interior of the guitar's strings and play a rhythm figure comprised of moving double-stops on adjacent strings. Figure 8-2 is a hard-rock figure that creates drama by moving a series of melodic-oriented double-stops up and down two strings, the 3rd and the 4th, over an open-A pedal. This is a great exercise to get your eyes and left hand used to playing accurately the up-the-neck frets.

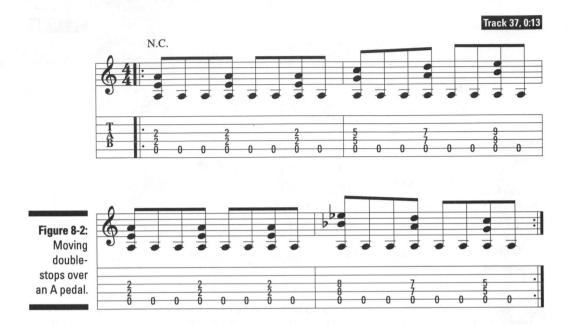

Track 37, 0:13

Figure 8-2: Moving double-stops over an A pedal.

Because Figure 8-2 creates an interplay between the open A string and the moving double-stops, try increasing that sense of delineation by applying palm mutes (see Chapter 5 for a detailed explanation on palm mutes) to the open A string and accents to the fretted double-stop notes. You can hear this effect on the CD performance.

After you've gotten a feel for what it's like to move around the neck, you can see that not only won't you get hurt, but also it's kind of cool to do. The next section shows some movable lead patterns that will get you sounding and thinking like a pro in no time.

Playing Closed-position Lead Patterns

Playing in closed position means that you employ no open strings to play your chords, melodies, or riffs. That might seem like a restriction, but it actually frees you from the tyranny of open position, allowing you to transpose instantly and easily. But getting comfortable playing all fretted strings takes a bit of an adjustment.

The first lesson about playing up the neck is that you can no longer rely on your dear friends the open strings. When you first learn the guitar, the open strings are like spin doctors to your politically incorrect blunders: They can shield your most embarrassing gaffes by running sonic interference. The open strings will ring through clearly while your fingers struggle with a tough chord change, muffling and buzzing their way to coherence.

But in up-the-neck playing, if you relax your left hand — even for the briefest moment — the sound disappears. So you have to be really sensitive to what's happening on both sides of the notes — the attack as well as the cut-off (the point your finger leaves the current fret to go do something else). And without the benefit of open strings, you have to actively work to get the notes to connect to each other smoothly. You do that by employing legato.

Letting notes ring for their full term is called playing *legato,* and after guitarists no longer have ringing strings to provide the sonic glue, achieving legato turns from a passive let-it-just-happen affair into a concerted effort.

So as you begin playing up the neck, in closed position, keep an ear out for making the notes ring for their full value. Don't let a note stop ringing until it's time for the new note to take over. Often that's as simple as leaving full pressure on your finger before releasing it at the last possible moment to play a new note on the same string (if the next note is lower), or placing an additional finger down on the same string (if the next note is higher). I call this the "lazy-finger approach" — where a finger doesn't move — or release pressure — until it absolutely has to. So you are hereby granted permission to be "digitally lethargic" and practice the lazy-finger approach to develop a legato technique on closed, or fretted, strings.

Learning to play patterns that employ no open strings has big-time benefits. Playing all-fretted patterns presents a clear advantage in one respect: The pattern can be transposed easily.

Playing in Position

So that you don't just go tearing up the neck willy-nilly, I need to define some zones, or positions, to give your up-the-neck forays some purpose. Guitarists don't just go up the neck because it's higher up there (although that's sometimes a desired result — to produce higher-pitched notes), they do so because a certain position gives them better access to the notes or figures they want to play. Going to a certain zone on the neck, to better facilitate playing in a given key, is called *playing in position.*

Positions defined

A position is defined as the lowest-numbered fret the left-hand index finger plays in a given passage. So to play in 5th position, place your left hand so that the index finger can comfortably fret the 5th fret on any string. If your hand is relaxed and the ball-side of the ridge of knuckles on your left-hand palm is resting near the neck, parallel to it, your remaining fingers — the middle, ring, and little — should be able to fret comfortably the 6th, 7th, and 8th frets, respectively. Figure 8-3 shows a neck diagram outlining the available notes of the C major pentatonic scale in 5th position.

Figure 8-3:
The available frets in 5th position.

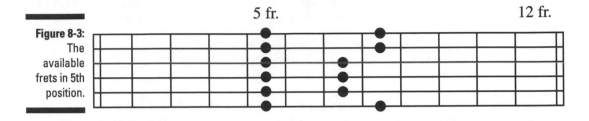

A firm position

Now that you have the answer to what playing in position means, the next question is what specific benefits playing in position brings — other than allowing you access to higher-pitched notes not available in open position? The answer is that certain positions favor certain keys, scales, figures, or styles, better than do other positions. Following are the three most common criteria for determining the best position in which to play a given passage of music:

✔ **Key:** The chief way to determine at what position to play a certain piece of music is by its key. To use the example in Figures 8-3 and 8-4, 5th position favors very much the major keys of C and F. If you have melodic material in the key of C or F, you'd be well advised to first try playing it in 5th position. Chances are, you'd find the notes fall easily and naturally under your fingers. The relative minors of C and F, A minor and D minor, also fall very comfortably in 5th position. This is no accident, because these minor keys share the same key signature, which means they use exactly the same *pitch class* (a term you learn in music school for collection of notes, not necessarily in any given order) as their major-key counterparts.

The pitch class of the C major and A minor pentatonic scale is A C D E G. The order of the notes changes depending on the context. For example, in the key of C, where the root is C, the notes read C D E G A. In A minor, A is the root, so the notes are ordered as A C D E G. After you start to play, however, the order becomes less important than the collection of notes (which is exactly the same for both keys), because life would be pretty boring if music was played in order of the notes in the scale or key from which they were derived.

✔ **From a scale:** A scale can be derived from a key, but often the scale you want isn't extracted from a traditional major or minor key. For example, the blues scale is one of the most useful scales in rock, but it's not pulled from an existing, major or minor key. So C *blues* is better played out of 8th position, not 5th.

✔ **From a chord:** Sometimes you may not care anything about scales or keys because you find a chord whose sound you can manipulate by pressing down additional fingers or lifting up existing fingers to create a cool chord move. The technical term for this is *a cool chord move*, and often the movement doesn't involve melodic or scalar movement, just a neat way to move your fingers that results in a nice sound (rock guitar moves are often discovered and adopted simply because they feel comfortable to perform or involve satisfying a natural impulse).

Using the Moveable Pentatonic Scale

Probably the greatest invention ever created for lead rock guitarists is the pentatonic scale, which I pay homage to in Chapter 6. Its construction and theory have spawned countless theoretical discussions, but for rock guitar purposes, it just sounds good, and I'm going to focus your efforts on figuring out as many ways to use it as possible. Though I define and apply a fixed, 5th-position version of the pentatonic scale to several contexts in Chapter 6, in this chapter I focus on moving it around the neck at will, changing the fingering to fit all sorts of different positions. And you can do this while maintaining the same notes in the same key.

Staying at home position

The main position for the pentatonic scale is placed in 5th position. This is the home position of the pentatonic scale in C major or A minor. For simplicity's sake, I use one scale, A minor, in my pentatonic studies for the remainder of Chapter 8. But be aware that most of the same qualities discussed can be applied to C major as well. Figure 8-4 is the A minor pentatonic scale in 5th position, shown in tab and a vertically oriented diagram.

Figure 8-4:
The A minor pentatonic scale in its home, or 5th, position.

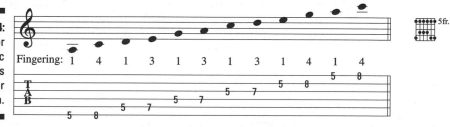

Although this scale looks to be positioned fairly high up the neck, only two of its notes — the 8th-fret C and 5th-fret A, both on the 1st string — are out of range in open position. The rest of the pitches can be found in other places in open position. For example, the 8th fret on the 2nd string is a G, which is the same G as the 1st string, 3rd fret — a note that's easily played in open position. So as you step through these notes in 5th position, be aware that you can play almost all of those same pitches in an open-position location as well.

The next step is to learn the various ways to play the same scale but in a different position, starting on a different note. This is known in music as an *inversion*. An inversion of something (a scale, a chord) is a different ordering of the same elements.

Going above home position

After the home position, you may feel restless and yearn to break out of the box. To extend your reach, learn the pentatonic scale in the position immediately above the home position. Figure 8-5 is a map of the A minor pentatonic scale in 7th position.

Figure 8-5: Notes of the A minor pentatonic scale in 7th position.

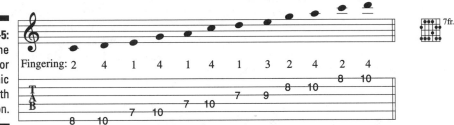

These are exactly the same notes (except the highest note, the 1st string, 9th fret, which is out of the home position's range) as those found in 5th position.

Dropping below home position

To apply some symmetry in your life, learn the pentatonic scale form immediately below the home position. Figure 8-6 shows the scale form immediately below the home position. It's played out of 2nd position and has one note on the bottom that the 5th position doesn't have, the low G on the 6th string, 3rd fret.

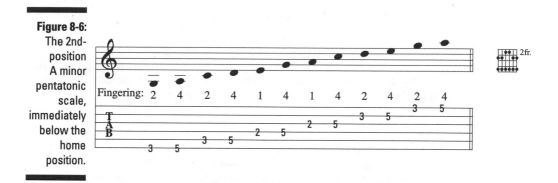

Figure 8-6:
The 2nd-position A minor pentatonic scale, immediately below the home position.

Take a moment and see what you have accomplished so far. You can now play one scale, the A minor pentatonic, in three different positions: 2nd, 5th (the home position), and 7th. If you look at the neck diagram with all three patterns superimposed on the frets, it looks like Figure 8-7. It's presented in two ways: as three separate but interlocking patterns (triangles, dots, and squares), and the union of those patterns, the actual notes available (as just dots).

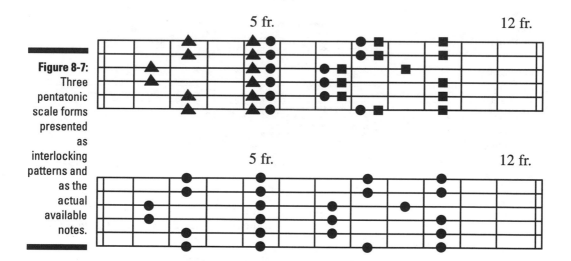

Figure 8-7:
Three pentatonic scale forms presented as interlocking patterns and as the actual available notes.

Note how the patterns "dovetail," or overlap: The bottom of the 5th position acts as the top of the 2nd position, and the top of the 5th position acts as the bottom of the 7th position. It's like Paul Simon once said: "One man's ceiling is another man's floor."

Moving between positions

Okay, so I've shown you the way to play a given pentatonic scale in three positions. Now it's time to put these patterns into motion by actually moving between them. This way you not only get to travel laterally, across the neck, but longitudinally, up and down the neck. Can you stand it?

The shift

Figure 8-8 shows two simple melodic segments that go from 2nd position to 5th position and 5th position to 7th position via a *shift*. To perform a shift, slide your left-hand finger from one fret to another above or below it, maintaining contact with the string. In the first segment, Figure 8-8a shifts up from the 5th fret to the 7th fret on the 3rd finger of the left hand, hitching a ride on the 5th string. Shifting this way takes you from 2nd position to 5th position. In Figure 8-8b, slide up on the little finger.

Figures 8-8a and 8-8b: A melodic figure that shifts on the fourth note of the sequence, going from the 5th string, 4th fret, to the 5th string, 7th fret.

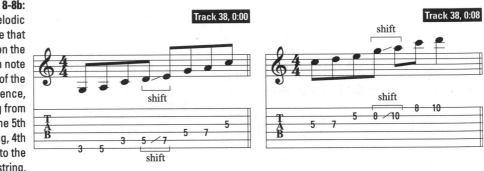

Sometimes the finger you slide up with is not the proper finger for that fret and string in the new position. But you can usually correct it easily enough on a subsequent move.

The slide, reach, and jump

A *slide* is one of two ways to shift positions while playing. A *reach* is the other. When you reach, either upwards or downwards, you stretch your hand out so that a left-hand finger can play a note out of position. You can always *jump* or *leap,* too, which just means that you don't leave any fingers down, or maintain any contact with the old position. Mostly, you just do whatever works.

Lateral vs. longitudinal

Figure 8-9 is an example of an ascending melodic line that illustrates the difference between playing laterally versus longitudinally. The first ascending and descending sequence takes you across the fingerboard in a stationary position. Then on the second ascent the line shifts to reach the upper notes, rather than playing to the upper strings on the same position. You have to play this one up to tempo to hear how the same pitches sound when played in two different places.

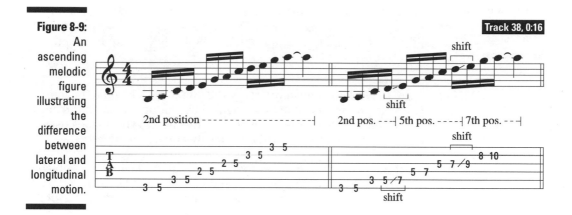

Figure 8-9:
An ascending melodic figure illustrating the difference between lateral and longitudinal motion.

Track 38, 0:16

Seeking Out the Five Positions of the Pentatonic Scale

Figure 8-10, for your amazement, lays out on one long neck diagram the five positions of the pentatonic scale. Although Figure 8-11 maps out the notes to only one key and its relative minor, you can fit this pattern to all 12 keys — and their relative majors or minors — simply by moving it up or down to the appropriate fret (for example, up three frets for E♭, down four frets to A♭, and so forth).

Almost as important, each of these patterns has an associated chord form. For example, the home position corresponds to an open position G chord. The scale just below the home position looks like an A chord. The position immediately above the home position is based on an E chord. The appropriate chords are also shown in Figure 8-10 relative to their corresponding scale forms.

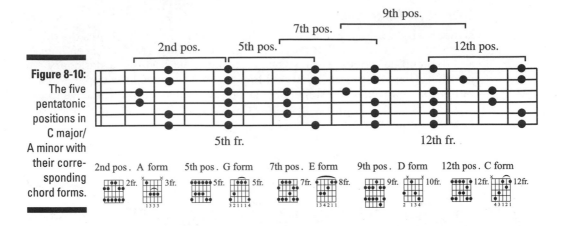

Figure 8-10: The five pentatonic positions in C major/ A minor with their corresponding chord forms.

You can begin to see how the many frets of the guitar neck begin to become demystified. This one scale occupies so many different positions on the neck. And this is only one scale, in one key, with only five notes. The shapes used to plot the notes help you to differentiate visually among the patterns.

With five positions of the same scale at your disposal, try Figure 8-11, which is a melody based on the pentatonic scale and can be played in all five positions. The rests separating the phrases should give you ample time to switch to the new position.

Chord licks, lead licks

In rock, a *lick* is a short, self-contained melodic phrase. This may sound suspiciously close to the definition of a riff, but there is a slight difference. While "riff" and "lick" are often used interchangeably, most guitarists agree that a riff is a repeated figure that can be used to form the basis of a song, while a lick is more of a melodic snippet, fleeting in nature, and is not generally used to form the basis of a rhythm figure.

Like riffs, licks are usually single-note affairs. But sometimes a lick can be chord based. If the distinction between a riff and a lick is a little fuzzy on the single-note front, it's even more obscure when dealing with chords. In other words, there's not much difference from a chord-based riff and a chord-based lick. It's sort of like distinguishing between good tequila and bad tequila: It's hard to do because the best tequila you've ever had in your life doesn't taste a whole lot different than the worst tequila you've ever had in your life.

Nevertheless, in an effort to pigeonhole, classify, and label all things musical, some famous chord-based licks throughout the history of rock and roll include the Doobie Brothers' "Listen to the Music" and "Long Train Running," Jimi Hendrix's "Hey Joe," "The Wind Cries Mary," and "Little Wing," and Led Zeppelin's "Stairway to Heaven" (the section right before the line "Ooh, and it makes me wonder").

Track 39

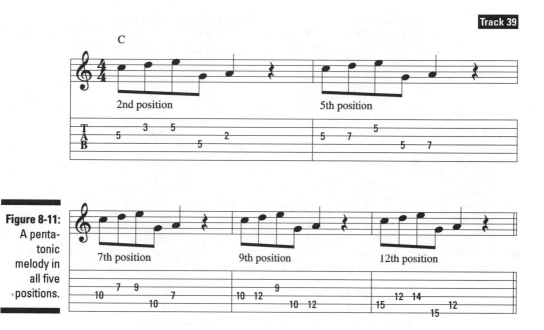

Figure 8-11: A pentatonic melody in all five positions.

In the Beatles' "Let It Be," lead guitarist George Harrison plays a terrific guitar solo in the middle of the song, based entirely in the C pentatonic scale. He shifts artfully between several different positions, proving he obviously had an advance copy (*way* advance) of *Rock Guitar For Dummies*.

Changing Your Position

What's cool about playing up the neck is how often you get to shift positions while doing it. And make no mistake, shifting is cool. You get to move your whole hand instead of just your fingers. That looks really good on TV.

Now that you've gone from one pentatonic scale position to another via a shift, you're ready to try some real licks. These licks are not limited to notes drawn from the pentatonic scale, as previous figures in the chapter were. Going forward, I'll allow the luxury of some chromatic (out of key) additions. You're playing real music now! Anything goes.

Licks that transport

Just like life, a lick can start you out in one location and take you to another unexpected place — often with delightful results. Figure 8-12 begins in 5th position, but quickly shoots up to 7th and finishes in 8th position with a bluesy flourish. The added chromatic note here is the flat five in A minor, E♭, which is called a *blue note* (so named because it is the note that creates a sad or blue sound). The left-hand fingering indications will help you to play this smoothly.

Track 40, 0:00

Figure 8-12:
A short blues lick starting in 5th position and ending up in 7th position.

Adding E♭ to the A minor pentatonic scale creates a six-note scale called the *blues scale.* In A, the blues scale is spelled A C D E♭ E G. The numeric formula (the "interval recipe," if you will) for the blues scale is 1 ♭3 4 ♭5 5 ♭7. The ♭5 can also be written as a ♯4, the ♭5's *enharmonic* equivalent. So applying this formula to a C major scale (C D E F G A B) produces C E♭ F G♭ G B♭, the C blues scale.

Of course, you can start high and end low — which might be bad in the world of finance or investments, but is perfectly fine in music. Figure 8-13 is a lick that begins in 5th position and takes an unexpected dip into 2nd position for some low-end gravity.

Track 40, 0:09

Figure 8-13:
A lick that dips down to 2nd position to get some "big bottom."

From the depths to the heights

For the ultimate exercise in shifting, try Figure 8-14, which starts in 2nd position, goes through 5th position, then 7th, and finally winds up in 9th — ending on a high, 12th-fret E on the 1st string. This allows you to "end on a high note" (albeit through low humor).

Figure 8-14: An ascending line that progresses through three position shifts.

Track 40, 0:18

Remember that although I've discussed different positions, various ways to shift, and five versions of the pentatonic scale, I've never left the key of C major/A minor.

Knowing Where to Play

After you get your hand moving comfortably around the neck, and you have a solid foundation in the A minor pentatonic scale and its different positions, try playing the pentatonic scale in its various forms in different keys. To do that, you must know how to place the scale patterns on the different regions of the neck.

Associating keys with positions

Some keys just fall more comfortably in certain positions than in others, so I'll start with the obvious, default positions for three common keys. Remember, any pentatonic scale satisfies two (related) keys: a major and its relative minor, or a minor and its relative major, depending on your orientation.

G positions

The home position for G major falls in open position or 12th position (which is exactly an octave higher). Because these are two extremes of the neck (and the open-position version defeats the purpose of this exercise), you might try to play G-based stuff out of 7th position. Figure 8-15 is a riff in 7th-position G major pentatonic (with one out-of-key note, the A♭ in bar 1), and its corresponding neck diagram.

Track 41, 0:00

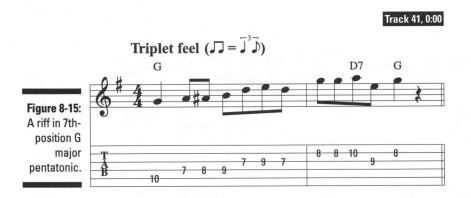

Figure 8-15: A riff in 7th-position G major pentatonic.

F positions

F is a common key for blues, especially if you jam with horn players. Figure 8-16 is a bluesy riff in F major, with an added flat 3, A♭. This riff sits well in 7th-position F major pentatonic. Note that because F is one whole step down from G, its five pentatonic scale positions are the same as the key of G, but shifted down two frets.

Track 41, 0:08

Figure 8-16: An F major lick with an added flat 3 in 7th position.

Note that even though this lick is in 7th position, it's in F, not G, and so uses a different pentatonic scale form than the 7th-position form designated for G or E minor.

F minor positions

The key of F minor (and its relative major, A♭) is the interval of a major 3rd (4 frets) lower than our dearly beloved A minor, so all of its pentatonic scale positions are shifted down four frets, relative to A minor. Its home position falls in 1st position, which means all subsequent positions are up from that. So even though the A minor example had a position lower than the home position, in the F minor example, that lower position gets "rotated" up the neck to the 10th position. Figure 8-17 is an earthy minor riff that takes advantage of its low position on the neck — the lowest possible closed-position pentatonic scale.

Track 41, 0:18

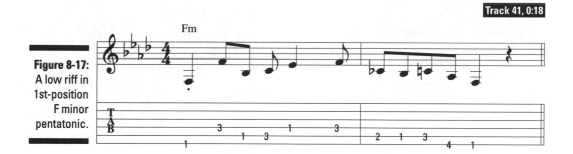

Figure 8-17: A low riff in 1st-position F minor pentatonic.

Placing positions

One great advantage to the guitar is that after you learn one pattern, in any key, you can instantly adapt it to any other key without much thought at all. Unlike piano players, flute players, and trombonists — who have to transpose, remember key signatures, and create different fingerings to play the same phrase in another key — guitarists just have to shift their left hand up or down the neck a few frets. But the pattern — what you actually play — remains the same.

It's as if you wanted to learn a foreign language, but instead of learning new words for all the nouns and verbs you know in English, you simply had to raise or lower your voice. Speak in a high, squeaky voice, and you're talking French. Say the same words in a deep, booming voice and you're conversing in Chinese. That's what transposing is like for the guitarist.

To help you know which positions are good for which keys, look at the table in Figure 8-18. This table is by no means exhaustive and by no means the final word on where to place your pentatonic positions. It merely gives you a jumping off point to know in what general vicinity to put your hands to improvise in, say, the key of A♭.

Major/minor key	Pentatonic pattern/fret #	Chord forms
A major/F# minor	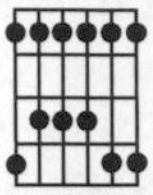 2nd fret	G/Em
B♭ major/G minor	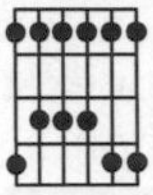 3rd fret	G/Em
B major/G# minor	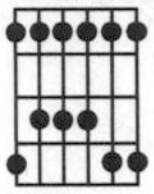 4th fret	G/Em
C major/A minor	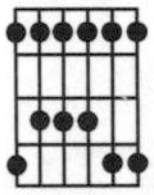 5th fret	G/Em
D♭ major/B♭ minor	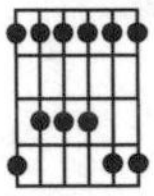 6th fret	G/Em
D major/B minor	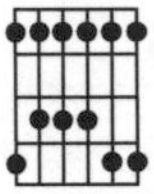 7th fret	G/Em
E♭ major/C minor	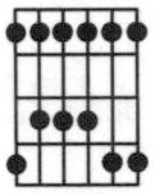 8th fret	G/Em
E major/C# minor	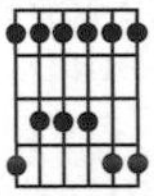 9th fret	G/Em
F major/D minor	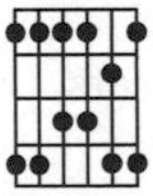 5th fret	C/Am
G♭ major/E♭ minor	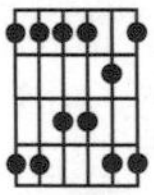 6th fret	C/Am
G major/E minor	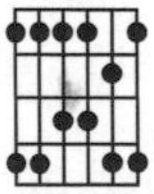 7th fret	C/Am
A♭ major/F minor	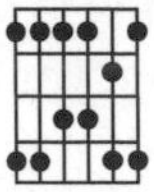 1st fret	G/Em

Figure 8-18:
A table showing the 12 keys and their relative minors, the fret number, appropriate pentatonic pattern, and chord form.

Putting the five positions into play

After you learn the pentatonic scale in five positions, you are more than 90 percent there, technically. The next hurdle is more mental than anything else. You simply have to be able to calculate where to play any given key, and which pentatonic pattern best suits your mood. Here are some exercises you can do to limber up your brain, learn the fretboard, and become acquainted with the differing characteristics offered by each of the five pentatonic positions:

- ✔ **Work out in different keys, spot transpose:** Don't just always play in A minor and C. Jam along to the radio, which often has strange (at least for guitarists) keys.

- ✔ **Arpeggiate the chords you're playing over:** Remember from Figure 8-10 that all these scale positions have associated chord forms. Try arpeggiating (playing one at a time) the notes of the chord whenever that chord comes up in the progression. This is a great way to break up linear playing, and it forces you to think of the notes of the chord, rather than playing memorized patterns.

- ✔ **Work out in different positions:** It's one thing to work out in different keys. It's another to work out in different positions. Make sure that you mix it up with respect to positions as well as keys.

We're all human and we tend to favor routines and like to tread familiar ground. With pentatonic scale patterns, the comfort zone lies in the home position and the ones immediately above and below. Make an effort to treat all the positions equally, however, so you can breeze through them on an ascending or descending line, without hesitating as to where the correct notes are.

If you work to become fluid in all keys, all positions, and all patterns, the neck becomes your musical magic carpet and can transport you as effortlessly as the breeze to magical lands.

The fret markers on the neck are not just there to look pretty. They make it easier to find positions up the neck. Use them!

Chapter 9

Playing Expressively: Making the Guitar Sing

*P*laying the guitar expressively — with passion, feeling and an individual voice — is how you evolve from merely executing the correct pitches and rhythms to actually playing with *style.* In rock guitar playing, the technical approach to expressive playing involves varied approaches to *articulation,* or the way in which you sound the notes. Hammer-ons, pull-offs, slides, and bends are all different articulations to connect notes together smoothly.

In addition to attacking, or sounding, the notes, you can add expression to already-sounded notes with *vibrato,* which adds life to sustained notes that would otherwise just sit there like a head of brown lettuce. You can also apply *muting,* where you shape the *envelope* (the beginning, middle and end) of individual notes, giving them a tight, clipped sound.

Applying varied articulations is how you play and connect notes on the guitar. It's what gives the music a sense of continuity and coherence — like well-expressed thoughts in a poem or song. If you master articulations and can weave them seamlessly into an integrated playing style, you can convince your guitar to do almost anything: talk, sing, cry, and even write bad checks.

In this chapter I examine the individual articulation techniques, apply them in idiomatic situations, and then work to play them together in a cohesive, integrated style. If any of the techniques seem a little hard to grasp, you can refer to *Guitar For Dummies,* which deals with each of these techniques in much more detail. If you already play guitar a little bit, however, you can probably absorb this collection of articulation techniques pretty quickly. In any case, this is the chapter where pitches and rhythms, techniques and form, actually become real music. Tell everyone within earshot to grab a hanky, because we're going to start wailing!

Bringing Down the Hammer-ons

A *hammer-on* is a left-hand technique where you sound a note without picking it. This makes a smoother, more legato connection between the notes than if you picked each note separately. In the notation, a *slur* (curved line) indicates a hammer-on.

To play a hammer-on, pick the first note and then sound the second note by fretting it with a left-hand finger (without re-picking the string). Figure 9-1 shows two examples of a hammer-on from a fretted note.

Track 42, 0:00

Figure 9-1:
A hammer-on from a fretted note.

 You can play hammer-ons in a variety of ways: from an open string to a fretted string, as double-stops, and in succession, or multiple times, where a hammer-on follows another hammer-on. But the technique is the same; you always sound the hammered notes by slamming down a left-hand finger (or fingers) without re-picking them with the right hand.

Idiomatic licks are musical phrases in a particular technique or style. Figure 9-2 shows a passage using different types of hammer-ons in a blues-rock groove.

Track 42, 0:07

Figure 9-2:
Various hammer-ons in a blues-rock groove.

The opening lick to Eric Clapton's "Layla" features a series of hammer-ons that gives the passage a facility and fluidity not possible if each note were to have been individually picked. Open strings help make this lick ring out and, along with the hammer-ons, give it an ultra-legato sound.

Having Pull with Pull-offs

A *pull-off* enables you play two consecutive descending notes by picking once with the right hand. To play a pull-off, pick the first note and then pull the fretting finger off to sound the lower note (another fretted note or an open string). Figure 9-3 shows two pull-offs: one from a fretted note to another, lower fretted note, and a double pull-off, where two successive notes are sounded.

Track 42, 0:16

Figure 9-3:
Two kinds of pull-offs to fretted notes.

Like hammer-ons, you can apply pull-offs in several different situations: You can pull off to either an open string or a fretted one; you can pull off two notes at a time (a double-stop pull-off); or you can have consecutive pull-offs (one after the other, with no picked note in between). You can even pull-off in a chordal context, in a reciprocal motion to hammering on within a chord position.

Figure 9-4 shows various kinds of pull-offs in a musical context.

Track 42, 0:23

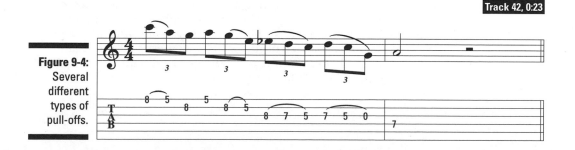

Figure 9-4:
Several different types of pull-offs.

Sometimes getting a clear, clean attack on a pulled note is difficult. If you find you can't get the second note to speak clearly, try "peeling" the finger off to the side as you sound the second note, rather than lifting it straight up. This enables you to create a sort of "left-hand pick" and provides a sharper attack to the second note.

Slippin' into Slides

Slides are one of the most expressive techniques available to guitarists because they allow you to sound the notes *in between* your two targets, or principal notes. Slides give your playing a slippery sound, and can help you produce an even more fluid sound to your lines than hammer-ons and pull-offs.

To play a slide, pick the note and then, while keeping pressure on the fretted finger, slide it up or down the string length to the second note. Do not pick the second note. Figure 9-5 shows two ways how a slide connects two notes.

Track 42, 0:34

Figure 9-5:
A slide allows you to connect two notes without having to pick the second note.

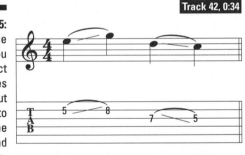

In addition to using slides to connect two notes, you can also employ them to enter into and slide off of individual notes, for a horn-like sound.

In addition to slides that connect two notes, you can play two other types of slides, known variously as *indeterminate slides,* and *scoops* (for ascending, and going into a note) and *fall-offs* (for descending and going out of a note). These slides decorate single, individual notes, and imbue them with the vocal- and horn-like characteristics where notes begin and end with a slight pitch scoop and fall-off. Figure 9-6 begins with an indeterminate slide and ends with a fall-off and in between are ascending and descending slides. Note that you can use a slide to facilitate a position shift.

Track 42, 0:41

Figure 9-6:
Various
slide
techniques
in a musical
passage.

Bending to Your Will

Bending strings is probably the most important of all the articulation techniques available to a rock guitarist. More expressive than hammer-ons, pull-offs, and slides, a *bend* (the action of stretching the sounding string across the fretboard with a left-hand finger, raising its pitch) can turn your soloing technique from merely adequate and accurate to soulful and expressive. Because the pitch changes in a truly continuous fashion in a bend (rather than in the discrete, fretted intervals that hammers, pulls, and slides are relegated to), you can really access those "in-between" notes available to horns, vocalists, and bowed stringed instruments. What's more, you can control the rhythm, or travel, of a bend — something you can't do with a hammer-on or pull-off. For example, you can take an entire whole note's time to bend gradually up a half step; or you can wait three and a half beats and then bend up quickly during the last eighth note's time; or you can do any of the infinitely variable ways in between. How you bend is all a matter of taste — and your personal expressive approach.

To play a bend, pick a fretted note and push (toward the 6th string) or pull (toward the 1st string) the string with your left-hand fretting finger so that the string stretches, raising the pitch. Figure 9-7 shows two types of typical bends in 5th position, on the 3rd string, 7th fret.

Track 43, 0:00

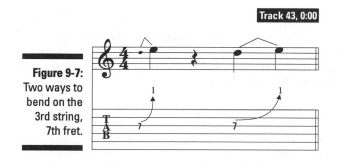

Figure 9-7:
Two ways to
bend on the
3rd string,
7th fret.

If you find it difficult to bend with one finger, try "backing up" the bending finger with another finger behind (toward the nut) it. For example, if you use your 3rd finger to bend (as you would when in 5th position and bending the 3rd string, 7th fret), you can use your 2nd, 1st, or even both your 2nd and 1st fingers help push the string.

To bend successfully and without pain, your strings must be of a light enough gauge that they will stretch easily as you push your fretting finger sideways. Electric guitars take gauges light enough to do this, whereas acoustic guitars usually don't. Also, the sustain factor in electric guitars allows the note to ring longer as the bend is applied, yielding a more dramatic effect. You also must practice bending in tune, where your bends go up exactly the interval the notation dictates (a quarter step, a half step, a whole step, etc.). In the notation, the distance of the bend is indicated by pitches in the music staff connected by angled (not curved) slurs, while the tab uses numerals and curved arrows.

Figure 9-8 shows a passage mixing two types of bends: an immediate, or instantaneous, bend and a bend in rhythm.

Track 43, 0:07

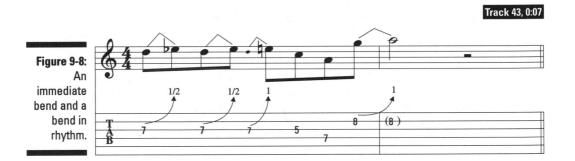

Figure 9-8: An immediate bend and a bend in rhythm.

Bend and release

In addition to the standard bend, where you push or pull a string to raise its pitch, you can play other bends to create different effects, such as a continuous up-and-down pitch movement through a bend and release. Figure 9-9 shows a *bend and release*, which consists of a picked note, a bend up, and then a release of that bend, which produces three distinct notes, but where only the first one is picked. Note the rhythm of the bent notes and that the notes change in sync with the chord changes.

Slide guitar

Many rock players love the sound of slides so much that they explore the style of playing called *slide guitar,* where the notes are *stopped* (they're not *fretted* in the traditional sense, but stopped at different points along the string length to produce different pitches) with a physical device called, appropriately enough, a *slide.* Slide guitar involves playing different notes and chords using a glass or metal cylinder placed over the left-hand ring or little finger. You can play both rhythm and lead using a slide, though it's usually best employed on lead breaks. Great rock slide players include Johnny Winter, Duane Allman, Danny Gatton, Bonnie Raitt, Warren Haynes, and the Wallflowers' Michael Ward.

Track 43, 0:16

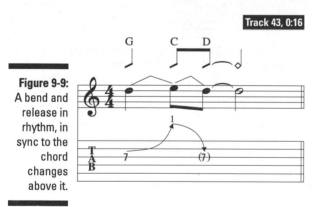

Figure 9-9: A bend and release in rhythm, in sync to the chord changes above it.

Pre-bend

Another variation of the standard bend produces a "downward bend" effect through a pre-bend and release, where the pitch appears to drop. A *pre-bend* is where you bend the note and hold it in its bent position before picking it. This allows you to then release the note after it's picked, creating the illusion that you're bending downward. This is sometimes called a "reverse bend," although that's technically a misnomer. You can only bend in one direction, with regards to pitch: up. By letting the listener hear the pre-bent note first, however, and then executing the release, you give the impression that you're bending (especially if you do it slowly) downward. Because pre-bends are a little trickier to set up, they are not as common as normal, ascending bends. But they are extremely powerful expressive devices and should be employed wherever you desire to create a "falling-pitch" effect.

Figure 9-10 shows a good example of how to use a pre-bend and release to fall into a note from above. Again, the note choice is dictated by the chord progression going on above it.

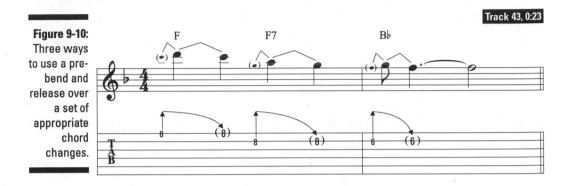

Track 43, 0:23

Figure 9-10:
Three ways to use a pre-bend and release over a set of appropriate chord changes.

The hardest part about performing a pre-bend is not technical but musical: You must bend up to the starting note — and it must be in tune — without your being able to hear it first. Because you can perform bends on a variety of different strings, on many different frets, and to different intervals (for example half-steps, whole steps, minor 3rds, and major 3rds), the pre-bend distances are all different. Still, through practice, you can learn to "feel your way" to an in-tune pre-bend and achieve remarkably consistent results.

Sounding a Vibrato That Makes You Quiver

Vibrato is that wavering, quivering quality that an opera singer or a power-ballad vocalist adds to a sustained note to give it a sense of increased energy or life. Some guitarists, such as Eric Clapton, are renowned for their expressive vibrato technique. The notation indicates a vibrato by placing a wavy line over a note.

You can create a vibrato several ways:

- ✔ By bending and releasing a fretted note rapidly (called "fingered" vibrato).
- ✔ By giving your whammy bar a shake.
- ✔ By applying electronic vibrato, through an external effect.

The bend-and-release, fingered approach to vibrato is the most common, controllable, and expressive, because, naturally, you use your fingers to execute it. To play a vibrato this way, bend and release the fretted string rapidly, causing the note's pitch to quiver. You determine the speed and intensity (how fast and how far you bend the note to achieve the wavering effect) by the context in which the vibrato appears. Slower music usually dictates a shallow and slow vibrato; faster music urges you to bend faster, so that the vibrato is detectable before the note changes pitch. The intensity of the vibrato is how subtle or obvious you want the effect to appear, independent of the speed.

Figure 9-11 shows a fingered vibrato, over a tied whole note. The notation indicates vibrato with a wavy line appearing above a note head and continuing through its duration.

Track 44, 0:00

Figure 9-11:
A vibrato
executed
with the
left-hand
fingers.

Guitarists often play a descending fall-off type of slide after a long held note with vibrato. Another trick is to allow a note to sound without vibrato, then to add some vibrato. This *delayed vibrato* is a standard technique for vocalists.

Adding Spice Through Harmonics

Harmonics are pure-sounding, bell-like tones that are often used to make a note sparkle or scream. You can play a *natural* harmonic, which involves open strings, or you can play a *pinch* harmonic, which is a type of "artificial" (so named because it uses a fretted, not an open, string) harmonic executed using both the right and left hands simultaneously. Natural harmonics are by far the easiest to execute, but they are limited in their pitch selection. Pinch harmonics take a while to master, but you can use them wherever you like and can produce virtually any pitch with them.

To play a natural harmonic, strike the open string and with the left hand, simultaneously touch it lightly (do not press down) above the 12th, 7th fret, or 5th fret (the 12th-fret harmonic is the easiest to play). Place your left-hand finger directly above the fret wire, not in the middle of the fret. Figure 9-12 shows a short passage using all natural harmonics derived from the 7th and 12th frets and played across several strings.

Track 44, 0:07

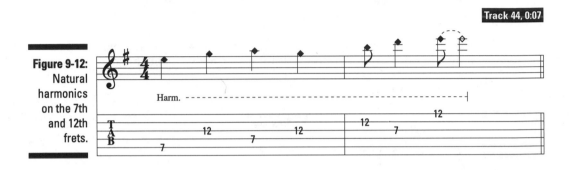

Figure 9-12: Natural harmonics on the 7th and 12th frets.

To play a pinch harmonic, fret the string normally, then strike it with the right hand and instantly mute the ringing string with your right-hand thumb. Move the right hand around slightly to different locations along the string length until you achieve the desired ringing sound. You need to practice this technique to become consistent at producing the harmonic every time, but it's a lot easier to do with high volume and distortion. Figure 9-13 shows a short blues-rock phrase highlighting a pinch harmonic. Listen to the CD to hear how the effect should sound, and then try to achieve similar results.

Track 44, 0:16

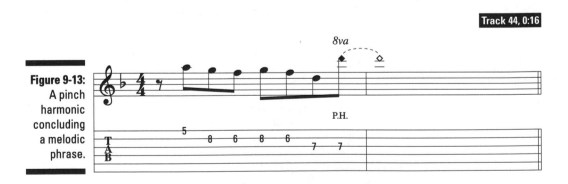

Figure 9-13: A pinch harmonic concluding a melodic phrase.

Passing the Bar Exam

You can skip this section if your guitar is not equipped with a whammy, or vibrato, bar. But if you've wondered what that skinny metal protrusion dangling off your guitar's bridge is for, you've come to the right section. The bar can be used to slacken the strings to cause a "dive bomb" effect, or to create a vibrato. If you press down or pull up on the bar, the pitch changes in accordance with the pressure apply. If you bear down on the bar, the effect is dramatic; if you just jiggle or "bounce" (lightly tap, allowing it to spring back) the bar, the effect is more like a shimmer, or dip. Figure 9-14 shows a passage that uses the bar to drop a string a whole step, allows it to return to pitch, gives the note a little "goose" with two bounces, and finishes up with vibrato.

Track 44, 0:25

Figure 9-14: Two different kinds of bar moves: a dip and release, and a bounce.

Putting It All Together

Figure 9-15 is "Just an Expression," a short solo piece, that employs several of the articulations explored in this chapter. Before jumping in and attempting to play this piece and all its required techniques, look at the song's notation. You see hammer-ons, pull-offs, slides, bends, and vibratos. Try to imagine what the song will sound like, when all the articulations are executed properly.

A good way to break this piece down into a practice routine is to separate it into three stages:

1. **Get all the notes down first.**

   Play the correct pitches in the correct rhythms with little or no attempt at executing the articulations or applying expression. In other words, it's okay to ignore the hammer-ons, pull-offs, slides, and bends, and so on, to just hear and play the song correctly.

2. **Employ the indicated articulations.**

After you know what the notes are and how they sound rhythmically, start employing the techniques one by one. If one articulation situation proves problematic, isolate that passage and practice it over and over. Then go back to playing the whole song and see if you can execute the problem passage as easily as you can play other parts of the song. Do this as many times as is necessary for the various techniques.

3. **Apply phrasing and a sense of cohesiveness to the song.**

After you can play the piece with all the articulations executed correctly, work to make the piece seamless, so that the phrases are smoothly connected to each other and the song flows. It is this last aspect that is the most elusive and difficult, but it's also what makes your playing achieve real expression and style. In any piece of music you tackle, keep working at step #3 to really internalize a piece and make it your own.

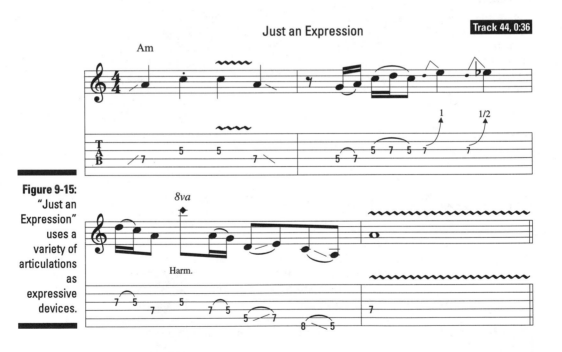

Just an Expression

Track 44, 0:36

Figure 9-15:
"Just an Expression" uses a variety of articulations as expressive devices.

Part IV
Mastering Different Rock Styles

"Now this little plant is called Emma. Emma blooms best to the scathing guitar riffs of Ted Nugent and Eddie Van Halen."

In this part . . .

Now it's time to put the air guitar away for good and get ready to play your own guitar in the styles of the most revered rock guitar masters in the world. Want to duck-walk to your rock roots? Look to Chapter 10 for coverage of the beginning of rock and roll and early masters such as Chuck Berry, Buddy Holly, the Beatles, the Rolling Stones, and more. Hooked on classics? Tune in to Chapter 11 for a look at the varied styles of the Who, Eric Clapton, Jimi Hendrix, Led Zeppelin, U2, and the Eagles. Want to bang your head and annoy your neighbors? Look no further than Chapter 12 for riffs in a variety of molten styles, from classic metalers like Black Sabbath and AC/DC to modern metalmeisters Metallica and rap-rockers Korn. And to smooth out the end of this part, Chapter 13 cruises and bops through progressive rock and jazz-rock fusion in the styles of Rush, Steely Dan, and Yes. Enjoy!

Chapter 10

Rock and Roll: The Early Years

• •

In This Chapter

▶ Playing barre chords in a rock style

▶ Playing early rock style lead guitar

▶ Combining single lines and chords

▶ Covering the styles of early rock greats

• •

*R*ock and roll was created from a hybrid of musical styles that included traditional blues, country and western, rhythm and blues (R&B), and mainstream popular music. Many rock pioneers, such as the Beatles, claim to have been influenced by the older blues players, yet their music was sunny, pop-ish, and of the stuff that made teen-age girls giggle, scream, and faint. No prison chain-gang song, field holler, or other traditional blues form could do that.

So clearly something else was going on. It was the mating of these raw but obscure (at least with regard to what was going on in the mainstream) forms that found the vast hordes of disaffected and rebellious youths searching for the Next Big Thing. They didn't find it completely in the movies or in matinee idols, but they did find all they could wish for — and then some — in music, and it was called rock and roll.

Early rock and roll songs clearly showed their roots, because a "universal rock style" hadn't yet developed. Like immigrants meeting in a new land, everyone was there to pursue a common purpose, build a common community, and speak a common language, but they all still carried with them habits and dialects of the Old Country from which they came. Buddy Holly and Elvis had clear southern roots (Texas and Memphis, respectively), and Chuck Berry and Bo Diddley were definitely a product of more northern climes (Chicago's Chess Records). Yet all were learning from each other, while converting listeners who heard them and influencing every guitarist who followed them. This early era in rock and roll was a musical melting pot of styles.

In this chapter I explore different rhythm and lead sounds of the early rock era (the mid-1950's through the early to mid-60's), visiting the styles and techniques that guitarists at the time were applying to this curious rock and roll hybrid. Following each musical figure, in this chapter and throughout Part IV, are bold-faced titles of two encapsulated summaries: *Music,* for the overall lasting musical influence of the guitarist that inspired the example; and *Technique,* for the techniques showcased in the musical example here based on that style.

It Don't Mean a Thang If It Ain't Got That Twang

In early rock guitar playing, guitarists didn't have a different *technique* so much as they had a new *attitude* and approach to playing over what popular music had seen previously. Before the super-distorted sound of Led Zeppelin and Cream, and while Pete Townshend was still discovering how to overdrive an amplifier, guitarists sounded kind of, well, *twangy*.

Despite the fact that a pickup increased a guitar's sustain (as I discuss in Chapter 1), the sound that people now associate with early rock is characterized by a sharp, strident quality and a rapid *decay* (the musical term for the time it takes a sounded note to die away). So the guitar sounds of Buddy Holly, the Beach Boys, Scotty Moore (Elvis Presley's guitarist), and Carl Perkins leaned toward fast and busy, rather than slow and lyrical, in large part because the short, clipped quality of the electric guitar sound suited that kind of playing.

Sending R&B Mainstream: Bo Diddley

One of the biggest influences in rock was rhythm and blues (or R&B), which would continue to develop on its own, but also had a profound effect on rock and roll. Some performers, such as pianist/vocalist Fats Domino, weren't really rock musicians, but enjoyed mainstream success because of R&B's close spiritual association with rock in those days (the mid- to late 50s), and because radio playlists and record-sales charts hadn't distinguished between the two genres yet.

However, one of the biggest influences in bringing the R&B sound mainstream was Bo Diddley. Born Ellas McDaniel in McComb, Mississippi, Diddley grew up in Chicago, where he moved at age five. He was a self-invented phenomenon who played a homemade rectangular-shaped guitar with his teeth and behind his back, and he brandished it in a sexually suggestive manner — all techniques that would be brought to high art by Jimi Hendrix. One of Diddley's best-known songs was an anthem he composed for himself, named after himself, and which used a syncopated rhythm that became synonymous with his name. That must be some kind of record: a person, song, and a rhythm, all having the same name.

(Buddy Holly composed "Not Fade Away," which was later covered by the Rolling Stones, using the "Bo Diddley Beat.") His homemade guitar also bore his name, so the list goes on.

Figure 10-1 is a rhythm guitar passage that employs the "Bo Diddley Beat." Note how "scratchy" the sound is, and how the left-hand mutes are actually written as X-shaped noteheads in the notation. Above the music are *rhythm slashes,* which show what the rhythm section does to accompany the guitar figure below it.

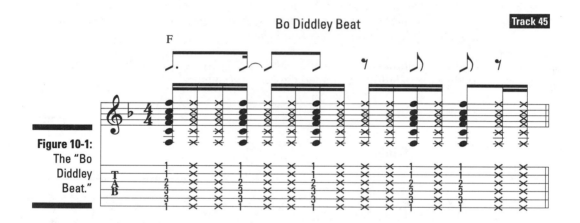

Bo Diddley Beat

Track 45

Figure 10-1: The "Bo Diddley Beat."

The rhythm Bo Diddley popularized is not some obscure, ineffable entity that only he knew how to create. It's a definite 16th-note-based pattern, consisting of a dotted-eighth note followed by a 16th tied to an eighth note, followed by an eighth note and ending with two eighths on beats 3½ and 4. Then the sequence repeats. The whole pattern is only two beats long.

Music: He immortalized the "Bo Diddley beat," and was copied by everyone from Buddy Holly to the Rolling Stones. He was also one of the early performers who helped bring R&B to mainstream audiences.

Technique: Here you use left-hand muting, syncopated strumming, scratches, and sounded notes to create the implied syncopation effect.

Giving Rock a Texas Twang: Buddy Holly

The southern United States still has a regional flavor when it comes to its native-born musicians producing music, but it was even more pervasive in the 1950s. Although the Deep South produced its own flavor of blues (the Delta blues being the most famous), "Texas twang" also had its place in rock development.

Everyone knows Lubbock-born Buddy Holly because of his unique status in rock and roll history: He was part of the trio of rock performers (along with Ritchie Valens and the Big Bopper) that went down in the tragic plane crash in 1959 (which was later immortalized in Don McLean's song "American Pie" as "the day the music died"). He also composed and sang some memorable songs, including "That'll Be the Day," "Not Fade Away," "Every Day," and "Peggy Sue."

Holly made a lasting contribution to rock guitar, however, in addition to achieving mythic status as a rock martyr: He was one of the first to popularize the Fender Stratocaster; he played, wrote, and recorded his own music with his own band (being one of the first to use multi-tracking in the studio to enhance his performances); and he played the featured guitar himself. And he did it all while wearing thick-framed glasses.

Figure 10-2 shows a blues turnaround with a distinctly Holly-like treatment, followed by a boldly strummed chordal statement.

Track 46

Figure 10-2: A bluesy double-stop riff and a featured chordal figure.

Music: Buddy Holly helped to popularize the Fender Stratocaster; wrote, multi-tracked, and played his own music; used a double-stop blues turnaround lick in "That'll Be the Day"; and played a rhythm guitar as featured "break" (the bona fide guitar solo would come later) in "Peggy Sue."

Technique: You can use either fingerstyle or a pick with fingers to play the triplets across alternating strings.

Bringing Doo-Wop Up Front

The sub-genre of rock known as *doo-wop* got its name from the sound of a group's background singers chanting "*doo-wop*" (and probably while performing some rudimentary ensemble choreography) behind a lead vocalist. But to musicians and guitarists, the term *doo-wop* conjures up a chord progression as well: the I-vi-IV-V, or the almost-identical I-vi-ii-V. (For more on how to interpret the roman numerals representing this progression, see Chapter 6.) This arrangement of chords is not unique to the doo-wop era (it exists in centuries-old classical music as well as music that followed doo-wop). But played with a certain lilt at a certain tempo, you just can't help (if you're a boy) slicking back your hair and pulling on a white t-shirt and leather jacket, or (if you're a girl) doing up your hair in a pony tail, donning a poodle skirt, and sporting saddle shoes. Man alive, those times were just a panic, weren't they?

But musically, you should tackle the I-vi-IV-V as a viable entity because this progression helps to illustrate a few different feels, and because it's what most music of that period sounded like. Plus, this progression is one infectious little bugger, so I don't think you'll mind going a few rounds with it. You can even construct your own song involving innocent and questioning teen-age angst (although I don't think the word *angst* existed in the '50s).

I-vi-ii-V: 12/8

The I-vi-ii-V progression is perhaps the most popular progression ever, next to the 12-bar blues. Strangely, it doesn't have a convenient name, except probably the not-so-pithy "doo-wop progression." Figure 10-3 is a passage in 12/8, which, despite its intimidating numbers, you play in an easy triplet feel. The Beatles' "This Boy" is a great example of the doo-wop progression given a sophisticated, post-doo-wop treatment. Here I've placed it in all barre chords for maximum left-hand control over the notes' ring-out (which you want to selectively shorten, or clip). It's in the key of D.

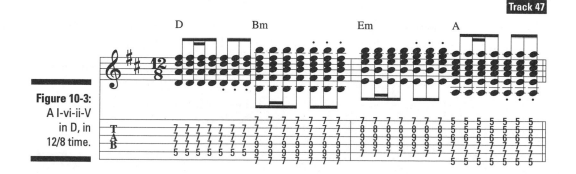

Figure 10-3: A I-vi-ii-V in D, in 12/8 time.

Track 47

Music: The I-vi-ii-V progression is the most popular chord progression in the early decade of rock and roll.

Technique: Use a relaxed up-and-down right-hand motion to smoothly execute the triplet-based strumming pattern, and add left-hand muting to break up the ringing strings.

I-vi-IV-V: Straight-eighth feel

A variation on the 12/8 I-vi-ii-V is the I-vi-IV-V, which you can often use interchangeably, the small difference usually explained away as compositional whim on the part of the songwriter. In Figure 10-4, it's placed in a straight-ahead 4/4 groove, with a heavy *backbeat* (emphasis on beats 2 and 4, usually reinforced by a cracking snare drum). The "chunk" of the backbeat can be further reinforced with either an accent on beats 2 and 4, or a percussive left-hand mute on either or both of these beats, which creates a *chak* sound. I've written in the *chak* here on bar 7, beat 4, but it's usually felt more than written for. If your drummer's cracking that snare on beats 1 and 3, he's either off by one beat, or he's been listening to too many Lawrence Welk polkas.

Music: The I-vi-IV-V is a variation on the most popular chord progression in the early decade of rock and roll (the I-vi-ii-V).

Techniques: To emphasize the heavy backbeat in this straight-ahead 4/4 strum, place accents on beats two and four and clip the sound slightly using left-hand muting.

I-vi-ii-V: Shuffle

The final in the "doo-wop trilogy" features a shuffle feel that mixes arpeggiations with full-chord strumming. With its shuffle subdivision, two-beat feel, and quirky blend of chords and notes, the figure conveys an almost playful, lighthearted spirit. Minor 7 chords also help jazz up the sound. Just the thing for the Eisenhower era.

Figure 10-5 has beats 1, 3, 4, and the offbeats of beats 2 and 4 (beats 2½ and 4½) played with single notes. The full chords fall on beat 2.

Music: I-vi-ii-V, with minor 7 chords on the vi and ii, is the favorite child of the '50s chord progression.

Technique: Work for a smooth transition when going between the chordal strums and arpeggiated notes in this hybrid accompaniment approach.

Track 48

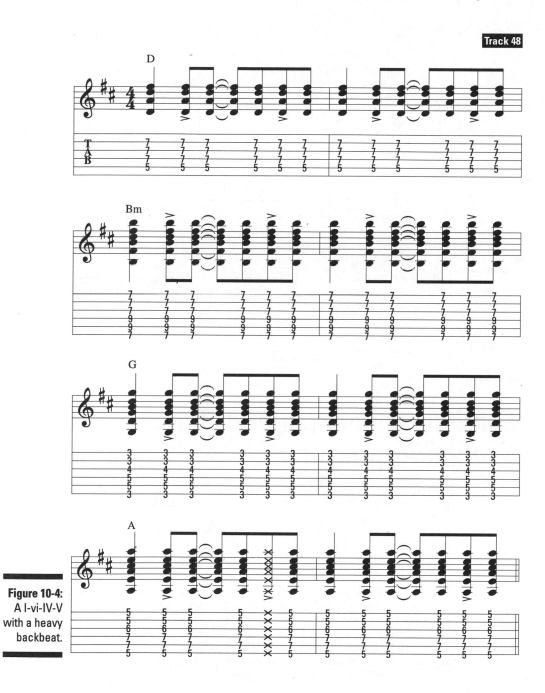

Figure 10-4:
A I-vi-IV-V
with a heavy
backbeat.

Figure 10-5: Mixing single notes and chord in a I-vi-ii-V shuffle.

Combining Country and Blues: Rockabilly Rhythm

The rockabilly sound combines country-influenced music with R&B, retaining the twang of the former and the swing of the latter. At Memphis's Sun Studios in 1954, a young Elvis Presley was loosening up with the band when producer/engineer Sam Phillips turned on the tape recorder — creating musical history. Scotty Moore, Elvis's guitar player at the time, played "That's All Right, Mama" with an urgent rhythm playing, adding chordal fills that just about, but didn't quite, explode into a lead break. This was the driving rockabilly rhythm that was spread through the era by such rockabilly greats as James Burton (who also played with Elvis), Jerry Reed, Carl Perkins, and even Chet Atkins. All had their own turn with the rockabilly rhythm lick.

Figure 10-6 shows a rockin' rockabilly rhythm progression in E. Notice the use of hammer-ons and how the partial barre in the 5th-position has to move quickly in and out of the D chord (played as a momentary A form).

Music: The rockabilly rhythm established the essential rockabilly strum, which simulated the engine of a chugging freight train.

Technique: This rhythm figure requires you to execute quick hammer-ons and a partial barre while within a chordal context.

Track 50

Figure 10-6:
A classic,
driving
rockabilly
rhythm
figure.

Creating Rock and Roll Guitar Style: Chuck Berry

More than any other guitarist, Chuck Berry defines the single point at which rock and roll guitar became a bona fide style. And he is considered a true innovator, a true hero, rubbing shoulders with the ranks of Eric Clapton, Jimi Hendrix, and Eddie Van Halen. Berry had down cold the entire ethos of rock and roll: the rhythm, the lead, the attitude, the understanding of lyrical double-entendre, and the stage moves (his famous "duck walk"). And he did it many years before any of these "guitar heroes" were on the scene, between 1957 and 1960.

Figure 10-7 is the familiar-sounding rhythm figure, which owes its signature sound to the movement of the chord's 5th degree momentarily up to the 6th degree, and then resolving back down to the 5th. You can play the 5-to-6 movement on the I, IV, and V chords, and in either a straight-eighth or shuffle feel. (The *5* and *6* refer to scale degrees of the chord — for more on this, see Chapter 7). It's sort of a stationary, one-note adaptation of the boogie-woogie line played by R&B pianists and bass players. Chuck Berry didn't invent this riff, but he sure made it popular, and it's often referred to in various appellations using his name.

> **Music**: The 5-to-6 rhythm figure is a stationary chordal figure with movement. It is also a variant and sometime substitute for the boogie figure.

> **Technique:** Hold your left-hand 1st and 3rd fingers stationary while reaching up with your 4th finger to momentarily fret the 6th degree of the chord. Be careful not to shift the already-fretted fingers as you fret and release the 4th finger.

Bo Diddley may have had a rhythm named after him, but Berry had a whole style, and a bevy of immortal songs, credited to him. He combined the 12-bar blues with country and blues licks, and he straightened them out and adapted them to his own driving, *chugga-chugga* style.

As a soloist, he was known for his signature use of double-stop 4ths (an interval of 2½ steps), shown here in Figure 10-8, in a 12-bar solo break. He also played almost exclusively out of the home position of the pentatonic scale. (For more on the pentatonic scale, see Chapter 8.)

> **Music:** Chuck Berry immortalized the double-stop figure in 4ths and created a signature sound for playing the 12-bar blues solo. He also got major mileage out of the 5-6 move, which he used in virtually all of his songs.

> **Technique:** In this miniature solo, you play repeated double-stops with both the left-hand 1st and 3rd fingers, and execute quick bends.

Copying a master

Countless guitarists from the early days copied Chuck Berry and knelt down and thanked their lucky stars for him (or they should have, especially after he made them all rich). Berry influenced the Beatles, the Beach Boys, the Rolling Stones, Eric Clapton, and Jimmy Page, many of whom either covered his songs or paid tribute to them in their own compositions or playing styles. Some of Berry's immortal songs included "Maybellene," "Johnny B. Goode," "Sweet Little Sixteen" (which the Beach Boys turned into "Surfin' USA" and later acknowledged Berry's music as the source), "Roll Over Beethoven" (covered by the Beatles), "Route 66," and "Reelin' and Rockin'."

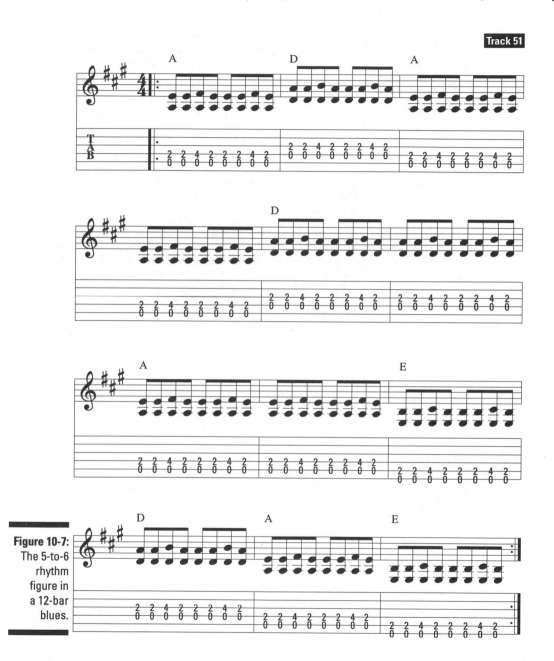

Figure 10-7: The 5-to-6 rhythm figure in a 12-bar blues.

Surf's Up

While doo-wop was an East Coast phenomenon, surf music, as played by Jan and Dean and the Beach Boys, was almost exclusively a West Coast phenomenon. (Have you ever tried hanging ten on New York City's East River?) But the so-called "surf" sound, characterized by twangy guitars, heavy reverb, and full-length instrumental songs, extended to the instrumental groups of the Ventures (with Nokie Edwards on guitar), the Surfaris (*Surf*-aris . . . get it?), Dick Dale (whose version of "Miserlou" enjoyed a revival in the movie *Pulp Fiction*), and, over in England, Hank Marvin and the Shadows.

The fascination with a featured, single-line-playing guitar extended beyond songs about sun and fun. Duane Eddy was a leader in the instrumental guitar arena with his contributions of "Rebel Rouser," and the "Theme from *Peter Gunn*." To modern ears, this proto-surf sound is almost cartoon-like, with its twangy single-note melodies, simply played, doused in reverb, and *sproinged* with the Bigsby bar (for more on a Bigsby, see Chapter 16). But this was instrumental rock guitar finding its sea legs (ouch!). But the guitar as a featured melody-playing instrument was now clearly established, paving the way for the guitar heroes of the mid- and late 60s.

Figure 10-9 features open-position chords strummed and lightly arpeggiated and mixed with barre chords for the strictly rhythm sections. The lead is based on a simple melody, played in eighths and quarters. You typically play a surf melody in open position, where the aggressively picked open strings add to the twang factor. Listen to the sound on the CD and notice that it's treated to an inordinate amount of reverb, and that the vibratos at the ends of notes are seasick swirly.

> **Music:** Surf music put unabashedly simple, guitar-driven melodies into the limelight — and onto hit records. It also established reverb as a way-cool effect.

> **Technique:** This passage features a lyrical open-string melodies played as featured part; use the whammy bar judiciously, to bring out a sustained note. (For more on the whammy bar, see Chapter 1.)

The British Are Coming, The British Are Coming

The so-called British Invasion was a clever catch phrase and headline dreamed up by some savvy media type to describe the flood of British rock bands that gained popularity in the early to mid-60s, the most famous being the Beatles from Liverpool. The *invasion* part comes from the fact that this flood of British bands took the United States, Canada, Australia, and any other English-speaking colonies by storm, immediately laying siege to their record stores and broadcast airwaves, and setting up occupying forces in their collective hearts. Think of the most famous of these bands: the Beatles, the Rolling Stones, the Who, the Kinks, the Animals, and the Yardbirds. They were all the rage, and the rest of the world couldn't get enough of this new, fresh sound. How did they do it? Was it something in that English water?

For guitarists, the British Invasion wasn't merely just a fashion trend in pop music. The British Invasion bands were the creative children of Chuck Berry, Bo Diddley, Buddy Holly, and other American bluesmen. They learned from the masters (and reverently acknowledged this) and then took guitar playing and rock and roll itself to the next level.

Figure 10-8:
A 12-bar
solo using
Chuck
Berry–style
double-
stops.

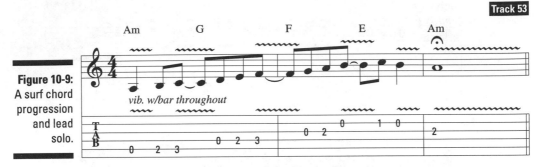

Figure 10-9:
A surf chord progression and lead solo.

The next section in this chapter covers the Beatles, the earliest of the three biggies to cross the Atlantic, who were really the bridge between early rock and classic rock. They did straight covers and knock-offs of Chuck Berry tunes, but they later transcended early rock and came to master just about any sub-genre in rock they touched, dominating the charts until they officially broke up in 1970. The Stones and the Who also made early forays into the United States and elsewhere, but reached the peak of their popularity a little later, more in the heart of the true era of classic rock.

The Beatles' "I Saw Her Standing There"

The rhythm riff to this early Beatles song is highly twangy and percussive-sounding. You just can't get this sound out of a barre chord, proving that open-position chords do indeed have their place in rock, not just as cowboy chords for folk songs. Figure 10-10 requires a tightly controlled rhythm guitar approach, using open-position chords, while "keeping a lid on them" through heavy left-hand muting. The harder you hit the strings, the more dynamic and choppy-sounding (in a good way) your sound is, but the more potential it has to get out of control.

> **Music:** The Beatles (in their early recordings) used open chords for a good *chak* sound, providing a brightness almost impossible to derive from barre chords.

> **Technique:** Here you can get really aggressive with your approach to left-hand muting, to produce a tight, punchy sound and to control the open, ringing strings.

Instead of just strumming, you can use a slow pick drag — either as an up- or a downstroke — to draw out the notes in a quick arpeggio. You can hear this technique on the CD, although it's not written into the music.

Melodic riffing à la the Beatles

Low-note melodies repeated over and over occupy an important place in rock songs of all genres, but because early rock started the whole thing rolling, I feature them here. Think of how surf guitar and early rock riffs were played, such as in the Beatles' "Day Tripper," or Duane Eddy's the "Theme from *Peter Gunn*" (a TV show about a private detective, for those too young to remember), or Roy Orbison's "Oh, Pretty Woman" (later covered by Van Halen). Figure 10-11 features some early rock-style melodic riffing, suitable for basing a song on (if I do say so myself).

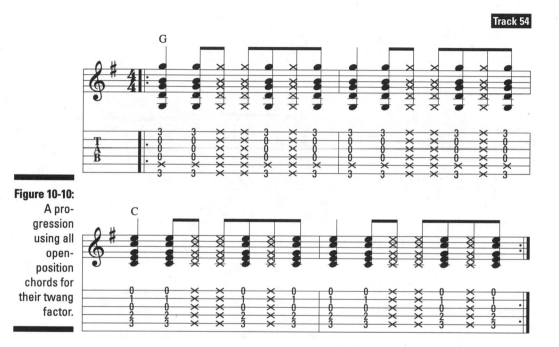

Track 54

Figure 10-10: A progression using all open-position chords for their twang factor.

Music: These songs were melodically inventive, yet simple enough to form a riff you could sing over. Many were even transposable up to the IV chord or other chords of the song.

Technique: The trick here is to blend the melodic material in with the background parts. (Try singing over this for extra points!)

Low- and high-note riffing

A different kind of single-note riff is not melodically based (such as in Figure 10-11), nor is it strictly a chord arpeggio. It's sort of like a *pedal,* where a low note sounds incessantly against a higher sequence of notes. But in this type of figure, the low notes act as part of the figure, interrupting the high-note activity to make themselves heard. The result, illustrated in Figure 10-12, is a quirky off-kilter figure, half melody, half bassline. You can hear this in the Rolling Stones' "Last Time," the Beatles' "I Feel Fine," and the Monkees' "Another Pleasant Valley Sunday."

Figure 10-11: Melodic, song-inducing riffs.

Figure 10-12: A low-note/high-note riff.

Music: Low- and high-note riffing ties a ringing open string against a moving upper line, creating a quirky syncopation effect — a uniquely guitaristic idiom, due to the juxtaposition of the low open strings and high-fretted upper strings.

Technique: Playing between strings in an eighth note rhythm requires a loose but controlled right hand. Work to get your wrist movements wide enough so that you can dart between the strings in enough time to play the notes in rhythm, but not so wide that you overshoot the intended string. You also must control the low open strings so that they don't ring out too much and bury the sound of the higher fretted strings.

Chapter 11

The Golden Age of Classic Rock

*I*n this chapter, I examine the more advanced approaches to two techniques I cover in Chapter 7: riffs and chord-based rhythm figures. Then it's on to the cool stuff: the classic rock masters! I will focus on Pete Townshend, Keith Richards, Jimi Hendrix, Led Zeppelin's Jimmy Page, Carlos Santana, the Allman Brothers, Lynyrd Skynyrd, ZZ Top, Stevie Ray Vaughan, Aerosmith, the Eagles, and U2.

Playing Advanced Riffs and Rhythm Figures

After the doo-wop and surf era, guitar sounds got thicker and less twangy. Thanks largely to the efforts of Pete Townshend of the Who and Keith Richards of the Rolling Stones — and to improving amp technology — guitarists now knew how to rely on the rhythm guitar to carry the entire band, acting in both a lead and rhythm capacity. Richards, Townshend, and the legions of those aspiring to be them, accomplished this by playing neither straight chords nor straight melody, but something in between: an integrated rhythm style incorporating chords, chordal embellishments, and single-note figures.

Helping their cause was the technological developments in guitar and especially in amp circuitry. (For more on amps, see Chapter 3.) Guitars just sounded better now when their notes were left to ring out more. Guitar amps were getting more powerful, and distortion was getting more musically usable and more pleasing to listen to. Taking a razor blade and cutting slits in your speakers or removing power tubes to give your amp a decent overdrive quality was no longer necessary. (Uh, you didn't hear that from me, okay?)

Riff-based rhythm figure

Figure 11-1 shows a riff-based figure that uses double-stops to help fill out the sound. Notice that this figure is played in open position, but that it incorporates *partial barres,* where the left-hand index finger holds down just some of the strings instead of all six. Figure 11-1 takes a single-line riff, such as the kind found in Roy Orbison's "Oh, Pretty Woman" (later covered by Van Halen) and fleshes it out with chordal figures and double-stops. At the progression's finish, notice the jump up to a snazzy E7#9 chord, a chord that would become one of Jimi Hendrix's trademarks, appearing prominently in "Foxy Lady" and "Purple Haze."

Track 57

Figure 11-1: Extended riff-based figure in A.

Chord-based rhythm figure

In addition to playing the running-eighth-note riff in Figure 11-1, you can also produce an advanced and intricate-sounding rhythm part by augmenting your chord playing to give it more activity. Figure 11-2 is also in the key of A, and, in fact, follows the same chord progression as in Figure 11-1, but achieves a sense of movement and variety through chordal embellishments. Dressing up an existing rhythm, or chordal, part is known as the fine art of *comping,* short for "accompaniment," and is a great way to give your playing some flair right within a background figure.

To move around the neck in different places while still playing over the appropriate chord, you can employ different voicings or *inversions.* An inversion takes the same notes and distributes them in a different order. An A chord is normally spelled A, C♯, E, with A as the lowest note (this is called *root position*). But if the chord is spelled (the technical term for indicating, in order, the notes of a chord) C♯, E, A, the chord is still A, just starting on the next tone up in the sequence. The ordering of C♯, E, A is known as the *first inversion A major chord.* I use inversions of chords in two places in Figure 11-2: at bar 3, on the descending D7 chord; and at bar 7, on the ascending A7 chord.

Studying the Classics: Classic Rock

Now I move on to discuss the individual styles of some of the greatest legends in rock guitar, in perhaps what is the greatest era of rock guitar.

The term *classic rock* cuts a wide swath through music history and is probably the category open to the most interpretation of any in rock. You can make a great game out of describing all the various sub-genres that can fall under classic rock — including blues-rock, garage rock, psychedelic rock, southern rock, glam rock, stadium rock, and so forth — but for the purposes of this chapter, I try to keep the list manageable, limiting the scope to include these principal sub-genres:

- ✔ British Invasion, as represented by the Who and the Rolling Stones.

- ✔ Early blues rock, as represented by Eric Clapton.

- ✔ The hard rock, proto-metal work of Jimi Hendrix and Led Zeppelin's Jimmy Page.

- ✔ The Latin-rock movement, dominated and solely occupied by Carlos Santana.

- ✔ The southern-rock stylings of the Allman Brothers and Lynyrd Skynyrd.

- ✔ The classic blues rock of ZZ Top and Stevie Ray Vaughan.

- The neo-classic riff-based rock of Aerosmith.
- The folk- and country-rock of the Byrds and the Eagles.
- Texture-based guitar rock, as represented by U2's The Edge.

Track 58

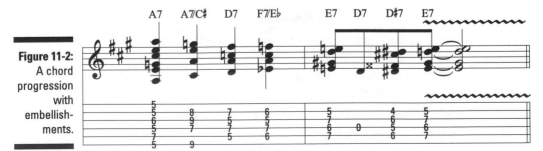

Figure 11-2:
A chord progression with embellishments.

All of these styles and artists came to fruition after the first onslaught of the British Invasion, in the period from about 1965 to 1975 (except for late-bloomer Stevie Ray Vaughan, whose debut album, *Texas Flood,* was released in 1983). In this incredibly short time, a mere ten years, the greatest practitioners of the instrument were rubbing shoulders with each other, sharing concert stages as well as an era, and producing some of the best and most diverse rock guitar work in rock's history.

The British Invasion

The influence of the best and the earliest band of the British Invasion — the Beatles — spilled over into the classic rock era and beyond. Because I cover the Beatles in Chapter 10, however, I am kicking off your stylistic exploration with the other two principal bands that came just slightly after the debut of the Beatles: the Who and the Rolling Stones.

Pete Townshend

You don't have to "carve" wailing leads to be a rock player, and no better testament to that is the Who's Pete Townshend. Townshend didn't play stellar lead, but he had the best rhythm sound in rock. In his hands — particularly that right hand of his — he elevated rhythm guitar to a high art. And it was great theater in the best rock tradition. No second banana was this rhythm-playing guitarist. To add emphasis or a sense of excitement, Townshend often threw in a quick 16th-note-strummed flourish with a quick down-up-down-stroked sequence in his right hand. Guitarists often describe this sound to each other as *chick-a-CHOW* (you won't find *that* in any college music-theory book). Even quarter notes would be treated to the "windmill," where Townshend would fully extend his long arm and make large sweeping circular motions, striking the strings as his hand passed his midsection. Figure 11-3 shows a rhythm guitar part in the Pete Townshend style with plenty of dynamics (loud vs. soft, active vs. sparse), plus some syncopations, both implied and actual.

> **Music:** Pete Townshend put rhythm guitar on par with lead guitar as far as an exciting and dynamic part. He defined the high water mark as far as rhythm playing.

> **Technique:** Use strong, quick right-hand strokes to execute the 16th-note-based full-chord strums.

Keith Richards

Keith Richards is a founder and musical anchor of one of the most enduring and successful rock bands of all time, the Rolling Stones. He is a highly original musician who plays chiefly rhythm guitar (the Stones employed a second guitarist for lead duties), tunes his guitar to a G chord when altered tunings were virtually unknown in rock guitar, and even removes his low E string to leave his low G (the detuned 5th string) as the lowest string — for satisfactory riffing.

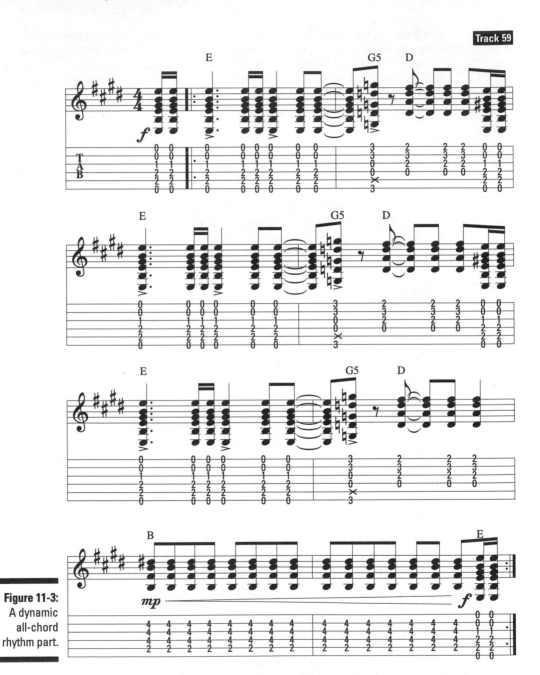

Figure 11-3: A dynamic all-chord rhythm part.

The riff to "Satisfaction" (1965) is arguably one of the most recognizable and classic of all time. It came to its composer, Keith Richards, in a dream. Unlike the more intricate and melodic riffs of, say, the Beatles, the riff to "Satisfaction" — along with its crude insistent lyrics brimming with sexual frustration — proved that rock and roll didn't have to use clever and inventive melodies to be effective. This riff was comprised of only three different notes having a range of 1½ steps. On paper (to coin a phrase), it didn't seem all that distinctive, and yet it launched a huge number one hit and was a harbinger of the future — of a rock and roll that was petulant and rebellious. Figure 11-4 features a simple, straight-forward and insistent single-note figure — with plenty of buzz-saw distortion thrown in for good measure.

> **Music:** The Rolling Stones presented rock and roll as it was meant to be: simple, grammatically incorrect, and immortal.

> **Technique:** Use a heavy, aggressive right-hand approach, and dial up some heavy distortion.

Track 60

Figure 11-4: A low-note riff reveling in its insistence and simplicity.

Chordal riffs

Keith Richards is a human riff machine, creating memorable hooks to such immortal songs as "Start Me Up," "Honky-tonk Women," "Jumping Jack Flash," "Last Time," and "Brown Sugar." The aforementioned songs all benefited from Richards's patented "chordal riff" approach, where the musical motion, interest, and impetus comes from not moving chords — nor single lines based on chords — but available movement within a left-hand chord form. Figure 11-5 is a blend of chordal riffs, played within a fairly stationary left-hand chord-form setting.

> **Music:** Keith Richards established the chordal riff, where simple static variations on chords created classic riffs for immortal songs.

> **Technique:** Learn the fingerings of these left-hand chord-form variations first, before applying the right-hand rhythm.

Track 61

Figure 11-5:
Chordal riffing inside assorted left-hand chord forms.

The Blues break through

One of the primary forces that defined the post-British Invasion classic-rock era was the maturing of the electric blues style, as typified by Eric Clapton, Jimmy Page, and Jimi Hendrix. Many of the previous British Invasion bands had readily acknowledged R&B and early rock greats Chuck Berry and Bo Diddley as influences, but either covered their material directly or ignored it completely in favor of a pop sound. But with the coming of age of Clapton, Page, and Hendrix, a new synthesis was taking place where the electric blues was about to enjoy not only a renaissance, but a transformation.

Eric Clapton

Eric Clapton got his start in the Yardbirds (as did jazz-rock pioneer Jeff Beck and Led Zeppelin guitarist Jimmy Page), but left to join John Mayall's Bluesbreakers where he honed his soulful and lyrical lead skills. He became a bona fide superstar of the guitar (and was the first "guitar god," a reputation buttressed when all over London subways and posters graffiti artists scrawled "Clapton Is God") and helped revive popular interest in many of the blues legends he drew inspiration from, including Robert Johnson, Blind Lemmon Jefferson, Son House, Skip James, and Elmore James.

Clapton earned the nickname "Slowhand" because of his supreme ease in playing and the effortless way he moved over the fretboard. Following his stint with the Bluesbreakers, he founded Cream, with bassist Jack Bruce and drummer Ginger Baker, often credited as the first true supergroup comprised of recognized virtuosos. The heaviness of their hit songs, including "White Room," "Sunshine of Your Love," and "Badge," helped to define the era of the "power trio" and to establish the blues as viable rock material, both creatively and commercially. "Crossroads," a song by Robert Johnson, captured in a live version on the album *Wheels of Fire* (1968), contains one of the greatest guitar solos of all time. Eddie Van Halen learned it note for note and, in concert, would drop it into a song's improvisational section as a tribute.

Figure 11-6 is a bluesy solo, employing many of the techniques Clapton used to infuse his solos with expression: bends, hammers, pulls, slides, and left-hand vibrato. Notice that much of this solo takes place comfortably in the home position of the pentatonic scale (see Chapter 7 for more on the pentatonic scale). This is the way Clapton played: not with gratuitous flash, but with restraint, precision, and taste.

> **Music:** Eric Clapton brought a truly lyrical blues lead style to rock, and established the guitarist as a frontman capable of garnering adulation previously reserved for singers.

> **Technique:** In this piece, executing correctly the pitches and rhythms is only part of the story. Focus on playing the line with expressiveness, working to make the bends smooth, seamless, and soulful.

Jimi Hendrix

Jimi Hendrix is hailed as perhaps the greatest rock guitarist of all time. He combined the best elements of electric blues, psychedelic abandon, sonic sculpting, and pure inspiration. Although he died at only the age of 27 (in 1970), his legacy is the most enduring (and studied) of any guitarist ever. He started off in the R&B circuit as a sideman, playing with the Isley Brothers and Little Richard, to name two, but quickly developed his own style and became a local legend revered for his other-worldly technique and far-out stage performances.

Hendrix was a superior showman as well as guitarist, and could play the guitar behind his back and with his teeth. Like Jimmy Page and Jeff Beck, Hendrix saw the guitar as a total sonic instrument and was a master of marshaling such effects as distortion, *feedback* (a high-pitched howl that occurs when you face the guitar's pickups directly at a cranked-up amp), and the wah wah pedal to conform to his vision. With his power trio, the Jimi Hendrix Experience (with Noel Redding on bass and Mitch Mitchell on drums), Hendrix recorded three albums, *Are You Experienced* (1967), *Axis: Bold As Love* (1967), and *Electric Ladyland* (1968), containing such classics as "Purple Haze," "Hey Joe," "All Along the Watchtower," "Little Wing," and "Voodoo Child (Slight Return)." Adding to his uniqueness was the fact that he played left-handed, but using a "flipped" right-handed guitar (usually a Strat), re-strung. So his strings were in the normal orientation (with the low E closer to the ceiling), but the tuning pegs, controls, bridge, and nut were all "upside down."

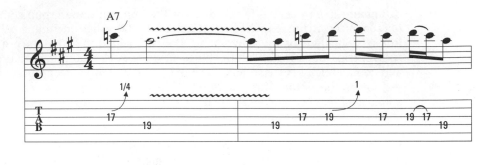

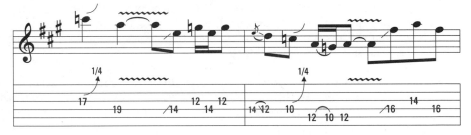

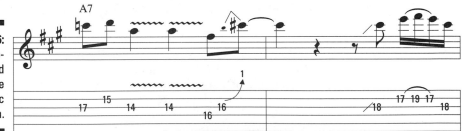

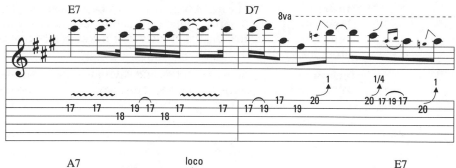

Figure 11-7 is a lead figure using several techniques of which Hendrix was an acknowledged master: blues playing, string bending, whammy-bar manipulation, and effects use (wah-wah pedal and distortion).

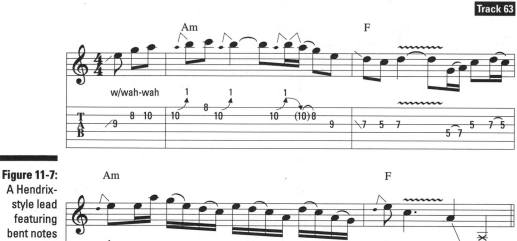

Figure 11-7: A Hendrix-style lead featuring bent notes and whammy bar moves.

Music: Jimi Hendrix brought together blues-based lead playing, inspired showmanship, avant-garde sound-production techniques, and a total approach to music making using the guitar never before realized through a single instrument.

Technique: Try getting the pitches and rhythms under your fingers first, before incorporating the bar moves. Then work to make the combination of blues soloing, whammy bar manipulation, and effects use as cohesive as possible.

Jimmy Page

Jimmy Page also got early professional experience in the Yardbirds, as did Eric Clapton and Jeff Beck. But Page was also a seasoned sideman and session player, and, perhaps because of this, was able to drive his band Led Zeppelin into producing the ultimate in finely crafted songs and perfectly orchestrated instrumental parts.

Although Page was a virtuoso, he never overplayed, preferring to showcase his genius through his composed riffs, arranging skill, or songwriting savvy. Page and company (John Paul Jones on bass and keys, John Bonham on drums, and Robert Plant on vocals) could seemingly take on any music form and make it work: traditional blues-based material ("Since I've Been Loving You"), Eastern-influenced music ("Kashmir"), folk influences ("Bron-Y-Aur Stomp") flat-out rockers ("Whole Lotta Love," "Heartbreaker"), trippy psychedelia ("Dazed and Confused") and epic anthems ("Stairway to Heaven"). Many people consider Zeppelin to be the prototype for a new category of rock and roll: heavy metal. (See Chapter 12 for more on heavy metal.)

If you had to pick one band from the entire classic rock era that encompassed everything — great blues-based guitar playing, immortal riffs, successfully eclectic material (from blues to folk to exotic to metal), and superior songwriting, it would have to be Led Zeppelin. No other band comes close in defining the classic rock era.

Figure 11-8 is a riff based on the Led Zeppelin sound — massively heavy, tinged with blues, and with a dash of the exotic thrown in.

Music: Jimmy Page used the guitar, studio production, and his songwriting talents to create the most versatile and popular hard rock band of the era. In doing so, he created the working prototype for heavy metal.

Technique: This is a good example of how to smoothly incorporate an exotic scale segment into a blues-based riff.

Latin rock: Carlos Santana

Mexican-born Carlos Santana rose to prominence in the early '70s, leading a big band that played Latin rock, but with a guitar sound so lyrical, so big, so mature, he became an unavoidable and irresistible influence for any other guitarist who heard him and every guitarist who followed him. Santana was equally at home playing in a flashy, virtuosic style as he was in a slower more soulful one, but it was his thick, creamy, blues-based sound that most people associate him with. His minor-key lines were especially achingly expressive. Through his hits "Evil Ways" (1970), "Black Magic Woman" (1970), and "Oye Como Va" (1971, written by Latin percussion great Tito Puente), Santana established himself as a true guitar hero along the lines of Clapton and Page.

Figure 11-9 is a lyrical, melodic line played over a Latin-rock-flavored beat. The progression here outlines the Dorian mode, which is like the minor scale but with a raised 6th degree. The quarter-note triplets (which are twice as long as eighth-note triplets, or three for every two beats) help lend an expressive, lyrical quality to the line.

> **Music:** Carlos Santana brought Latin-rock into the mainstream. He defined a voice that was lyrical and bluesy, but not derivative of Clapton and other blues rockers.

> **Technique:** This passage emphasizes the lyrical, expressive phrasing inherent in Latin rock. Isolate and practice the slow quarter-note triplets, and play along with the CD, if necessary, to make sure you're counting them accurately. You execute the embellishments (a quick flourish to dress up a note) with a quick hammer-on and pull-off movement.

Track 64

Figure 11-8: A heavy low-note riff, followed by a blues-based solo riff.

Figure 11-9:
A minor-key,
Latin-
flavored
lead line.

Southern rock

Southern rock is a freewheeling mix of country, R&B, gospel, blues, and bluegrass that gained huge popularity in the early-to-mid-'70s, largely due to the efforts of bands like Buffalo Springfield, Poco, the Marshall Tucker Band, Lynyrd Skynyrd, the Allman Brothers, Molly Hatchet, and Pure Prairie League. Southern rock didn't sport the over-the-top distorted guitar sound that emerging metal bands (like Led Zeppelin) favored, preferring instead to couch their guitar efforts in more melodic and laidback settings. Harmonically, southern rock trafficked in major and minor chords, basic progressions, and pentatonic scales. The music was quite accessible, both from a listening perspective as well as a playing one. But it highlighted the guitar, in both the rhythm section and as the featured soloist, and so attracted the best instrumentalists of the day. The southern rock of this period paved the way for one of the biggest bands of the '70s, superstars the Eagles.

Allman Brothers

Formed by two brothers, Duane on guitar, and younger brother Gregg on keyboards, the Allman Brothers hailed from Georgia and defined the southern rock sound of the early '70s. The twin guitars of Duane and Dickey Betts were an unbeatable combination: Duane had the mature blues sound and expert slide technique (he was an accomplished session player who played on Eric Clapton's Derek & the Dominos' record *Layla and Other Assorted Love Songs,* among several other recordings) and Betts was the master of major-pentatonic playing and composing hooky major-scale riffs. They combined equal amounts of classic blues, straightforward chord progressions, and easy country-pop melodies, but they could also rock out and entertain rock concert audiences with extended, 20-minute jams.

Figure 11-10 is in the style of their upbeat sound, as evidenced by songs such as "Blue Sky" and "Rambling Man," which has one of the great solos of all time in the full break by Dickey Betts. The freewheeling break here is based entirely in E pentatonic major and features some very country-like bends, in the style of Dickey Betts.

> **Music:** The Allman Brothers synthesized diverse elements of R&B, blues, and rock into the southern rock sound.

> **Technique:** This passage features major-pentatonic soloing and two position shifts. Be sure to execute the slides with smooth motions, and make sure you play them precisely in rhythm, especially when shifting positions.

Lynyrd Skynyrd

Like the Allman Brothers, Florida-based Lynyrd Skynyrd were known as a southern rock band but were more regional and aggressively southern than the Allmans. Their southern-fried, twangy-guitar sound was enhanced by a unique approach: Whereas most bands had either one or two guitars, Skynyrd boasted three (Allen Collins, Gary Rossington, and Ed King later replaced by Steve Gaines), a trend followed by the Eagles and others a little later. "Freebird" (1973) and "Sweet Home Alabama" (1974) were Skynyrd's biggest hits, the latter probably *the* emblem of southern rock idealism. Other well-known hits containing their infectious, good-time sound included "Gimme Three Steps," "Tuesday's Gone," "Simple Man," and "What's Your Name." In their songs, the guitar has a particularly sharp, in-your-face sound, placed refreshingly out front in the mix.

Figure 11-11 is a riff in the southern-rock style of Skynyrd, featuring open-string riffs and double-stops. The passage calls upon both the blues and major scales to create the mix of blues and country.

> **Music:** Lynyrd Skynyrd brought twangy, triple-guitar-driven, good-ol'-boy grooves into the southern-rock forefront.

> **Technique:** This double-stop and single-note riff combines notes from major scale and blues scale.

The lyrics in "Sweet Home Alabama" include a reply to Neil Young for his song "Southern Man," a scathing indictment of southern racism. In the Skynyrd song, the band challenges Young by name, singing, "Well, I heard Mr. Young sing about us. Well, I heard old Neil put us down. . . ."

Track 66

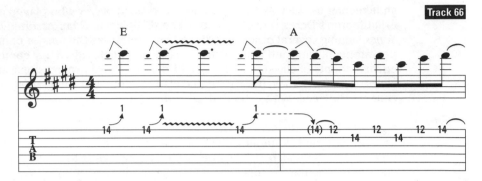

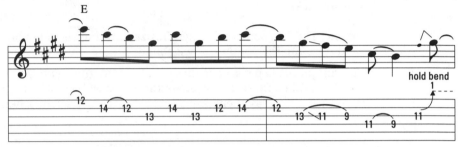

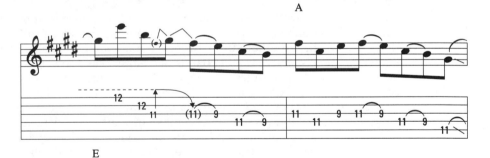

Figure 11-10:
An E pentatonic major passage in a southern rock style.

ZZ Top

ZZ Top was another band boasting a strong southern regional influence: Texas. But this was not the same Texas-style music of Buddy Holly; this was much more hard-edged and raw. ZZ Top wasn't the first band to electrify blues and bring it into the mainstream, but they had longevity and staying power and defined the Texas "swamp-boogie" sound with such hits as "La Grange" (1973), "Tush" (1974), and the greasy and fluidly tasteful guitar of Billy Gibbons. One of Gibbons's trademark techniques is the "pinch harmonic" — an artificial harmonic formed by stopping the string immediately after striking it with the right hand, causing a bell-like note to ring out. (For more on harmonics, see Chapter 9.)

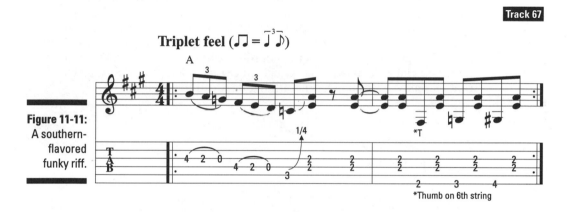

Figure 11-11: A southern-flavored funky riff.

Figure 11-12 starts with a low, growling rhythm riff and is capped off by a bent-string lick that includes a pinch harmonic. You may have to move your right hand around over the string area over the pickups to find just the right spot to make the note ring clearly. Make sure you have a lot of distortion in your sound; it helps to bring out the harmonic.

> **Music:** ZZ Top popularized the swampy Texas-boogie sound with slick production and expert songwriting.

> **Technique:** This example contains two ZZ Top hallmarks: a chord-based boogie pattern and a pinch harmonic in a blues-solo context.

Later blues influence: Stevie Ray Vaughan

Although primarily considered a blues guitarist and coming later than classic rock's acknowledged heyday, the brilliant Stevie Ray Vaughan simply demands inclusion in any discussion about rock, because he played with as much exuberance and abandon as any rock player since Hendrix. He revived the dying blues movement in the early '80s, after, improbably, getting his professional start as a sideman with the godfather of glam, David Bowie. He was profoundly influenced by Jimi Hendrix and often performed a solo tour de force of Hendrix's famed instrumental ballad "Little Wing." Vaughan was himself an inspiration to fellow-Texan and guitar great Eric Johnson (discussed in Chapter 18), as well as any rock player who's ever heard him and tried to fuse together the already-close sensibilities of electric blues and rock. He fronted his own band playing inspired rhythm as well as lead and was at the height of his career before his tragic death in a helicopter crash in 1990.

Figure 11-13 is a rhythm riff in the style of Stevie Ray Vaughan that features a hard-swinging rhythm part punctuated with short single-note phrases, followed by an aggressive lead phrase. The key here is to dig in on the notes, with both the right and left hands, especially on the lead parts. Part of what gave Vaughan his sound was that he strung his guitar with heavy-gauge strings. This produced a big, fat tone, to be sure, but required him to really attack the guitar aggressively to subordinate the string tension that fought him, especially when bending strings. But you could see in his performances that he enjoyed working hard at it, that he loved the struggle.

Track 68

Figure 11-12:
A blues-based boogie riff, with a pinch harmonic.

Track 69

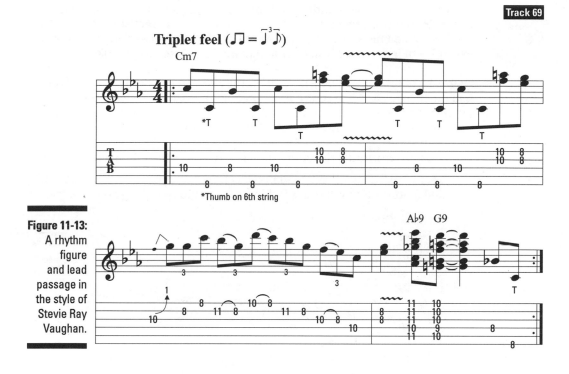

Figure 11-13: A rhythm figure and lead passage in the style of Stevie Ray Vaughan.

Music: Stevie Ray Vaughan brought unprecedented rock-like technique and new musicality to electric blues, showing the new way to play the blues like rock.

Technique: This rhythm figure features hard-swinging chordal riffs. Make it punchy, and really dig in with both your right and left hands, just like Stevie did.

Neo-classic rock: Aerosmith

Aerosmith might conveniently be classified as neo-classic rock, because their infectious riff-based rock and roll came at a time when more progressive styles of rock were in vogue. But Aerosmith, led by the twin talents of frontman Steven Tyler and guitarist Joe Perry (and supported by fine rhythm guitar playing by Brad Whitford), were so good at their game, they defied critics, won over audiences, and made classic hits of songs such as "Sweet Emotion," "Dream On," and "Walk This Way," which was so funky, it was covered by rap group Run DMC and turned into a big hit — again.

Because they are raw-sounding and riff-based, Aerosmith has been compared to the Rolling Stones and the Yardbirds. Joe Perry is a great soloist as well as riffmeister, and his short break in "Walk This Way" ranks as one of the finest examples of improvised lead over a frenetic, 16th-note-based funk feel.

Figure 11-14 is a funky single-note riff in the Joe Perry style. The wide skips and quick lead passage require that you don't keep your fingers on the frets for very long. You must be able to "hop off" the notes almost as soon as they have sounded to be in position for hitting the following notes.

Music: Aerosmith reinstated riff-based rock as viable, hit-making music.

Technique: This riff and lead break is based in a pentatonic blues scale and features funky, darting 16th-notes and a loopy string-bending lick.

Track 70

Figure 11-14:
A funky
single-note
riff and lead.

Fusing Country and Rock Lead Styles: The Eagles

Country music (also known by the more archaic term "country and western" as in the old joke, "I play both kinds of music: country *and* western") can be described as folk music on electricity. While that's not a completely accurate statement, country music is closely related to folk, especially comes to guitar solos, which are major-scale based and feature lyrical string bending reminiscent of the pedal steel guitar. Fusing folk (and its electrified cousin, country) and rock brought country lead guitar into a rock context. At the same time that southern rock was developing, popularizing bands such as Marshall Tucker ("Can't You See" and "Heard It in a Love Song"), the Allman Brothers and Lynyrd Skynyrd were putting a southern feel into rock, folk was putting bluegrass-oriented riffs in songs like the Eagles' "Take it Easy" and Pure Prairie League's "Aimee." Clarence White, a guitarist in the Byrds was also a bluegrass flatpicker, and one of the most revered instrumentalists in the genre. (White's career was cut short when he was tragically struck by a car and killed loading equipment into his car in 1970.)

Stylistically, if you take acoustic bluegrass lead, electrify it, and throw in some string bending and pedal-steel-guitar emulations, you have the basis for a country- or folk-rock lead sound. Ironically, the earliest and best practitioners of this new style were not from the South, but from California, including Linda Ronstadt and her band, J.D. Souther, Jackson Browne, and the biggest country/folk-rock of them all, the Eagles.

The Eagles were one of the most successful bands of the '70s, let alone the folk-rock genre. Their smooth, string-bendy lead styles were "required repertoire" for aspiring guitarists of the time. The easy California-based sound of the Eagles defined the folk and country rock genre (the two terms, *country rock* and *folk rock* were now used interchangeably), and to date, no band in the genre has surpassed them in record sales or hit songs. The smooth leads that graced such hit songs as "Take It Easy" and "Peaceful Easy Feeling" are stellar examples of country rock lead.

Figure 11-15 is a straight-four groove with a solo in the style of the Eagles, featuring a country-rock melodic approach and pedal steel-like bends. Note how the bent notes are slower and lyrical, and that often another note is played while the bend is sounding. Note too, that you play this solo out of a major pentatonic pattern, not the blues, or minor, pentatonic pattern in the same key.

Music: The Eagles codified the easy southern-California folk and country sound into some of the most popular music of the '70s, and made it essential for every guitarist to learn bluegrass- and pedal steel-type bends.

Technique: Practice smoothing out the slowish bends so that they are precisely in rhythm and accurately in tune. It's harder to play a slow bend than a fast one.

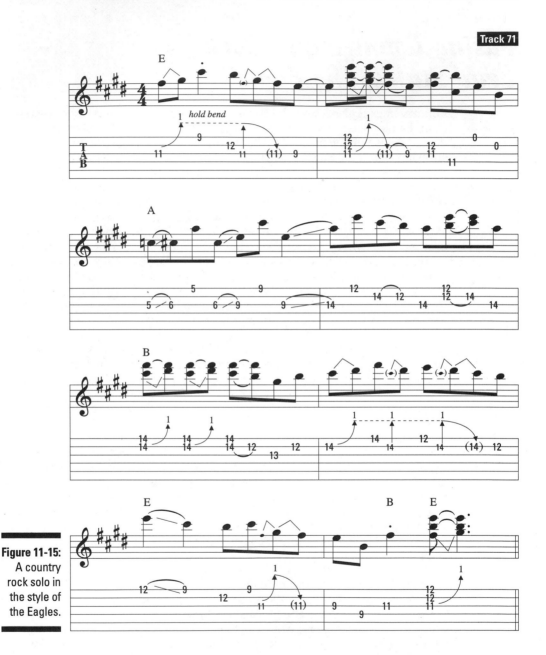

Figure 11-15:
A country rock solo in the style of the Eagles.

When former James Gang guitarist Joe Walsh joined the Eagles, the union seemed odd to people who knew both Walsh and the laid-back Eagles personnel, but the joining of Walsh's harder-edged blues soloing and Don Felder's easy melodic styles rendered one of the group's best-known hits, "Hotel California." Besides being a great song and perfectly constructed, it also features some amazing arranged guitar parts, twin leads, and inspired improvised solos. Along with "Stairway to Heaven," "Crossroads," and "All Along the Watchtower," "Hotel California" goes down in the annals of guitar playing as one of the all time classics.

Going to the Edge: U2's Guitarist Brings Epic Textures

Hailing from Dublin, Ireland, U2 was one of the biggest bands of the '80s, packing stadiums and creating multi-platinum-selling albums such as *War*, *Unforgettable Fire*, *The Joshua Tree*, *Rattle and Hum*, *Achtung Baby*, and *Zooropa* (the last two albums released in the early '90s). *The Joshua Tree*, released in 1987, was Number One on the U.S. record charts for nine weeks and produced two of their most well-known singles, "With or Without You" and "I Still Haven't Found What I'm Looking For." The band won two Grammy Awards that year, including Album of the Year. The band's success continues with their most recent Grammy Awards (2001), Song of the Year and Record of the Year, for "Beautiful Day" off the album *All That You Can't Leave Behind*, released in 2000.

U2's guitarist David Evans, known as The Edge, is a strikingly original player whose style is difficult to categorize. The Edge is the master of treating the guitar as an ensemble instrument and a leader in the group of expert effects users and minimalists that includes Brian May of Queen, Andy Summers of the Police, Adrian Belew of the Talking Heads and King Crimson, and Robert Fripp of King Crimson. Like any great, multifaceted band with a long and productive career, U2 has contributed stylistically to many genres and influenced a whole generation of guitarists, irrespective of stylistic preference.

The Edge uses signal processors and effects to high art, and it's often hard to tell that what you're listening to is even a guitar. He leads guitarists to think of the instrument as a tool for creating texture rather than just as a weapon with which to pound out chords or as a device for taking the obligatory single-line solo. The Edge was a lightning bolt of creative inspiration to rock, making the guitar important again in rock in ways no one imagined, and may be the most original and important guitarist of the '80s.

Figure 11-16 is a rhythm figure in the style of The Edge, utilizing some of his hallmarks: an arpeggiated treatment of an exotic chord progression, a deftly placed harmonic, and a reliance of outboard effects to achieve a rich, textured approach to rhythm-track layering.

> **Music:** The Edge brought a sense of grandeur to arena rock by using simple and subtle techniques that, when woven together, created a huge edifice of sound.

Technique: Let the arpeggios ring out as long as possible, and play exactly in rhythm so that the delay repeats stay in sync with the played notes. Work to make the final harmonic speak out amongst the normally picked notes.

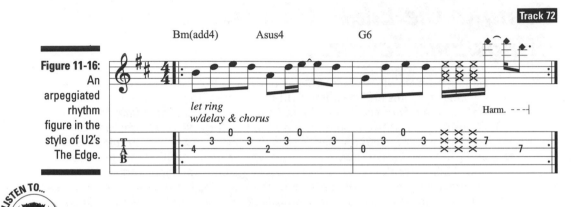

Figure 11-16: An arpeggiated rhythm figure in the style of U2's The Edge.

Anatomy of a guitar orchestration

To hear an absolutely astounding approach to rock guitar orchestration, check out U2's "I Still Haven't Found What I'm Looking For," from *The Joshua Tree.* The song opens with vaguely familiar-sounding percussive 16th notes, bouncing between the left and right speakers in a stereo pan, which you realize is muted guitar through a digital delay. After a few bars, a tambourine joins in, also in 16th notes. Two additional guitars enter, one playing power chords in double whole notes (one strum left to sustain over two entire measures), and another playing intervals of a perfect 5th in 16th notes, which creates an open sound. Then the bass and the drums join in. With the texture complete, the vocals enter, and this scheme continues throughout the first two verses and the chorus.

An interlude section follows the second verse, in which the Edge introduces an acoustic guitar

and an additional rhythm guitar, playing subtle ringing chords to outline the harmonic movement in the accompaniment underneath. In the third verse (beginning with "I have kissed honey lips. . . . ") the rhythmic activity becomes more pronounced, more driving.

Throughout the song, the accompaniment not only builds in rhythmic activity and layers, but in volume and sonic intensity as well. By the time the final-verse vocals are singing in four-part harmony, you realize the band has "terraced" — or built layer by layer — a massively huge sound using simple parts. These parts are, in and of themselves, unobtrusive. When taken as a whole, however, they provide a structure for this anthem on the proportions of a musical cathedral.

Chapter 12

Heavy Metal

* *

In This Chapter

▶ Playing electric lead and rhythm guitar

▶ Using multi-string rock licks and bends in solos and learning hard-rock power chords

▶ Playing in the style of Black Sabbath, Deep Purple, Van Halen, and Metallica

* *

Despite the current popularity of heavy metal, its roots actually go back to the beginning of rock 'n' roll (and even probably before). Among the first heavy rockers were the Kinks, the Who, and the Rolling Stones', who introduced fans to such future metal trademarks as guitar feedback, power chording, and distortion.

In 1966, Clapton formed Cream, the famed super-trio that quickly convinced the world that something heavier was on the way via great albums such as *Disraeli Gears* and *Wheels of Fire.* The development of heavy rock took another step forward the following year when psychedelic guitar genius Jimi Hendrix arrived on the scene and blew all his competition off the stage at the legendary Monterey Pop Festival. Then in 1968, Jeff Beck and Rod Stewart set the whole thing off with the Jeff Beck Group's *Truth,* which contained the basic blueprints for loud-'n'-raunchy rock.

But Led Zeppelin was hot on their heels and, right after their first album came out in January, 1969, heavy metal was a rock-and-roll reality. Afterwards came a steady stream of metal masters, from early supergroups such as Deep Purple, AC/DC, Iron Maiden, and Black Sabbath to later innovators such as Van Halen, Thin Lizzy, and UFO, and then on to various stars of the early-MTV era such as Whitesnake, Scorpions, Judas Priest, Dio, and Ratt. Later came Guns N' Roses, followed by the "thrash" assault of Metallica and Anthrax, as well as the alternative "Seattle Sound" of Stone Temple Pilots, Alice in Chains, and Soundgarden. More recently, hip hop-influenced metal bands have arrived such as Limp Bizkit and Korn. What a long, *strange* trip it's been.

Bring on the Metal

The signature sound of heavy metal guitar is *distortion,* which is the sound of an electric guitar being overdriven and contorted into a high-volume crunch. With this tone within their reach, metal guitarists are able to create sustained string bends, feedback, power chords, and many other distortion-induced effects. Long gone was the clean "twang" of early rock players. Heavy metal was distorted, loud, and featured oppressively huge rhythm guitars and wailing lead guitars. This was a welcome change for disaffected youths who could "bang their heads" (thus the moniker *headbanger* to describe a heavy metal aficionado) to the overwhelming guitars and vocalists keening about the apocalypse.

Back in the early days of this genre, the main requirement for the guitar player was to be loud — being *good* wasn't a necessity yet. For example, neither guitarist Leigh Stephens of Blue Cheer (a power trio that briefly hit it big in 1968 with a version of Eddie Cochran's "Summertime Blues") nor Erik Brann of Iron Butterfly ("In-A-Gadda-Da-Vida") were particularly good players. But their example — brazen young guitarists with plenty of hair and attitude — set the stage for the next, and far more musically accomplished, generation of metal players. Quality soon became as important as quantity, and, in short order, metal players became adept at blues-scale improvisation, fast technique, and a professional tone. Although people have often criticized metal guitar for its noisy solos and the musical ignorance of its players, it has still produced many of the greatest guitarists in rock-and-roll history.

Black Sabbath's skull-crushing riffs

Led Zeppelin (covered in detail in Chapter 11) may have been the driving force behind 1970s heavy metal (as well as the springboard for other subgenres in rock, such as hard rock and arena rock), but few would dispute Black Sabbath's place in the grand metal pantheon. In contrast to Zep's global palette of classic- and hard-rock textures, the members of Sabbath distilled a grim view of reality (perhaps inspired by their working-class upbringing in Birmingham, England) and turned it into something darker, more sinister sounding than anything Page or Plant could ever come up with. Fronting Black Sabbath was the twin force of vocalist Ozzy Osbourne and guitarist Tony Iommi. Although Ozzy was barely a singer in technical terms, he proved a devastatingly effective and even charismatic frontman. Iommi, who could turn the basic power chord into a towering wall of doom and gloom, was a surprisingly nimble soloist as well.

Iommi's combination of distorted, two-note power chords and fast pentatonic-based solos (on a Gibson SG guitar) truly helped carve out the sound of early metal. Iommi uses this signature approach on such classic Black Sabbath tracks as "Paranoid," "War Pigs," "N.I.B.," and the FM radio staple "Iron Man."

In all, Black Sabbath was a group who played a brand of rock and roll that was grimy, violent, and full of darkness. As such, you can see why contemporary thrash acts such as Metallica and Megadeth preferred the killer riffs of Sabbath over the polished guitar licks of Led Zeppelin. The typical Sabbath riff and lyric may have reflected a bleak outlook on life, but for a lot of folks, that reflected their reality, too. No one ever said life was a bowl of cherries.

Figure 12-1 shows a power-chord riff that is very much in the style of Iommi — simple, heavy, and menacing. Amazingly, Tony himself is a very sweet-natured, charming man in person. Just goes to show that you can't judge a metalhead by his riffs.

> **Music:** The classic Sabbath sound is a dark, menacing heavy metal with a take-no-prisoners attitude.

> **Technique:** Use simple root-fifth power chords and punch them up with downstrokes and plenty of distortion.

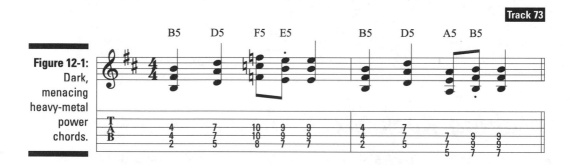

Figure 12-1: Dark, menacing heavy-metal power chords.

Ritchie Blackmore's baroque blast

Deep Purple was another top metal band of the 1970s, inspiring everyone from Judas Priest to Yngwie Malmsteen. Purple guitarist Ritchie Blackmore is just as influential, being the first major player to meld a heavy guitar tone with classical technique and harmony. He also follows Jimi Hendrix's example and uses a Stratocaster through Marshalls to create more distinctive sound (where most early metal players preferred a solidbody with humbuckers, such as a Gibson Les Paul).

Deep Purple's most celebrated song is "Smoke on the Water," a 1972 hit with dead-simple riffs and slippery Blackmore solos. Other key tracks — such as "Strange Kind of Woman," "Mistreated," "Woman from Tokyo," and "Burn" — also display Blackmore's patented guitar method: fast hammer-on runs, violent vibrato bar jerks, and melodic phrasing throughout.

One of the best examples of his classical side is on "Highway Star" (from *Machine Head*). Here, Blackmore weaves quickly picked intervals based on

Bach into his lead. The lick in Figure 12-2 offers a simplified Baroque-era-influenced phrase in the Blackmore tradition. Try it slowly at first and then bring it up to speed.

Music: Blackmore took classically influenced melodies and passages and put them in a metal setting.

Technique: Exercise cleanly articulated alternate ("up and down") picking to help this lick deliver the goods.

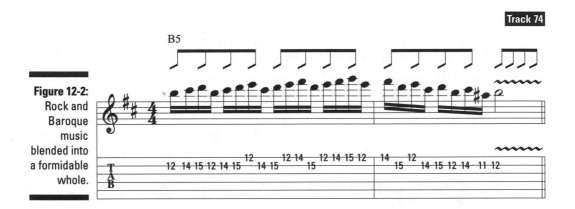

Track 74

Figure 12-2: Rock and Baroque music blended into a formidable whole.

Making Rock Stars: The Arena-Rock Era

As the 1970s rolled on, heavy metal became big business and took on a more formulaic style. Albums became high-production affairs, all featuring the prescribed number of screaming guitar solos, slick recording techniques, and loads of back-room marketing by the record company suits. When a popular band was ready to release a new LP (remember what those are?), a track or two would be flagged for heavy promotion on FM radio stations around the country. To back it, the band would hit the road on an endless tour of stadiums, outdoor festivals, or coliseums (more often than not pro hockey or basketball venues, few of which were conducive to good musical acoustics). But the formula worked, and when a band had a hot song backed up with a hot concert performance, those vinyl LP records flew off the shelves, turning bar bands into millionaires and, needless to say, *rock stars.*

KISS my axe!

For many rockers, KISS remains the ultimate heavy-metal band. With Kabuki-like makeup, smoke bombs, and flaming guitars, KISS has been a smash since the mid-1970s, thanks to their three-chord anthems and over-the-top live shows. On guitar, frontman Paul Stanley is the king of the power chord, with leadman Ace Frehley dropping simple, but effective Clapton-style licks on top. Frehley is no virtuoso, but he has a solid sense of pentatonic blues soloing, as well as heavy-metal showmanship. Plus, the KISS repertoire is full of really good, hook-laden songs.

Figure 12-3 is a an Ace Frehely-style lick that combines a little Chuck Berry, a little Eric Clapton, and a little Jimmy Page into something very typical of the mid-1970s. Remember to close your eyes and add some soul when you play it.

"Fig.1" appears in the first two bars and then repeats as the backup to the solo. So the music actually indicates two guitars: the rhythm part which is written out in the first two bars and then recalled (but not notated) in bar 3, and the lead guitar, which begins in bar 3.

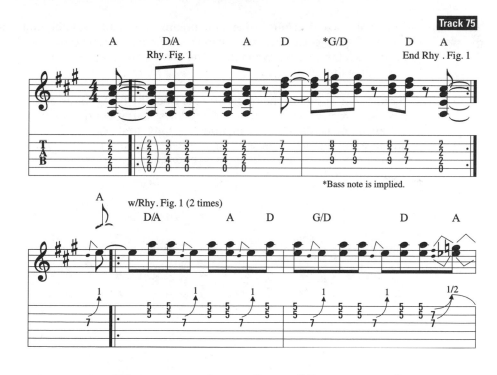

*Bass note is implied.

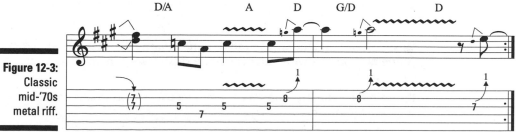

Figure 12-3: Classic mid-'70s metal riff.

Music: KISS popularized the brutish hard rock of the post-Led Zeppelin school.

Technique: Start off this roots-based passage with Chuck Berry-style double-stops and continue with more multi-string bends before climaxing with avibrato on the A.

Boston's FM-friendly riffs

Led by guitarist Tom Scholz, Boston's forte is a catchy combination of Led Zeppelin-styled riffs with the smooth vocal harmonies of L.A. rock. Part of the band's brilliance is due to Scholz's technical expertise in the recording studio — he is able to capture guitars on tape with dazzling clarity and punch.

Scholz also uses various homemade preamps, equalizers, echo units, and power attenuators to beef up Boston's studio guitar tone (some of these products later became available to the public, such as the fabled Rockman portable guitar amplifier).

"Long Time" is one of the classic tracks from the first Boston album. Besides having a great solo from original co-guitarist Barry Goudreau, an important guitar theme is repeated throughout the song, first played on acoustic guitar and later on distorted electric. Figure 12-4 is a chord progression very much in the Boston style, with the electric chords being strummed just like you would an acoustic guitar.

Track 76

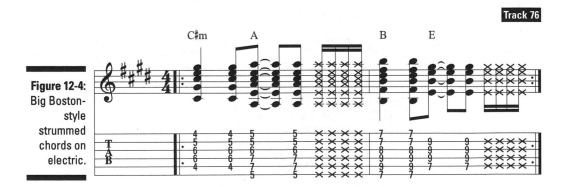

Figure 12-4: Big Boston-style strummed chords on electric.

Music: Boston led the way in radio-friendly hard rock that mixed Zeppelin-style riffs with California-style (lush, sweet, multipart) vocal harmonies.

Technique: Strum the chords on your electric as you would on an acoustic for maximum effect.

Van Halen's sonic revolution

Rock guitar was getting pretty stale and boring in the late '70s, with most rock guitarists relying on the same pentatonic-blues scales for their solos that Clapton, Beck, Page, and Hendrix had introduced a decade earlier. Then came Van Halen. Fronting his band of the same name, Eddie Van Halen strapped on a homemade Strat-style electric and blasted out solos of fluid hammer-ons, crazed whammy-bar dives, and a wacky two-handed striking technique.

Perhaps the most obvious trademark of the Van Halen style is the two-handed tap (where notes are sounded using the right hand fingertips to slam the string onto the fretboard, rather than brushing the strings). A right-hand tap is always followed by a right-hand pull-off, either to a fretted or an open string. Then a left-hand finger hammers and pulls off as well (see Chapter 9 for more on hammer-ons and pull-offs). This alternating of right- and left-hand hammer-ons and pull-offs produces a strikingly fluid sound and enables the guitarist to play wider intervals than possible with conventional left-hand technique.

Figure 12-5 is an example of right-hand tapping technique over an eight-bar, classically constructed chord progression. The taps arpeggiate the chords in a smooth and fluid manner that conventional techniques couldn't emulate.

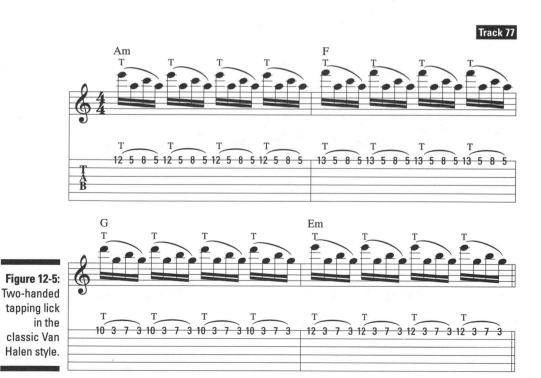

Figure 12-5: Two-handed tapping lick in the classic Van Halen style.

Music: Eddie Van Halen brought a virtuosic technique that provided a flashy and fluid solution to playing arpeggios.

Technique: Employ two-handed tapping, where a right-hand finger hammers, or taps, a string against the fretboard and then pulls off to a fretted or open string.

Angus Young's bar-room crunch

During the 1980s, when speed and virtuoso technique dominated most rock guitarist's styles, the Australian band AC/DC rocked the globe with clean power chords, economical rhythm arrangements, and aggressive, blues-based solos.

With his brother Malcolm playing kick-ass power chords, Angus Young relies on slow solos and Chuck Berry-style double-stops in solos to hard-rocking anthems such as "You Shook Me All Night Long," "Highway to Hell," and "Shoot to Thrill." The key to emulating Angus's solos is not to listen to other metal players, but instead blues guitarists such as B.B. King, Eric Clapton, or Stevie Ray Vaughan, all to get a feel for bending strings with soul.

Figure 12-6 shows a simple, bluesy lick in the style of Angus Young. Here again, the emphasis is on feel over speed.

Track 78

Figure 12-6:
Straight-ahead
blues-rock.

Music: AC/DC provides a fresh, raw sound for their version of straight-ahead blues-rock.

Technique: Uses bluesy string bends to convey the line's earthy character.

Introducing the Euro-Metal Invasion

Towards the end of the 1970s, European players began raising the bar of hard rock and heavy metal guitar, adding classically inspired melodic and harmonic techniques. Before then, the pentatonic "blues" scale or the funky Dorian mode (a minor scale with a raised 6th degree) was used in many solos. The new players supplemented these scales with the natural minor scale, as well as other exotic and jazz-based scales. This new breed of advanced guitarists included the guitarists in bands such as Iron Maiden (Dave Murray and Adrian Smith), Judas Priest (KK Downing and Glenn Tipton), Motorhead (Fast Eddie Clarke), Def Leppard (Phil Collen and Steve Clark), Thin Lizzy (Scott Gorham, Brian Robertson, and Gary Moore), and Scorpions (Uli Jon Roth, Rudy Schenker, and Matthias Jabs). These bands later influenced such '80s "hair bands" as Whitesnake, Tesla, Mr. Big, Winger, and Ratt.

The most influential Euro-metal guitarist of all time is Michael Schenker, who has played with UFO, Scorpions (also featuring his brother Rudolf), and his own Michael Schenker Group. Unlike Eddie Van Halen and his smorgasbord of tapping (see the Figure 12-5 for more on tapping) and whammy bar licks (see Chapter 9 for more on the whammy bar), Schenker possesses a flawlessly fluid technique, spicing up his leads with his lightning-paced picking runs and soulful string bends. In fact, most of the Euro-metal players mentioned in this section champion such novel techniques as *legato* hammer-ons and pull-offs to add new melodic fire to the music, as well as plenty of speed — indeed, many of these new players can pick like the devil!

Figure 12-7 is a typical lead in the Euro-metal style, played, not surprisingly, using a scale that is neither major nor minor: The Mixolydian mode.

Note how the solo takes the string-bending technique that is common to blues solos and converts it into a tool for conveying a more classical-like idea.

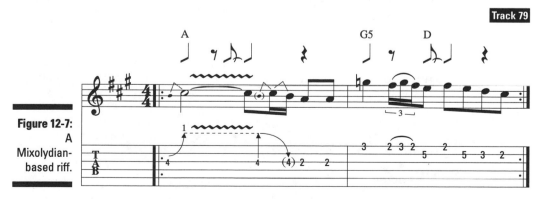

Figure 12-7:
A Mixolydian-based riff.

Music: The heavy sound of Led Zeppelin and Deep Purple is characterized by a classical sense of drama.

Technique: This passage is fast and furious, and relies on the Mixolydian mode to create a darker texture.

Putting Fans in the Stands: Heavy Metal Hits the '80s

After the 1980s rolled around, heavy metal went from a popular rock idiom to mass global entertainment thanks to MTV and the enduring influence of show-biz-savvy acts such as KISS and Alice Cooper. Live performances became highly theatrical, with huge stage sets and multiple laser lights. As metal players in this decade learned, no matter what happens backstage, "the show must go on!"

Randy Rhoads's metal attack

Next to Eddie Van Halen, Randy Rhoads was the hottest metal guitarist of the early 1980s. In the albums he cut with Ozzy Osbourne — *Blizzard Of Ozz* and *Diary Of A Madman* — Rhoads had proved himself a brilliant player, creating rhythms and solos that used two-handed tapping, classical influences, and plenty of double- and triple-tracked parts. He was a true phenomenon, but his career ended suddenly when he was killed in a freak plane accident in March 1982. Nevertheless, Rhoads was hugely influential on later metal guitarists of the 1980s.

Figure 12-8 is inspired by Rhoads's "Crazy Train" riff. It uses distorted power chords and concludes in a low lead lines, jumping between major and minor tonalities. Like the guitarist himself, this pattern has a little bit of everything.

Music: Rhoads combined Euro-metal with U.S. fretboard gymnastics.

Technique: Use a galloping rhythm approach on the open A string with three-note chords sprinkled on top. The riff ends in a minor lick on the low E string.

Yngwie Malmsteen, the Swedish speed demon

While most heavy rock guitarists of the 1980s were duping Van Halen's two-hand tapping tricks, Swedish phenom Yngwie (pronounced "Ing-vay") Malmsteen sped across the fretboard of his modified Fender Stratocaster with classically inspired phrases of startling agility. As his fame grew, new terms for his style were hatched: *Bach 'n' roll*, *neo-classical metal*, and perhaps most prevalently, *shred*. Malmsteen released his first solo album in 1984, under the name *Yngwie J. Malmsteen's Rising Force*. Containing classical-metal instrumentals, each track displayed his fast modal runs, sweep picking, diminished scales, high bends, tremolo dives, and clean classical passages.

Figure 12-9 shows an arpeggiated riff that reveals Malmsteen's frequent use of diminished chords (exotic-sounding chords that can be applied in many contexts). Here in E minor, I use a diminished chord arpeggio over a B7 chord.

> **Music:** Yngwie's use of classically influenced harmonies, such as the diminished chord used here, helped pundits coin the moniker "Bach'n' roll." Dramatic heavy metal is used to display how to use the diminished scale to resolve a chord.

> **Technique:** Apply alternate picking to insure clarity and evenness in the arpeggio.

Metallica's thrashing riffs

Taking Black Sabbath's dark, cynical view of the world and updating it for a modern metal audience with a hefty dash of punk rock, Metallica has become the most popular metal band of the last 20 years. Their albums instantly turn platinum upon release and their concerts are inevitably sold out. Great albums abound, too, such as their self-titled 1991 record (the so-called *Black Album*), which churned out metal anthems such as "Enter Sandman" and "The Unforgiven."

Powering the band is frontman James Hetfield, whose blitzkrieg rhythm guitar parts truly shape the Metallica sound. His signature guitar style involves incredibly fast strumming of root-fifth power chords, a style that has become known as "chunking." Completing the "guitar battery" is lead guitarist Kirk Hammett, whose blistering lead runs, thorough command of compound meters, and soulful blues approach have helped make Metallica the most successful metal band of our time.

You can drop the low E string to a D, creating an even deeper, heavier tone when chunking. Figure 12-10 is a "drop D" riff that captures the ferocity of Hetfield's approach in its rhythmic intensity and savage tone. Happy chunking!

> **Music:** Metallica's speedy metal style blends heavy rock with punk energy.

> **Technique:** This galloping riff requires fast but controlled strumming on the bottom three strings, emphasizing downstrokes.

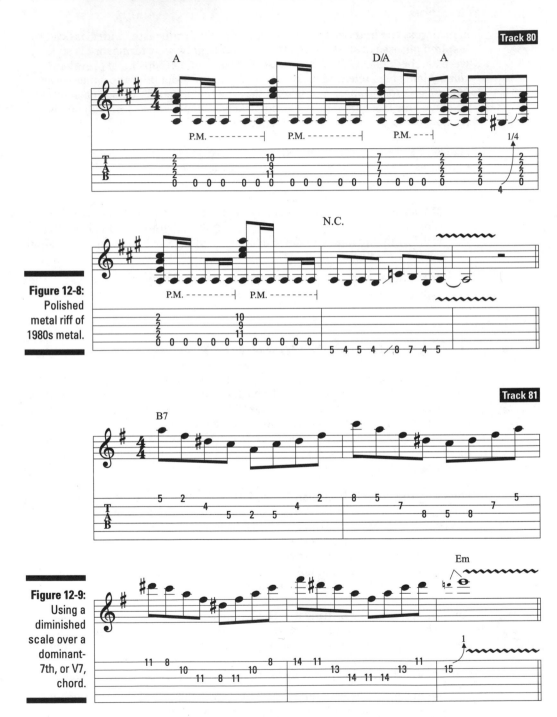

Figure 12-8: Polished metal riff of 1980s metal.

Figure 12-9: Using a diminished scale over a dominant-7th, or V7, chord.

Figure 12-10:
Speed metal
that blends
heavy rock
with punk
energy.

Raging into the New Millennium

As the 1990s got underway, the glitziness of old metal disappeared and was replaced with a darker, heavier sound, largely inspired by Metallica and other thrash bands such as Megadeth and Anthrax. Also during this time, the riff-oriented Guns N' Roses, fueled by the virtuosic blues-based guitar of Slash, seemed to inherit the hard rock mantle — and the penchant for popular success — from Aerosmith. Hip-hop also began to play a larger role in metal, converting songwriting sensibilities from melodic to rhythmic. Some metal bands even used rap DJs to add scratch-record effects over the din of cranked-up amps. Indeed, this wasn't your father's brand of heavy metal.

Dimebag Darrell's speed-metal frenzy

Following Metallica, Pantera led the next generation of thrash and speed metalers, thanks to guitarist Dimebag Darrell's furious chops and frontman Phil Anselmo's brutish lyrics. In the process, they became the most successful thrash-mongers to emerge in the 1990s. Other heavy bands of the era were Prong, Danzig, and Dream Theater.

Figure 12-11 is a tremolo-bar squeal that Darrell uses frequently. With plenty of distortion on, depress your whammy bar all the way, flick the open G string with your left hand, and as you bring the bar back up, gently touch a natural harmonic note on the 3rd fret of that string. If you touch the harmonic directly on top of the fret, you'll hear a wild, screaming harmonic. Check it out!

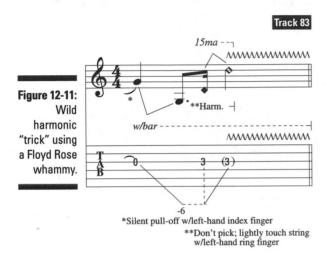

Figure 12-11: Wild harmonic "trick" using a Floyd Rose whammy.

Track 83

*Silent pull-off w/left-hand index finger
**Don't pick; lightly touch string
w/left-hand ring finger

Music: Pantera's crazed post-modern metal fuses thrash and hardcore into a dangerous new sound.

Technique: This riff uses heavy distortion, a natural harmonic on the 3rd fret, and a Floyd Rose-type whammy bar to create this stunning keening effect.

Alice in Chains

One of the heavier Seattle bands, Alice in Chains is famous for their dark, brooding metal in the tradition of Black Sabbath and Metallica. Guitarist Jerry Cantrell's playing is more soulful than virtuosic, not to mention super heavy, like Tony Iommi's or Soundgarden's Kim Thayil. His riffs and chord progressions also reflect a more melodic 1970s rock style. Cantrell also has an acoustic dimension, adding a lighter side to the Alice in Chains sound.

The lick in Figure 12-12 features an electric guitar strummed like an acoustic for the brooding-sounding rhythm part, and angst-ridden bent double-stops in the lead part wailing above.

Music: Alice's dark and moody rock is part grunge, part metal.

Technique: Use conventional strumming for rhythm and apply unison bends to convey a sense of unease and foreboding.

Figure 12-12:
A moody grunge lick.

Korn-ography

Here in the 21st century, Korn guitarists Munky and Head have completely reinvented heavy metal guitar. Where solos and power chords were once the hallmarks of the metal guitarist, these two create interlocking rhythm parts to create complex grooves. Using 7-string guitars, they also use "noise" as part of their sound arsenal, employing various types of feedback, whammy tweaks, scrapes, snarls, and white noise to drill their message home. Indeed, some Korn songs sound more like construction sites than the music of a rock band!

Figure 12-13 shows a riff and a sample of their approach to off-the-wall guitar groovedom.

Music: Korn is a leading band that creates hip hop-inspired modern metal with an emphasis on the groove.

Technique: Strive for an articulate and defined right-hand approach and string muting to deliver the full rhythmic effect.

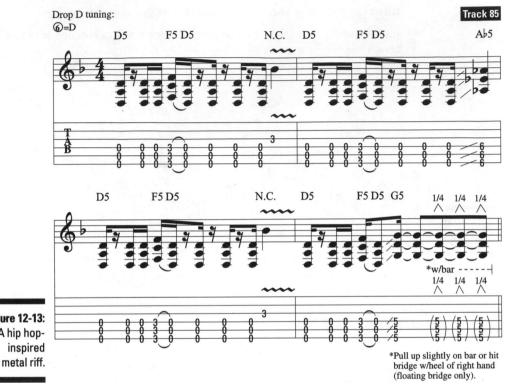

Figure 12-13:
A hip hop-
inspired
metal riff.

Chapter 13

Progressive Rock and Jazz-Rock Fusion

● ●

In This Chapter

▶ Playing beyond the blues scale

▶ Exploring new flatpicking, fingerstyle, and string-bending ideas

▶ Adding jazz-based phrases to a rock solo

▶ Playing in the style of Yes, Pink Floyd, Rush, Al Di Meola, and Pat Metheny

● ●

*T*wo of the biggest guitar categories in the 1970s rock were *progressive rock* and *jazz-rock fusion*. In the '60s, heroes such as Jimi Hendrix, Eric Clapton, and Jeff Beck had established "lead guitar" as a dominant rock voice, and many of the newer jazz-rock and progressive-minded guitar players took that concept forward by forming groups that were either completely dominated by guitar or wholly instrumental.

In this chapter, I show how jazz-rock fusion actually employs new scales and chords into rock, while progressive rock deals more with grand settings and complex musical forms, similar to symphonic movements.

Welcoming the First Wave of Progressive Rock

The first progressive rock artists exploded out of England during the period from 1968–1970. In this group are such legendary acts as Pink Floyd; Yes; Emerson, Lake & Palmer; and Genesis. During this fertile period, guitar style and technique took a quantum leap forward, as players such as Yes' Steve Howe and King Crimson's Robert Fripp sidestepped the blues-based Hendrix/ Clapton approach and instead invented very novel ways of playing rock guitar. In rock guitar, it was truly the beginning of a whole new ball game.

Just say Yes: Steve Howe's eclectic mastery

One of the finest players of the progressive-rock movement, if not in all of rock history, is Steve Howe. As guitarist for Yes, he joined classical, jazz, ragtime, rockabilly, country, blues, and various other guitar styles into his own individual brand of guitar playing. For a good part of the 1970s, many people considered him to be rock's best guitarist, and he frequently won guitar polls.

Perhaps Howe's best-known lick is in the 1972 Yes single, "Roundabout," the band's first major U.S. hit (from the album *Fragile*). One of the most captivating aspects of the song is Howe's simple but memorable intro — a blend of 12th-fret harmonics and hammer-on licks performed on a nylon-string guitar. The riff soon became a staple in the vocabulary of every beginning rock guitarist.

Figure 13-1 shows another Steve Howe staple — the double-stop-6th. A variation on Wes Montgomery's octave solos, Howe frequently slides these intervals up and down the fingerboard on either the high E and G strings or B and D strings, though I play it here on adjacent strings, the high E and B.

The music actually indicates two guitars: the rhythm part which is written out first and then recalled (but not notated), and the lead guitar, which, in this example, begins in bar 3.

> **Music:** Howe's playing in the early days of Yes mixed jazz, country, classical, and ragtime into a new rock style.
>
> **Technique:** This riff integrates a two-string double-stop approach into rock soloing.

The spectral guitar of Genesis

Before they became pop superstars, Genesis recorded some of the most beautiful progressive music of the 1970s, much of it created by their guitarists, Steve Hackett and Mike Rutherford (who doubled on bass). A unique soloist, Hackett is known for his haunting melodies that are embellished with volume swells and occasionally, two-handed tapping (he pioneered the technique in rock music long before Eddie Van Halen did). His best solos are in "Watcher of the Skies" (where he plays melodic background phrases, swells, and delivers a searing fuzz solo) and in "Firth of Fifth," which contains a long lead, filled with more swells, hammer-on trills, and linear melodic patterns. On many Genesis records, Rutherford can often be heard contributing acoustic and electric 12-string arpeggios (keyboardist Tony Banks also picked up a 12-string acoustic from time to time, too).

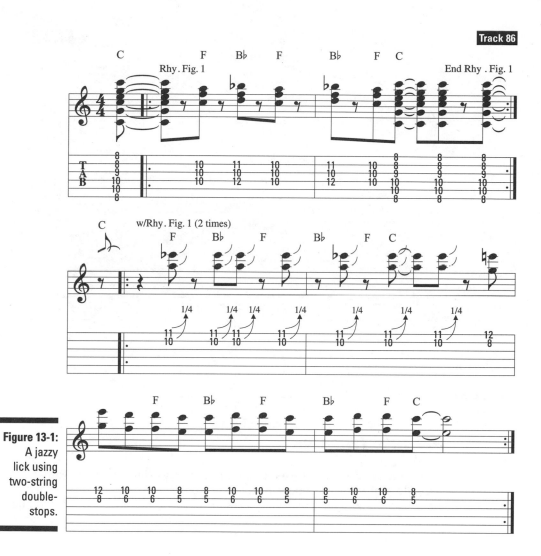

Figure 13-1:
A jazzy
lick using
two-string
double-
stops.

The passage in Figure 13-2 brings to mind the ethereal sound of early Genesis. It features a soft background of arpeggios (chord tones played one note at a time, not strummed all at once) and mesmerizing lead lines accented with a subtle whammy bar effect.

Music: The guitarists of Genesis created a mysterious, ethereal atmosphere avoiding obvious rock-guitar clichés.

Technique: You achieve power and drama in this simple melody by executing strong whammy-bar jiggles. If you don't have a whammy bar, you can simulate this effect with an electronic vibrato or chorus pedal.

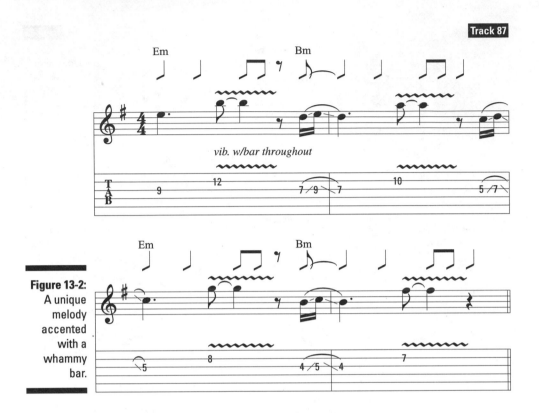

Figure 13-2:
A unique melody accented with a whammy bar.

Fripp's trip

Saying that King Crimson was the first progressive rock band and Robert Fripp its first guitarist of note is not unreasonable. Playing his trademark black Gibson Les Paul Custom, Fripp's ferocious guitar assaults mix a refined classical-fretting technique with an inventive use of unusual scales (at least for rock) and meter (or time signature) changes.

Although most of the songs on the band's 1969 debut, *The Court of the Crimson King,* primarily feature gentle keyboards and acoustic guitar-oriented ballads, they are offset by "21st Century Schizoid Man," an abrasive rocker highlighted by Fripp's off-the-wall power chords and solos. Over 30 years later, Fripp and King Crimson continue to provoke audiences with their daring, offbeat brand of progressive rock.

The lick in Figure 13-3 is classic Fripp, using heavy distortion and the neck pickup of an electric guitar to create a fat, thick tone and notes that slide up and down the fretboard. In many ways, it sounds more like an Indian sitar than a normal guitar. Like Fripp himself, the more exotic and unusual the lick the better.

Track 88

Figure 13-3:
An unusual
lick
involving
notes that
slide up the
fingerboard.

Music: King Crimson's progressive rock often danced on the edge of the
avant-garde.

Technique: This passage requires that you slide notes up the neck in an
unusual, original way.

Pink Floyd's space blues

If Pink Floyd is the ultimate "space rock" band, then David Gilmour is its
quintessential pilot-soloist. While other progressive rock players exude strange
and exotic influences in their solos, Gilmour is on the traditional side, more of a
bluesy guitarist in the mold of Eric Clapton than a sonic revolutionary.

Nevertheless, his haunting solos help define the Floyd sound as much as the
obscure lyrics and ethereal synthesizer parts do. Listen to "Time" (from the
mega-platinum *Dark Side of the Moon*), where Gilmour cuts an echoey lead
laced with plenty of string bends. "Shine On You Crazy Diamond, Parts I-V"
(from 1975's *Wish You Were Here*) includes a series of soulful solos over a
basic minor-blues backbeat. His best-known break, however, is in the power
ballad from *The Wall*, "Comfortably Numb." Technically, it's a basic blues-rock
solo, but one that's elevated to operatic proportions due to a highly dramatic
chord progression.

In Figure 13-4, you can hear an approximation of the bluesy nature of David Gilmour's guitar style. Again, the secret to its success is that it's in a "space rock" context, however, not a conventional blues one. Imagine B.B. King jamming with Yanni and you'll get the picture.

Track 89

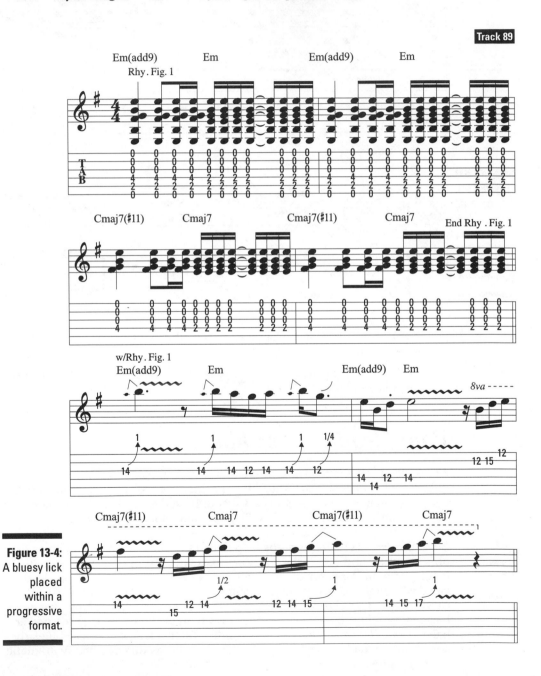

Figure 13-4: A bluesy lick placed within a progressive format.

Music: Gilmour successfully blended bluesy guitar in progressive-rock format.

Technique: This riff underpins straight blues-rock guitar with a dreamy art-rock chord progression.

Acoustic art-rock: Emerson, Lake & Palmer

One of the most elegant players on the progressive scene, Greg Lake can do it all: play electric, acoustic, and bass guitar; sing; produce; and write many of Emerson, Lake & Palmer's best songs. Although his instrumental work has often been subordinate to Keith Emerson's over-the-top keyboard antics, beautiful guitar parts abound on ELP albums such as *Tarkus* and *Brain Salad Surgery*. In particular, Lake contributes brilliant acoustic passages to "Lucky Man," "In the Beginning," and "The Sage," which contains a virtuoso solo performance. You can hear his most memorable electric parts in the suite "Karn Evil 9," as well as in the gentle ballad "Still You Turn Me On."

Figure 13-5 is a riff that brings to mind the acoustic arpeggios in "The Sage." You can play the notes either with a pick or fingerstyle. Try both and see which technique better suits your playing style.

Figure 13-5: A haunting arpeggio of simple chords.

Music: Greg Lake brought an elegant classical-like approach to pop music.

Technique: Play arpeggiated, ringing notes to create a full-sounding effect.

Joining Two Rock Styles: Progressive Meets Heavy Metal

It's not surprising that as progressive rock and heavy metal both took off in the 1970s that they would eventually crossover over. Bands such as Jethro Tull, Mountain, Kansas, and Rush successfully mixed the muscular guitar thump with the lighter keyboard textures of art rock.

Into the limelight with Alex Lifeson of Rush

A powerhouse player, Alex Lifeson remains among the most innovative rock guitarists of the last three decades. His work with the Canadian power trio Rush is marked by blazing melodic solos, shimmering rhythm parts, and a frequent use of "modulation" effects, such as chorus and echo. Some of his best electric solos are in tracks such as "La Villa Strangiato," a complex instrumental, and "Limelight," which includes tasteful tremolo bar effects and a strong sense of melody.

In addition to his fiery lead work, Lifeson is also a skilled rhythm guitarist and, like the Police's Andy Summers, makes extensive use of chorus effects in his arpeggiated chord progressions. He is equally at home with electric, acoustic, or classical guitars. A veritable jack of all guitar trades, Lifeson often pushes the envelope of rock guitar — if not licks and stamps it, too!

Figure 13-6 concentrates on Lifeson's unique chord parts. Instead of block barre chords, Lifeson often lets the upper E and B strings ring open, making his 6-string guitars sound like 12-strings. Add a chorus pedal to heighten the effect.

Music: Rush featured distinctive rhythm guitar parts as well as progressive leads.

Technique: Strum your electric like an acoustic to make the open strings really ring out.

Songs from the wood: The riffs of Jethro Tull

Martin Barre joined Jethro Tull in 1969 and has been their electric guitarist ever since. His tough guitar work is all over early '70s hits such as "Cross-Eyed

Mary," "Locomotive Breath," and the FM-radio anthem "Aqualung." His solo on "Aqualung" is particularly noteworthy because it possesses a melodic sense rarely shared by his hard-rock brethren. But Barre is also known for his killer riffs, usually played on a Gibson or Hamer solidbody going through a tube amp stack.

Figure 13-7 is a riff in the classic Martin Barre style: simple, distorted, and full of visceral punch. Make sure to mute the strings completely for the "scratch" effects.

Figure 13-6: Airy electric chords that use ringing open strings and a full strumming technique.

Figure 13-7: A heavy rock riff with an unusual non-diatonic note at the end.

Music: A Tull-like progression in the style of a classic piece of early-'70s hard rock riffery.

Technique: Play simple power chords decisively and with aggressive downstrokes.

Hitting the Charts with Jazz Rock

The 1970s saw an unprecedented rise in the popularity of jazz-rock guitar. During this time, several paths were being blazed: the smooth "L.A." jazz-pop sound, as characterized by Steely Dan, the soulful syncopations of veteran jazzer George Benson, and the mellow instrumental jazz of guitar virtuoso Pat Metheny. Incredibly, all these different subgenres seemed to spring on the scene nearly simultaneously, and all developed independently of each other. Then just when things seemed to be getting too "jazzy," a young phenomenon named Steve Lukather brought the L.A. sound back to arena rock sensibilities. In this section, we cover some of the representative artists who contributed to this fertile and varied period of jazz-rock guitar.

Steely Dan's elegant jazz-pop

Steely Dan is often referred to as "the thinking man's rock band," thanks to their sophisticated arrangements and rich, image-filled lyrics. Another of their strengths has been the use of L.A.'s top session musicians on many of their albums. Great guitarists such as Jeff Baxter, Denny Dias, Rick Derringer, and Dean Parks have recorded with them, but perhaps none more famous than Larry Carlton, a.k.a. "Mr. 335" (so known for his trademark Gibson ES-335 semi-hollowbody guitar).

For much of the 1970s, Carlton was a studio musician who played on hundreds of classics albums, including those by the Crusaders and Joni Mitchell. In sessions for Steely Dan, his guitar work dominated their 1976 jazz-rock classic, *The Royal Scam*. His sinewy leads in the Steely Dan hit "Kid Charlemagne" brought fusion to the masses and gave many guitar-heads their first taste of the two-handed tapping technique. The first solo is composed of single-note runs, bends, and a deft "tapped" note at the end, while the second sports an exciting blast of pure improvisation. Other important players that helped formulate the California school of fusion were studio cat Lee Ritenour and Robben Ford — a bluesy, soulful player that has performed with Miles Davis, George Harrison, the Yellowjackets, and his own band, the Blue Line.

Figure 13-8 shows a simple jazzy lick of the type that Larry Carlton might lay over a sunny Steely Dan tune. Note the slurred note into the B, which adds to its sophisticated feel.

Figure 13-8: This lick mixes an interesting combination of slurs, chromatic licks, and bluesy bends.

Music: The deft production techniques of Steely Dan and their legion of top-call guitarists blends jazz and pop into an infectious brew.

Technique: This riff uses some syncopated rhythms subtle articulations to achieve a cool, sophisticated sound.

The soulful jazz of George Benson

One of the most successful guitarists in jazz history, George Benson scored big-time after he crossed over to pop in 1976 (he had been recording largely straight-ahead jazz albums since the mid 1960s). He landed giant hits with "This Masquerade," "Breezin'," and "The Greatest Love of All," later a hit for Whitney Houston. The smashes continued into the '80s with "Turn Your Love Around" and "Give Me the Night." Most recently, Benson has returned to jazz for a series of big band recordings.

In addition to being a great singer, Benson is a world-class guitarist, able to blend jazz, pop, and funk into one thrilling style. He often sang in unison with his nimble guitar lines, a technique not unheard of in jazz, but new to jazz-rock guitar. This *scat* (using nonsense syllables like "do" and "dah") singing is a Benson hallmark. Add to that his near-perfect technique, and you clearly have one of the most formidable players on the planet. And he's a great singer to boot — some guys have all the luck.

In Figure 13-9, play the notes in the first three bars on the offbeats to generate a funkier feel. The last bar features a simple slurring of notes that Benson often uses.

Track 94

Figure 13-9:
A simple lick
that deftly
blends jazz
and funk.

Music: In Benson's hands, jazz, funk, and pop merge for an intriguing contemporary treat.

Technique: Play this riff with crisp, syncopated picking and toss in slurs in the last bar.

Pat Metheny's sophisticated jazz-pop

Pat Metheny is another of those rare "jazz superstars." With his radio-friendly Pat Metheny Group, the guitarist ranks as one of the most commercially successful jazz guitarists performing today. Although his guitar style is rooted in traditional jazz (he grew up listening heavily to Wes Montgomery and Jim Hall), Metheny also uses pop and worldbeat music as vehicles to express himself. Conversely, the guitarist also records experimental jazz albums with various partners such as avant-garde saxman Ornette Coleman and drummer Jack DeJohnette.

For guitars, Metheny plays an archtop hollowbody and uses a clean tone like a standard jazz player. But his tone is highly untraditional, relying as he does on a smooth stereo chorus effect and non-standard chord progressions to realize his creative ideas. His rock, pop, and ambient, pre-New Age compositions, however, put "jazz guitar" in a whole new context. He's a well-known purveyor of the guitar synthesizer, too, and has created a singular tone based on the trumpet work of bop legend Miles Davis. Metheny was also one of the first players to get a chorus pedal and put it to work.

Check out Metheny's deft melody-making and chord work in "Phase Dance" from the superlative *Pat Metheny Group* (1977) to hear why he became such big news in the commercial jazz world — and why he's influenced so many guitarists on the rock 'n' roll side of the fence. Figure 13-10 is a progression that modulates from D major to D minor, with a lyrical melody placed on top. The chords are simple yet powerful, and the melody, although not jazzy in the traditional sense, shows a jazz-like intelligence in the way it interacts with the chords underneath.

> **Music:** One of Metheny's hallmarks was using a major-to-minor modulation to create a more interesting melody.

> **Technique:** This riff combines single-note picking in the lead part with two-note double stops in the rhythm part.

Toto's Steve Lukather: Rock monster

When studio players such as Larry Carlton and Lee Ritenour performed more as solo artists and less as session players in the late '70s, a hole was left for an ace rock guitarist. It didn't take too long for that space to be filled and soon the studio set was abuzz with the name of 19-year-old Steve Lukather. Landing a prestigious spot with singer Boz Scaggs, then at the peak of his career, Lukather quickly parlayed this position into many studio dates with other artists.

Figure 13-10: A progression that combines single-note picking with double stops.

Eventually, "Luke," as he's commonly known, lent his scorching guitar solos and rhythm riffs to records by everyone from Michael Jackson to Paul McCartney and hundreds, if not thousands, more (that's Luke playing bass and rhythm guitar on Jackson's 1983 smash "Beat It" — Eddie Van Halen plays the solo).

Luke's contribution to the studio work is that he brought the tone of hard-rock guitar into the soft-pop world of the L.A. studio scene. In short, he was the first guy to show up at a session with a Les Paul and a Marshall stack (along with plenty of reverb and echo effects), and literally "crank it up!" His playing can also range from blistering hard rock to screaming jazz-fusion, funk, and pop. And through his work with the band Toto, he's been all over the radio and concert stages for the last 20 years, singing and playing on singles such as "Rosanna," "99," and "I Won't Hold You Back." (And you can forget about Frank Sinatra or the Beatles. Toto is hugely popular in Europe and, in fact, Austria's *X-Act* magazine recently voted Lukather as their "Artist of the Century.")

Figure 13-11 shows a classic Lukather-style lead over a pop groove. Note that it blends a heavy-rock tone with melodic phrasing. Also pay attention to the half-step bends, somewhat of a rarity in rock circles.

> **Music:** Lukather and his disciples synthesized jazz melodicism with a hard-rock tone.

> **Technique:** Warm up your left-hand fingers to successfully deploy these long full- and half-step bends in a rock melody context.

Looking at the Legends of Jazz-Rock Fusion

Although there are dozens of brilliant fusion guitarists, among the most influential were John McLaughlin, Jeff Beck, and Al Di Meola. During their jazz-rock heydays, all three created albums that crystallized the marriage of jazz and hard rock, a sophisticated sound that nonetheless was perfectly at home on the rock concert stage. Sure, it wasn't Duke Ellington, but for stoned-out '70s audiences, it was a tad more lofty than Grand Funk Railroad and fit perfectly into a decade when the musical credo was "anything goes, dude."

Pure virtuosity: John McLaughlin and Al Di Meola

Few modern guitarists can claim to be the best in their particular genre — for jazz-rock guitarists, though; John McLaughlin and Al Di Meola are no doubt two of the world's finest. Both players have set new technical and virtuosic standards over the past 30 years and made countless brilliant recordings, too.

McLaughlin's early claim to fame was playing with Miles Davis on Davis's 1970 *Bitches Brew* album, an early attempt at electric fusion. The following year, he formed the Mahavishnu Orchestra, a dazzling jazz-rock outfit that added hard-rock sonorities to the fusion soup, replete with screaming guitar solos and heavy, aggressive riffs. Mahavishnu's first two albums, 1972's *Inner Mounting Flame* and 1973's *Birds of Fire*, really set the blueprints of jazz-rock guitar. Instead of a traditional jazz hollowbody guitar, McLaughlin strapped on a Gibson Les Paul Custom and EDS-1275 doubleneck (one 6-string neck and one 12-string neck), plugged into a Marshall, and added hard-rock scorch to the graceful sounds of fusion. The result was nothing short of revolutionary, as the band pummeled their way through masterpieces such as "Birds of Fire" and "Meeting of the Spirits."

Track 96

Figure 13-11:
Melodic lead lines with interesting full- and half-step bends.

Adding fuel to the fire was the virtuoso's dazzling technique. Over 10 years before anyone had heard of that shredding entity called "Yngwie," McLaughlin was tearing up the fingerboard with his blitzkrieg alternate-picking technique and forever changing the face of modern guitar playing (for more on Yngwie Malmsteen, see Chapter 12). In 1974, McLaughlin shifted gears completely and created Shakti, an all-acoustic band of Indian musicians that was just as groundbreaking as Mahavishnu. Since then, he has led a breathtaking solo career that has touched on genres from funk to flamenco and everything in between. The man never sits still and is still as vital a player today as he was 30 years ago.

By 1976, fusion was picking up speed fast. And speaking of *fast,* another great titan was emerging at this time: Al Di Meola. Barely 20 years old, Di Meola had joined Chick Corea's great fusion band, Return To Forever, when he was 17 and still a college student, and then launched his solo career in '76. The next year, he released the seminal *Elegant Gypsy,* which included the historic acoustic duet with flamenco player Paco de Lucia on "Mediterranean Sundance." But Al made his mark more as an electric soloist, combining McLaughlin's speedy chops with meticulously clean technique and Latin-fired inspiration. The rocker "Race with Devil on Spanish Highway" is a great example of Di Meola in his prime. The riff is part hard rock, part fusion, and part flamenco, but all topped off with the fastest, cleanest guitar riffs anyone had ever heard. For a while, he was considered the greatest guitarist on the planet and, looking back, understandably so.

In Figure 13-12, you get a sense of the Di Meola's "electric flamenco" approach, applied over a very common Spanish-style chord progression. The key to this speedy run isn't really playing fast, but synchronizing your picking and fretting hands to play 16th notes articulately and precisely on the beat. Start playing the figure slowly and then gradually increase the tempo to faster and faster levels. Stop only when your fingers start to smoke and keep a fire extinguisher on hand!

> **Music:** Heavily influenced by Latin music forms, Di Meola blends rock and flamenco into a viscerally exciting style of fusion.

> **Technique:** Exercise precise flatpicking and observe strict alternate (up- and downstroke) picking.

Jeff Beck's jazz comeback

Ten years after joining the Yardbirds, Jeff Beck made a huge comeback in the spring of 1975 with his first fusion album, *Blow by Blow.* It was an instrumental tour de force that blended rock ("Highway Jam"), fusion ("Scatterbrain"), R&B ("She's a Woman"), and funk ("You Know What I Mean") styles. Produced by

George Martin (who produced all the Beatles records), *Blow by Blow* sailed up the album charts and re-established Beck as rock's premier guitar player and a major force in the new jazz-rock universe.

The British guitarist followed this up with yet another chart-topper in 1976, *Wired*. This time, Beck brought onboard drummer/composer Narada Michael Walden and synthesizer master Jan Hammer (both former members of John McLaughlin's Mahavishnu Orchestra). *Wired* had a more electronic vibe than *Blow by Blow*, as shown on tracks "Blue Wind" and his electric version of Charles Mingus's be-bop classic, "Goodbye Pork Pie Hat." Together, *Blow by Blow* and *Wired* remain timeless milestones in the history of jazz-rock fusion.

Figure 13-13 is a collection of Beck-style licks that reveals how the guitarist ably blends major and minor scales into an interesting, offbeat sound. The scale pattern he uses over this E9 chord vamp is based on a minor pentatonic scale, but uses a major 3rd and major 6th to, dare I say, *jazz* things up. Try it.

Music: Beck's funky and dazzling playing represents the apex of mid-'70s "funk fusion."

Technique: This riff allows you to blend major and minor scales to create some novel soloing ideas.

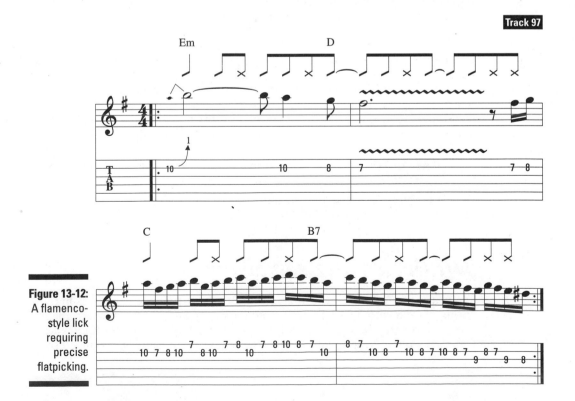

Figure 13-12: A flamenco-style lick requiring precise flatpicking.

Progressive rock enjoys a sort of timeless popularity, and is immune to the fickle trends of other rock subgenres. Many fusion and progressive rock band enjoy steady record sales and sold-out concert dates. Table 13-1 presents ten essential fusion and progressive rock albums that no record collection should be without.

Figure 13-13:
A solo lick combining major and minor scales.

Table 13-1	Ten Essential Fusion and Progressive Albums			
Band/Artist	*Guitarist*	*Album Name*	*Year*	*Impact*
King Crimson	Robert Fripp	*Court of the Crimson King*	1969	Avant-garde invades the mainstream
Mahavishnu Orchestra	John McLaughlin	*Inner Mounting Flame*	1972	Introduced modern fusion
Yes	Steve Howe	*Close to the Edge*	1972	Eclectic virtuosity
Billy Cobham	Tommy Bolin	*Spectrum*	1973	Created funk-fusion guitar
Genesis	Steve Hackett	*Selling England by the Pound*	1973	Ethereal and haunting electric guitar
Pink Floyd	David Gilmour	*Wish You Were Here*	1975	Blues meets progressive rock
Return to Forever	Al Di Meola	*Romantic Warrior*	1976	Speedy Latin-fusion guitar
Jeff Beck	Jeff Beck	*Blow by Blow*	1976	Fusion guitar masterpiece
Bruford	Allan Holdsworth	*One of a Kind*	1978	New virtuosic legato technique
Dixie Dregs	Steve Morse	*Dregs of the Earth*	1980	Southern-fried fusion on overdrive

Part V
Becoming a Gearhead

In this part . . .

There's a lot of gear out there. But, hey, that's half of the fun of playing guitar — getting to play with all the cool stuff that goes with it! Whether you're looking to buy your first electric guitar or your fifth, Chapter 14 helps you sort all the different types of guitars available, plus discusses which amp is best for what style of playing. And to round out the chapter, I give you some tips on shopping for these two big purchases. Chapter 15 gets you going on essential stompboxes — effects, that is. Effects and signal processors can give your sound a whole different personality, and you have more options than a start-up dot-com. Check out this chapter to define, or to blow the doors off, your individual sound. Sure, rock guitar is about strutting your stuff and pushing the envelope, but you don't need to be strutting to the repair shop while pushing your broken-down amp. Chapter 16 gives you all the info you need to know to keep your gear in shape and humming, from wielding the tools of the trade to performing your own repairs to safely storing your equipment.

Chapter 14

Gear Lust: Assembling Your Dream Rig

In This Chapter

▶ Exploring guitars: their types, their construction, and their components

▶ Discovering amps and their characteristics

▶ Putting together the ultimate rig

*U*nless you're completely committed to a career as an air guitarist, your most important decision as a player is choosing a guitar and an amp. Notice how I included both guitar and amp in the same sentence: Your amplifier is as much a part of your instrument as the piece of wood you hold in your hands. The amp is your guitar's voice and your window to the world.

Rock music is an eclectic genre with rebellion at its roots, so there is no right way to get a "rock" sound. There *are,* however, some conventions worth considering. For example, most rockers favor solidbody electrics — at least for the bulk of their playing — but can use semi-hollowbody or even amplified acoustic guitars on occasion. In rock, every rule has *several* exceptions. A guitar associated with one style may suddenly become the rage with another — such as when Nirvana's Kurt Cobain used a Fender Jaguar, which had always been considered a tame guitar best suited to surf music, to create the musical beast known as *grunge.* But if you're creating the Guitar Solo of Doom or the definitive rock-polka sound, you need to have two essential elements: a guitar and an amp. And the choices you make here can influence the sound just as much as your own playing technique. This chapter presents the myriad of choices and options you have when embarking on the quest for your sound.

Getting What You Want Out of a Guitar

You can always tell a novice guitar buyer. He'll walk into a shop and say: "I want to buy an electric guitar." That's a little like strolling into a restaurant and saying "I want something to eat." Electric guitars are like nourishment:

You'll find *haute cuisine* and fast food, with many variations of each, and plenty of options in between. Any of these meals can satisfy your hunger, but the trick is to choose the dish which best suits your palate.

Electric guitars can be divided into basic categories, defined, by one archetypical guitar, a model that has become so popular that it's widely imitated. Four of the most notable archetypes for electric guitars are the Fender Stratocaster, the Fender Telecaster, the Gibson Les Paul, and the Gibson ES-335, all of which are shown in Figure 14-1.

Figure 14-1:
Four archetypical guitars. From left: Fender Stratocaster, Fender Telecaster, Gibson Les Paul, and Gibson ES-335.

Each of these guitars has a unique body shape and tone. They're not the only important guitar models, but they've been so influential that their names have become generic terms, used to describe guitars by other manufacturers in the same way Kleenex has come to mean any facial tissue. For example, you may find a Yamaha guitar with a *Strat* (short for *Stratocaster*) shape, or an Ibanez guitar with a *335* design. Other important archetypes include the Gibson Explorer, Flying-V, and the SG.

When you're evaluating a guitar, breaking the instrument down into components and features can help. Four factors stand out as primary:

- ✔ Body style and wood
- ✔ Neck and fingerboard dimensions and wood
- ✔ Bridge, nut, and tuning system and their materials and components
- ✔ Electronics

Understand how these interact, and you're on your way to making an informed purchase.

Checking out the body

The body contributes to the instrument's tone. Luthiers (a.k.a. the folks who build guitars) use a range of materials to create the guitars, including *tonewoods* such as alder, ash, mahogany, maple, koa, and others, as well as synthetic materials. Each of these materials has unique resonating property and so makes the guitar sound different. Try guitars of different composition — you may find that two similar models, one made of alder, the other ash, sound completely different.

Hopefully, you'll be spending endless hours playing your guitar, both at home and on stage. The instrument should feel comfortable in both sitting and standing positions and should afford you easy access to all the frets. Plus you should feel cool and look cool playing it.

Body style

Electric guitars come in three main categories:

- ✔ **Solidbody:** The solidbody — so called because its body is made of wood with no holes in the top or in the body's interior — is by far the most common type of guitar used in rock. Solidbodies offer great sustain and resist feedback at high volume. Examples include the Gibson Les Paul and SG (which actually stands for "Solid Guitar"), Fender Stratocaster and Telecaster, Paul Reed Smith Standard, and many, many more.

- ✔ **Hollowbody:** Hollowbodies are more often associated with jazz than rock, although exceptions do exist (Ted Nugent, for example, uses a hollowbody Gibson Byrdland, and Steve Howe of Yes was famous for playing a Gibson ES-175). Because they resonate more than solidbodies, hollowbodies are prone to feedback at high volumes. They also have less sustain than solidbodies, and so produce a "woodier" sound.

- ✔ **Semi-hollowbody:** A semi-hollowbody is a solidbody guitar with one or more acoustic chambers. The chambers add acoustic resonance and depth to the tone, but the guitar's solid nature keeps the resonance under control and lessens the chance of feedback. The Gibson ES-335 is the most popular example, but Rickenbacker, Guild, Ibanez, and others have contributed important semi-hollowbody designs. Hollowbodies are extremely versatile guitars, used for early rock, jazz, jazz fusion, funk, and country.

Cutaways

Most guitar terms describe what's there, not what's missing, but cutaway is an exception. A *cutaway* is a section of the guitar's body that has been removed to allow easier access to the upper frets. Most electric guitars have at least one cutaway; guitars that have two cutaways are known as *dual-* or *double-cutaway* models. Figure 14-2 shows a variety of cutaway styles. Note that some of the dual cutaway designs have cutaways of equal depth on both the treble and bass sides of the neck. Others have *offset* cutaways — the treble-side cutaway is deeper than the neck-side cutaway.

Figure 14-2:
Three different cutaway styles (from left): The single cutaway of a Fender Telecaster, the offset dual cutaway Fender Stratocaster, and the equal dual cutaway Gibson SG.

Weight and balance

Weight and balance are other important factors. When you're test-driving a guitar, don't just play it sitting down; strap it on, stand up, see how well it balances against your body. Make sure that the guitar's weight won't be a burden over the long periods you'll be wearing it in action.

Testing the neck and fingerboard

The neck is the most important part of your guitar because it's the channel between your hands and the strings. The neck must fit your hand like that eleven-year-old pair of sneakers that you simply refuse to throw out even though it clears the room each time you lace 'em up.

The ideal neck is as personal a choice as selecting your ideal mate. And that analogy is far from idle: You'll be wedded to that neck, for better or worse, for as long as you have your guitar (though the type of neck knows as a *bolt-on* neck can be replaced fairly easily). Like the body, the neck and fingerboard (and the decorative inlays used for fret makers) are made of a variety of materials that contribute to their feel and their tone. Most common are maple and mahogany (for the necks), and maple, rosewood, and ebony (for the fingerboards). Try guitars with each material — you may be surprised at how much it affects your technique and tone. Look for evenness of color, grain, and texture, and be sure to check for cracks. Most important, the surface should feel comfortable under your fingers as you move them around.

Measurements

Like you, every guitar neck has a set of measurements — vital stats that give you a clue about how the guitar will perform. You should be able to reach across to all six strings without straining and run your hand up the length of the neck without getting caught in the guitar's body or the neck joint. The neck should be stable (if it moves around, the guitar will go out of tune) and straight. Action (the distance of the strings to the fretboard) should be comfortably low, but not so low that the strings make a buzzing sound when you finger them. An explanation of each measurement follows:

- **Nut width:** The neck's width at the nut has a major impact on its feel. A wider neck makes you stretch further to reach across the strings, but leaves more room for your fingers.

- **Scale:** The distance between the nut and the bridge is one of the most important factors in a guitar's feel and sound. The most common scales are 24 ¾" (also known as *Gibson scale* because it's the common measurement on Gibson guitars) and 25 ½" (known as *Fender* scale because it's found on most Fender guitars). Longer scale guitars exert greater tension on the strings when they're tuned to pitch, making the strings feel tighter than they would on a shorter scale model. But while shorter scale guitars can be easier to play (thanks to the reduced string tension and the slightly smaller distance between frets), they offer a less percussive tone than their longer-scale counterparts.

- **Radius:** The *radius* is the curvature of the fingerboard. The larger the radius, the flatter the neck's surface. Radii can run anywhere from 7.5" (very round) to 16" (quite flat), but 12" is most common. The ideal radius is generally a matter of taste, but roots rockers have traditionally favored rounder necks because such necks are more comfortable to chord, while metal and neo classical players seem to like the flatter feel because it better suits a more virtuosic style of playing.

- **Shape:** When guitarists talk about a neck's *shape* they're referring to the back of the neck — the place where you put your thumb, palm, and that little flap of skin between thumb and index finger. Necks can be round at the back, flat, or can have a sharp *V* shape. There was a time when each manufacturer built all its necks to one shape, but these days you can find a variety of shapes for many models.

✔ **Frets:** Electric guitars generally offer between 21 and 24 frets. The more frets, the more notes you can access; a neck with 24 frets yields two octaves per string. You'd think you'd always want to have more frets, but in practice, most players are comfortable with 22 — the extra frets can be hard to reach and they also leave less room on the body for the neck pickup. Frets (and I'm speaking of the actual fret *wire* here) also come in a number of gauges: thin, medium, and jumbo being the most common. Each gauge has various advantages and disadvantages associated with it in regard to string-bending range and intonation. Which frets you like, however, is largely a matter of personal choice and tradition.

Bolt-on necks, set necks, and neck-throughs

Guitar necks can connect to the body in three different ways. As the name implies, *bolt-on* necks are bolted to a socket on the body, a design that lets you remove the neck easily for service and adjustment or even replacement. Bolt-on designs are common on solidbodies, especially Fenders.

Set neck designs are more traditional than bolt-ons. The neck is glued to the body in a permanent joint. Examples include the Gibson Les Paul and the Gibson ES-335.

With *neck-through* designs, the neck and the body are made up of one piece of wood, eliminating the neck joint. Usually, the neck forms the center of the body; separate *wings* are attached on each side of this center block to give the body shape. Because there's no neck joint, neck-through designs allow easier upper fret access. Neck-throughs have a particularly slick feel that appeals to many players tackling the more virtuosic forms of rock. If you plan to do a lot of higher-fret playing, and do it at lightning speeds, check out the playability that neck-through designs offer.

Tuning into the hardware

The bridge, nut, and tuners — also known as the *hardware,* or the *string path* — play a vital role in shaping a guitar's tone and musical capabilities. You should think of these three components as one system of interconnected parts.

Bridges

Although many different bridge systems exist, they fall into two categories: floating bridge and fixed bridge.

Floating bridge systems sit on springs, allowing you to change the pitch of the strings with a lever called a *vibrato bar* or *whammy bar* (see Chapter 9). A variety of systems exist, including *non-locking systems* (sometimes called *vintage* style because they were first available in the 1950s) and *locking systems* that feature clamps at both the bridge and the nut (called *Floyd Rose* systems after their inventor, though some non-Floyd Rose systems exist). Locking systems stay in tune better than their non-locking counterparts, but they're more difficult to set up and can alter a guitar's tone. Still, if you're heart's set on working your whammy, the Floyd's tuning stability can't be beat.

A *fixed bridge* stays in the same position at all times. It lacks the pitch-altering capabilities of a floating bridge, but it also provides a more stable tuning environment.

Nuts and tuners

The guitar's nut may not be high on your list of spectacular features, but its vital to an instrument's performance. Like bridges, nuts fall into two categories:

Standard nuts come in different materials, such as nylon, other synthetics, and brass. Nylon yields more of a traditional guitar sound, while brass helps increase sustain. When checking out a guitar, look to see that the grooves of the nut haven't been filed too deep, so that the strings sits too low on the fretboard, creating a potential for buzzing.

A *locking nut* clamps down on the strings so that they cannot move (and therefore, can't become hung up or snagged). This clamp, which is used in conjunction with a Floyd Rose-type bridge, helps keep the string in tune under heavy whammy duress. A locking nut usually signifies a higher-end rock-style guitar, and assumes a floating, Floyd Rose-type bridge down below.

Tuning machines, or tuning keys, also come in two types (the guitar is a veritable Noah's Ark): standard and locking. *Locking tuners* hold the string in place for the same reason locking nuts do — to prevent string hang-ups and slippage — and locking tuners do improve the tuning stability of non-locking tremolo systems.

When you evaluate a guitar, always test the nut and tuners by bending the strings, working the vibrato bar, and de-tuning and retuning the guitar. Don't worry if the salesperson looks at you like you just stepped on his hamster — he may have spent his morning getting the thing in tune. If you have trouble tuning the instrument, move on.

Trying out the pickups and electronics

Electric guitars wouldn't be very electric without electronics (say this ten times fast for extra credit). The pickups and switches that form your guitar's inner guts link your playing to your amp — and to your audience. Figure 14-3 shows a typical guitar control layout with the parts labeled, including the pickups (Stratocaster only), volume and tone controls, and selector switch (Stratocaster only).

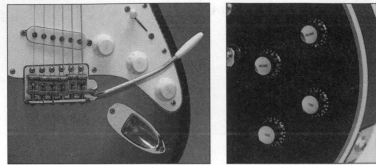

Figure 14-3:
The control layout of a Fender Stratocaster (left) and a Gibson Les Paul (right).

Pickup primer

Although you can choose from literally hundreds of pickups (for more on pickups, see Chapter 1), you can divide them into two groups: *Single-coil* (such as those skinny pickups you see on Strats and Teles), and double-coil, or *humbucker,* pickups (like the fat ones you find on a Les Paul). These are known as *magnetic pickup* because they're made of magnets. An example of a non-magnetic pickup is the *piezo* pickup. This was first developed to amplify acoustic guitars and is still used primarily for that purpose, but lately it has become a popular feature on hybrid electric guitars such as the Parker Fly and the Hamer Duo Tone. Magnetic pickups handle traditional electric guitar sounds, while the piezo produces a tone reminiscent of an acoustic-electric guitar.

Single-coil pickups sound brighter and more "articulate" than humbuckers, but they're noisier and generate less output. By using two specially wired coils, the humbucker design cancels out the hum (electronic noise) generated by single-coil pickups. And because they use two coils (and, therefore, a greater number of wire winding), humbuckers offer greater output (so they're louder) and a more pronounced midrange than single coils, albeit with less clarity in the treble range. There are also single-coil-sized pickups called *stacked humbuckers* that offer humbucking features but retain the tone and footprint of the traditional single-coil. And, there are humbucking pickups that can operate in both dual- and single-coil mode, offering the best of both worlds (via a switch called a *coil tap* or *coil cut*).

A pickup's placement on the body influences how it will sound. The same exact pickup will sound different simply because of where it's placed under the area of the vibrating strings. Because the pickup in the *bridge* (or *rear*) *position* sounds brighter, it's often called the *lead* pickup. The mellower sounding *neck* (or *front*) *position* is sometimes referred to as the *rhythm* pickup. The same is true for your own playing, too: Place your hand near the bridge for a brighter sound (for when you're playing lead), or place it up nearer to the fingerboard for a mellower sound (for when you're playing rhythm). You can, however, use either pickup to play anything you want (although I'd appreciate it if you refrain from playing "Stairway to Heaven" when I'm around). Some pickups, such as those on the Telecaster shown in Figure 14-4, are specially designed to go in one or the other position.

Figure 14-4:
The Fender Telecaster uses different types of pickup in the neck and bridge positions.

Pickup configurations

You can use pickup configuration as shorthand to describe an electric guitar. A traditional Strat, for example, has three single coil pickups controlled by a five-way switch (for selecting the individual neck, middle, and bridge pickups, or the neck and middle or bridge and middle combinations), so you can say "Strat configuration" to indicate a guitar with three single-coils. You can use the neck, middle, and bridge pickups individually or combine the neck or bridge pickup with the middle to create a distinctly modulated sound.

The Les Paul Standard is equipped with two humbuckers controlled by a three-way switch (which selects the two individual pickups, or the two in combination). You can isolate each pickup or combine both for a bright, jangly sound. This is referred to as the "humbucker configuration" or the "Gibson configuration."

Many guitars, such as the one shown in Figure 14-5, employ both single-coil and humbucking pickups. This popular hybrid configuration, sometimes referred to as the "Super Strat," offers single coil neck and middle pickups (which yield the classic Strat sound) and a humbucker in the bridge (for a more powerful lead sound). Plus, a coil tap switch on the bridge-position humbucker, allows it to mimic a three-single-coil pickup sound. (Purists will argue that nothing sounds like a three-single-coil pickup sound other than three true single coils. These purists will say that even though you're only using one of the coils of the humbucker, the other coil's magnets still pull on the strings, which a true single-coil wouldn't do. Purists have *a lot* of time on their hands.)

Figure 14-5:
The "Super Strat" combines single coil and humbucking pickups.

In many catalogs, spec sheets, and product reviews, pickup configuration is indicated by a series of letters — *S* for single-coil and *H* for humbuckers. A guitar with three single-coil pickups would be *S/S/S,* a guitar with two humbuckers would be *H/H,* and a guitar with two single-coils and one humbucker would be *S/S/H.*

Common controls and special electronics

The typical electric guitar has very simple circuitry. The main controls include a *toggle switch* or pickup selector (used to activate the different pickups), one or more *volume controls,* and one or more *tone controls,* which are used to reduce (or *roll off*) a pickup's treble frequencies. Usually, the tone controls are *passive,* which means that they can only attenuate (reduce in level) the signal from a maximum position. They can't actually boost the pickup's volume and tone beyond its natural, unfiltered state. Some guitars include additional switches for coil-tapping and other configurations of a pickup's basic wiring.

Active electronic systems use a battery-powered preamp (which fits snugly inside your guitar) to pre-amplify and shape the pickup's signal. They offer quiet performance, powerful output, and sonic versatility unavailable in traditional passive designs. Unlike passive controls, an active system can boost as well as cut volume and tone.

Deciding among guitar variations

Most electric guitars are six-stringed instruments, but a number of alternatives exist. These variations share the main design elements described earlier in this chapter, although individual components may be altered to take advantage of the guitar's unique features. Some of the most popular variations on the electric six-string guitar include:

✓ **Seven string:** The seven-string guitar, like the one pictured in Figure 14-6, has an additional low B string on the bass side of the neck. This trait makes the seven-string popular with hard rockers such as the bands Korn and Limp Bizkit, who use the lower string to create grinding riffs.

✓ **Twelve string:** The jangly sound of an electric 12-string helped power 1960s folk rock bands such as the Byrds. The strings are arranged in pairs: the lower four pairs in octaves, the upper two pairs in unison.

✓ **Baritone guitar:** A cross between a guitar and a bass, the bari has six strings, but they're tuned a fifth lower than those of a conventional guitar. Baritone guitars have longer-scale necks (which facilitate the playability of the lower-tuned strings) than conventional guitars and are extremely popular for doubling (recording over a traditional guitar part).

Figure 14-6: Thanks to its ability to produce bone-crushing riffs, the seven-string guitar has become popular in hard rock circles.

Choosing the Perfect Amp to Give Your Guitar Life

As I discuss at the beginning of this chapter, choosing the right guitar is only half the battle. An amp makes your guitar come alive. The following list outlines some of the key features and traits that you find as you shop for an amp. Keep in mind that an amp, like a guitar, is a musical instrument. The spec sheet only tells part of the story. When you shop, let your ears decide which amp is right for you.

You can divide amp circuitry into four main categories:

✔ **Tube amps:** The first guitar amps were built in an era when vacuum tubes powered all electronics. Solid-state technology took over most of the electronic world, but tube amps remain popular, thanks to their ability to saturate, or overdrive. Tube overdrive is the signature sound of rock guitar, and the appeal of a quality tube amp can't be beat for warm sound and vintage tone.

✔ **Solid-state amps:** Tube technology may be popular, but solid-state circuits are more cost-effective to build and therefore buy, which is one reason that solid-state amps proliferate despite the popularity of tubes. Another reason for their popularity is the success that designers have had in emulating tube performance with solid-state circuitry. They're also less fragile (no glass tubes to break) and require little or no maintenance. Solid-state amps may not have the warmth and authenticity of a tube amp, but they are extremely versatile, capable of producing a wide range of sounds. They tend to run a little cheaper than tube amps.

✔ **Hybrid amps:** Amps that combine tube and solid-state circuits are known as *hybrids*. The tube circuit — found in the preamp stage — provides the core of the sound, while a solid-state power section keeps the cost (and the amp's weight) down to a manageable level. Hybrid amps enjoy the best of both the tube and solid-state worlds, and are extremely popular for their wide range of sound and tube-like tonal characteristics.

✔ **Digital amps:** Until recent years, the word digital was poison to guitarists. But developments in digital modeling technology have changed all that. A digital modeling amp uses software to re-create (or model) the sound of a tube (or solid-state) amp. Unlike traditional tube and solid-state amps, which are designed to deliver a signature sound, a modeling amp can emulate the sound of many different amps and are programmable. Digital amps offer the best of solid-state reliability and add a whole new dimension in their emulation of other amps. Plus they usually boast a wide range of onboard effects. Some find the emulation properties of digital amps unconvincing, but for many playing situations (in a noisy club, buried in the mix of a recording session), it's close enough.

Configurations and features

Be they tube, solid state, or digital, amps come in three physical configurations, which are shown in Figure 14-7.

✔ *Combo amps* such as the Fender Twin Reverb and the Vox AC-30, house the electronics and the speaker or speakers in a single cabinet.

✔ *Head and cab* configurations — also called *head and stack* or just *stack* (because you stack the head onto the cabinet) — or *piggyback* designs (such as the Marshall stack and the Mesa Triple Rectifier), house the amp's electronics (called the *head*) and the speakers (called the *cabinet*) in separate components. Because they're much bulkier than combo amps, stack systems are usually used in situations that call for high volume.

You can describe the configuration of both combo and stack speaker cabinets the same way — by listing the number and size of the speakers. For example, a 4 x 12 cabinet has four 12" speakers and a 2 x 10 cabinet has two 10" speakers.

✔ *Rack* systems take the modular approach a step further. A *preamp* shapes the tone, a separate *power amp* amplifies it, and a *speaker system* carries it to the audience. Rack systems can get very elaborate, with the preamp feeding one or more stereo effects processors, stereo power amps, and banks of speakers. Rack systems allow you to mix various components together and are extremely popular for session players because of the versatility they offer.

Figure 14-7:
Amp configurations (from left to right); combo, head and cab/stack, and rack system.

Key features

Once upon a time, an amp had only one channel, a single volume control, and a minimal set of tone controls. More elaborate designs offered primitive effects such as spring reverb and tremolo. Today's amps have none of these limitations. You'll find multiple channels, onboard EQ, built in effects, and effects-loops for interfacing with outboard processors. Here's a quick rundown of some key features:

✔ **Power rating:** Power is one of the most misunderstood and controversial aspects of amp features. Not all manufacturers use the same method to rate their amps' power out, which is one reason why a 100-watt Marshall may sound twice as loud as a 150-watt amp by another manufacturer. As a general rule, high-wattage amps are marginally louder than lower wattage amps. The main advantage of a high-wattage amp comes in *headroom,* or the ability to increase gain (or volume) before distortion. A Fender Twin Reverb, for example, will sound much cleaner at medium volume than the lower-wattage Fender Princeton. Because saturation is such an important element in creating great guitar tone, an amp with too much power can be a liability if your gig doesn't allow you to turn it up to its full potential. So be realistic: Some of the biggest guitar sounds come from smaller amps that are turned up to their saturation point. Higher wattage amps are more expensive than lower-wattage amps, regardless of other features.

✔ **Channel switching:** A channel-switching amp offers two or more preamp circuits, or channels. Each channel has separate gain controls, so that you can set one channel for clean sounds, the other for overdriven, or distorted sounds. Channel can be changed via a switch on the amp's control panel or via a footswitch that plugs into the amp's back panel. (See Chapter 3.)

✔ **Effects loop:** An effects loop lets you plug an external effects device into your amp's signal chain. See Chapter 3 and Chapter 15 for more on effects loops in amps.

✔ **Onboard effects:** A growing number of amps (including tube and solid-state designs) offer onboard digital effects processors. These save you the trouble of carrying separate effects around with you, but are often less flexible than outboard effects processors. For more on effects, see Chapter 15.

Putting It All Together

Is one type of amp suited to one type of guitar? The official answer is: That depends. Many of rock's classic sounds were created with very specific combinations of a guitar and amp. The Gibson Les Paul and Marshall stack, the Fender Stratocaster and the Fender Twin Reverb, the Fender Stratocaster and the Marshall stack, the Rickenbacker 360 and the Vox AC-30 are four of the most popular combinations of all time.

But these are simply starting points in the quest for tone. Strat players influenced by Jimi Hendrix have used Marshall amps for generations, Les Pauls sound great through AC-30s, and Rickenbackers produce wonderful jangle through Twin Reverbs. Multiply these choices by the hundreds of guitars and amps available, and you can see that there are endless possibilities for finding a classic tone — or creating one of your own.

Table 14-1 shows some famous combinations. Use these as a jumping off point for creating your own sounds.

Table 14-1	Common Guitar and Amp Combinations		
Guitar	*Amp*	*Style*	*Artist*
Fender Stratocaster	Fender Bassman	Texas blues	Stevie Ray Vaughan
Fender Stratocaster	Fender Twin Reverb or Fender Dual Showman	surf	Dick Dale
Fender Stratocaster	Marshall 100-watt amp	Hard rock	Jimi Hendrix, Ritchie Blackmore
Gibson SG	Marshall 100-watt amp	Hard rock	AC/DC
Ibanez K-7 7-String	Mesa Triple Rectifier	Heavy metal	Korn
Super Strat, Peavey EVH Wolfgang	Marshall 100-watt amp Peavey 5150	Heavy metal	Eddie Van Halen
Fender Telecaster	Roland JC-120	New wave	The Police's Andy Summers
Rickenbacker 360/360-12	Vox AC30	Folk rock and pop	Tom Petty, The Byrds' Roger McGuinn
Fender Stratocaster	Vox AC30 with custom effects rack	Arena rock	U2's The Edge
Paul Reed Smith Santana Signature Model	Mesa Boogie Mk-I	Blues rock	Carlos Santana
Gibson ES-335	Custom rack system	Jazz rock	Larry Carlton

So, how do you choose? You could simply scope out the details of your favorite guitarist's rig and buy the same exact stuff. You *may* even find that you're able to achieve a similar tone that way. But beware: When it comes to tone, heaven is in the details. Your idol's guitar may be equipped with custom parts; his amp may have been *hot rodded* (electronically altered to offer more gain or a different tone); he may even rely on effects, or studio tricks, to get his sound.

Remember that the most essential component in any rig is you. Your touch is just as important to your tone as your gear. Conventional wisdom is a good starting point, but the best way to find your ideal rig is by careful testing, listening, and patience. A credit card with plenty of headroom — at least 100 watts or more — can also be useful.

Buying tips

Once you know some terminology, you're ready to go out and ask for what you need. The following tips can help you stay happy with your purchase *after* you get it home from the store.

✔ **Bring another guitar player with you.** An objective set of ears is always a good thing, especially when they're attached to an experienced player who knows what to look for in a guitar and an amp. Make sure to let your friend play the guitar while you step back and listen. Also, your friend has your best interests in mind and knows your tastes, which can't necessarily be said of the salesperson.

✔ **Check the controls first.** Don't be afraid to ask the salesperson what each control does, how the pickups are configured, and what special features (such as coil-splitting or channel switching) the guitar or amp offers. Make sure each of these works to your satisfaction.

✔ **Be thorough.** You may have your heart set on that sunburst Les Paul hanging in the corner next to the Dimebag Darrell cutout, but don't restrict yourself. Try *all* the Les Pauls in the store, as well as a sampling of other guitars. Guitars are made of wood, so individual examples of the same model can look, feel, and sound different.

✔ **Stick to the familiar.** Always test new equipment in as familiar an environment as possible. If the store has an amp just like the one you have at home, use that to test the guitar — even if there's a better sounding model available. If you're testing an amp, bring your own guitar to the store.

✔ **Ask about service.** Guitars and amps are like cars — they take a lot of wear and tear, and they require regular tweaking. If you're new to playing an electric guitar, it's especially nice to be able bring the guitar back a month after purchase for a free setup. Just be sure the repairperson doesn't try to add five quarts of oil to your cherry Les Paul.

Chapter 15

Wild and Crazy Sounds: Effects

* *

In This Chapter

▶ Knowing your effects

▶ Defining effects parameters

▶ Connecting effects

▶ Organizing your effects

* *

*H*ow many times have you heard a professional guitarist's tone and thought, *Why can't my playing sound like that?* Aside from talent (which you've got) and practice (you're diligent, right?), top guitarists understand how to make their tone come alive through effects. The guitar and the amp are important, but what goes in between — the effects — can be the difference between nirvana and narcolepsy.

Effects are devices that electronically alter, in strange and wondrous ways, the sound coming out of your guitar. Effects go between your guitar and amp and are built for modularity, meaning you can put as many as you want, or in whatever order you want, to achieve slightly different variations in sound. You can think of effects like a train: The guitar is the engine and the amp is the caboose. In between, go the box cars, which can be placed in any number and in any order and still form a train. Because effects are modular and self-contained, you can mix and match to your heart's (and wallet's) content.

Effects alter the relationship between a guitar and amp, adding another layer of sonic potential in between. Best of all, effects let you play the role of sound designer. The right processors can fortify an anemic sound or morph a mundane tone into an otherworldly swirl.

Identifying Effects

Effects can generally be broken down into four divisions:

> ✔ **Gain based:** These effects act on the volume or signal level and respond in various ways. They include distortion, compressors, volume pedals, and gates.

  ✔ **Tone based:** These effects — which include graphic and parametric EQ, wah-wah pedal, and auto-wah — affect the tonal color, such as the bass and treble content.

  ✔ **Modulation:** The most "effectlike" of the effects, modulation effects generally do something strange to the sound, such as make the guitar sound like it's swirling or under water or wavering. These effects include chorus, flanger, phase shifter, rotating speaker, tremolo, and vibrato.

  ✔ **Ambience:** Ambience effects provide an acoustic space or environment and include reverb and echo (referred to as *delay* by musicians).

Some effects, such as flanger, wah-wah, and delay, are obvious to the ear. But others, such as compression, reverb, and even distortion, are core elements of your tone, so you might not always notice these as "effects." But used artfully, or sometimes even just correctly, they can take you to tonal utopia. Even if your personal style doesn't call for mind-altering sound, you need to understand what the core effects can do for you.

Choosing an Effects Format

Guitar effects come in four basic formats:

  ✔ Individual, single-function effect pedals, or stompboxes
  ✔ Floor-mounted multi-effects units
  ✔ Rack-mounted processors
  ✔ Effects built into an amp or preamp

Stompboxes

Individual effects pedals, or *stompboxes,* are the most common type of guitar effects. They're the masochists of the electronic world because you literally stomp on them with your feet to turn them on and off. Their greatest strength, besides (hopefully) their ruggedness and affordability, is modularity: A typical stompbox may produce only one or two effects, so you can mix and match your favorites to create your ideal system — even if the individual components are made by different manufacturers. Virtually all stompboxes run on 9-volt batteries or an optional AC power supply (some purists insist that batteries "sound" better, but if you use your effect often, the power supply will save you money). Most stompboxes work best when you place them between the guitar and the amp in your signal chain (I take a closer look at signal chain a little later in this chapter).

A stompbox's battery will drain any time something is plugged into the device's input — even if the effect appears to be turn off. Always unplug the input cable of battery-powered effect when it's not in use. And to prevent a loud (and potentially speaker- or eardrum-damaging) *pop*, turn your amp off, put in standby, or turn down the volume all the way before unplugging any cables.

Floor-mounted multi-effects

Floor-mounted multi-effects combine a number of popular effects into a single, integrated package that sits on the floor, underfoot. You then have any number of closely spaced pedals that you can hit to activate any effect singly, or change all the effects at once by changing presets. Any floor-effects unit covers the basics — such as distortion, compression, chorus, reverb, and delay — but some include advanced features such as amp modeling (see Chapter 14) and auto-accompaniment. Their biggest advantage is convenience — because all effects reside in one unit, you have less to set up on stage, no wires to plug and unplug between units, and all the effects run off of one central power supply. They even let you store your favorite settings as "presets" for later recall — a big advantage over manually operated traditional stompboxes.

Rack-mounted effects

When something is "rack-mounted" it means it sits in a cabinet-like rack. A rack allows you to place several effects devices in one housing and control these effects by attached foot pedals. In rack units, the brains sit in the rack at the back of the stage (or even offstage) and a small pedal or series of pedals resides near the guitarist's foot. (In floor-mounted effects, the brain and pedals are all in one unit that resides underfoot.) As a rule, a rack-mounted version of an effect will be more powerful and of higher quality than a similarly named one that exists in floor-mounted or stompbox form.

Built-in effects

The effects built in to amplifiers were once limited to onboard reverb and tremolo, but full-featured onboard processors are becoming more common, especially with the emergence of digital amps and preamps. Some amps offer a full complement of effects, including distortion, compression, modulation, delay, reverb, and beyond, while others concentrate on modulation and spatial effects and leave the distortion and compression to you. Again, convenience comes at the expense of flexibility — built-in effects can sound great, but you're stuck with the ones in your amp. Still, you don't have to use the built-in ones if you don't want to.

Coming to Terms

Here are some key features and controls common to all effects:

- ✔ **Input:** Where the signal enters the effects processor or signal chain.
- ✔ **Output:** Where the signal leaves the effects processor.
- ✔ **Parameter:** An element of the effect that you can control using an external device, such as a continuously variable knob.
- ✔ **Control:** Knobs, faders, foot pedals, and buttons that all exist for one purpose — to let you tweak your effects to your heart's desire.
- ✔ **Bypass:** Removes the effect from the signal path.

The bypass button might be the most important off all effects controls. The bypass switch allows the signal to pass through without processing the sound. It allows you to compare (also called "A/B" in musicians' lingo) the unprocessed sound with the processed sound.

Processing Gain-based Effects: Overdrive, Distortion, and Fuzz

In an early draft of *Romeo and Juliet,* Shakespeare wrote: "That which we call a fuzz by any other name would sound as sweet." The line was later changed by a militant florist, but the Bard's essential point still holds true today: No matter what your processor calls distortion (the terms *fuzz, distortion,* and *overdrive* are often used interchangeably, though subtle differences exist and are defined in the following sections), it must produce one or more of the core effects. All the world's a sound stage, and each effect has a role to play in your tone.

Though the terms are often used interchangeably, knowledgeable guitarists do make distinctions between the different types of the gain-based processing effect where the signal strength overwhelms the circuitry's capacity to reproduce it exactly. Though the term "distortion" is used generically to describe this effect, it also has a connotation when used to describe the differences between fuzz and overdrive. Take a moment to sort out these terms on the guitar player's level.

Distortion, in the generic sense of the signal getting electronically corrupted, is the signature sound of rock and roll. Can you imagine classic riffs such as the Rolling Stones' "Satisfaction" and AC/DC's "Back in Black" without a little *crunch*? The notes would be the same, but the musical statement would lose all its power, danger, and excitement.

Distortion boxes add *gain* to your guitar's signal. So much gain, in fact, that the circuit can't handle it any more. The resulting "overdrive" makes the circuit *clip,* or distort.

Since guitarists often use the terms overdrive, distortion, and fuzz interchangeably, and no clear-cut definition of each variation exists, you'll find overdrive units that can achieve fuzz-like effects, and vice versa. Always listen before you buy.

Distortion devices typically offer three controls:

- **Drive** (or gain) determines the amount of distortion.
- **Tone** (sometimes called EQ, for equalization, or filter) lets you shape the bass and treble content.
- **Output** (or level) determines the final, overall volume of the signal coming out of the box.

Overdrive

Overdrive is the mildest and most natural sounding of the three distortion types. The best models, such as the classic Ibanez Tube Screamer, shown in Figure 15-1, emulate the characteristics of a tube amplifier — some even have actual tubes built into their circuitry. The sound, rich in even harmonics, is warm and full. Use overdrive for blues and classic rock as well as pop lead sounds and hard rock rhythm sounds.

You can use an overdrive pedal as a clean boost by setting the drive control low and the output control high. This is a great way to saturate your tube amp without adding too much coloration to your tone.

Distortion

Distortion, in the sense that it's compared with fuzz and overdrive, is an exaggerated, edgier form of overdrive. Distortion boxes, such as the Boss Metal Zone in Figure 15-2, produce a brighter, more cutting tone. Use them for hard rock and metal rhythm and lead sounds.

Distortion pedals carry all kinds of creative names, such as "Grunge," "Metal," and "In Your Face, Whimpering Slug." These names can give you a clue to the pedal's tone, but you still need your ears to judge. Remember the adage "One man's metal is another man's grunge."

Figure 15-1:
Although its
circuitry is
solid-state,
the Ibanez
Tube
Screamer is
a classic
effect
known for
its smooth,
tube-like
overdrive.

Figure 15-2:
The Boss
Metal Zone
offers
extremely
high gain
and built-
in EQ.

Fuzz

Fuzz boxes, which were among the earliest guitar effects, take you to the extreme edge of distortion. Their bright, buzz-saw-like tone is *the* choice for classic '60s sounds. Pedals that specialize in fuzz don't do a very good job of simulating the natural distortion of a tube amp; however, you *can* simulate a fuzz tone with a conventional distortion box by turning up the gain control and setting the tone for the brightest possible sound.

Turning It Up, or Down: Dynamic Effects

Dynamic effects include compressors and gates, which respond to and act on your signal's volume. These devices "read" the signal, and their behavior changes depending on how loud or soft you play.

Compressors

A *compressor* reduces the difference between the softest and loudest parts of the signal, by *attenuating* (a fancy way of saying "making quieter") any signal that is louder than a specified threshold.

By thus *squashing* the signal — and then boosting its overall output — a compressor makes quiet notes seem louder (but keeps loud notes where they are). One byproduct is an apparent increase in sustain as the note dies out, so a guitarist often uses a compressor as a *sustainer.*

Compressor parameters include:

- ✔ **Threshold:** The level at which the compressor starts working. Signals below the threshold are unaffected; signals crossing the threshold are attenuated.

- ✔ **Ratio:** The amount of attenuation after the signal goes over the threshold: the higher the ratio, the greater the gain reduction.

    At a 2:1 ratio the compressor allows the signal to go 1 dB (decibel, a unit of loudness) for every 2 dB of gain. A 4:1 ratio means that for a signal that increases by 4 dB, only 1 dB registers at the output.

- ✔ **Attack time:** The amount of time it takes the compressor to kick in. Slow attack times allow some or all of the initial *transient* (the percussive-like attack portion of the string strike) to sneak through, which is often desirable.

✔ **Decay time:** The amount of time the compressor keeps working after the signal has fallen below the threshold.

✔ **Output:** The overall, final output volume after compression. This is sometimes called "make-up gain," because it's used to add back in any volume lost or reduced during the compression process.

Don't worry if your guitar compressor's controls are labeled a little differently than the parameters previously listed. Some compressors will not have all those parameters, either (for example, those with a fixed ratio or no decay time adjustment). Some simple stompbox compressors have only two controls. You'll see things like *sensitivity* for threshold, *sustain* for ratio, and so forth. This is all just part of living in that quirky universe known as Effects Land. Many guitar compressors also include a tone control — useful because the compressor can rob the signal of highs.

Use a compressor to add sustain and emphasize the attack of clean lead sounds. Country players use compressors to create that "chicken-pickin'" sound, a percussive style of playing that emulates the sound of a clucking fowl (as opposed to that of a plucking fool, which, as a guitarist, you never want to be). Compressors are also great for clean rhythm sounds because they can bring out the individual attack of every note in a chord. Figure 15-3 shows a popular compressor, the Boss CS-3, whose controls govern compression and sustain.

Figure 15-3:
The Boss Compression Sustainer CS-3.

If you set the compressor for a high ratio, you may actually throw your signal out of balance — power chords may sound quieter than single notes. You can get more natural results by bypassing the compressor whenever your playing goes on the offensive.

Gates

Like compressors, gates control signal levels. But instead of reducing dynamic range, gates shut down any signal that falls below the threshold.

Use a gate after distortion and EQ (tone control device, explained later in the chapter) in your signal chain to reduce unwanted noise, such as the fuzzy whooshing sound generated by the effects themselves when you're not playing, or the hum from your pickups. Because gates shut down the audio path when not enough signal exists to "open them," they're sometimes referred to as *noise gates*. You can also apply a gate to other effects, such as delay and reverb to give them an unnatural "slamming shut" sound.

Gates are great for keeping unwanted noises from reaching your audience, but they can cut off quiet notes against your will. Make sure to set the *threshold* (the control that determines when the effect kicks in) low enough that *all* the notes you play can come through. If you're playing a particularly delicate passage, bypass the gate.

Playing by Ear: Tone-based Effects

Tone-based effects include anything that alters the bass and treble content of your tone, whether it's a passive filter, such as turning up the high frequencies, or a dynamic setting, as in a foot-operated wah-wah pedal. Strictly speaking a tone control is a volume control on only a certain part of a signal's frequency range, but humans don't hear a perceptible change in signal level, just a change in the quality of the sound. Tone-based effects include EQ (the musicians' term for "tone control") and other filters.

EQ

EQ — short for *equalization,* or equalizer — shapes your guitar's tone by boosting and cutting specific frequencies. With equalization, you can bring out the highs and pump up the bass, or cut out the midrange for the "scooped" sound used by bands such as Metallica. The tone controls built into your guitar and amp are examples of EQs, but these have fewer features than the outboard models you find on the floor effects or in rack effects.

EQs are sometimes called *filters,* because they block, or filter, certain frequencies while letting others pass through. Never use an EQ filter in your coffee maker — unless it's well grounded.

Frequencies are expressed in Hertz (Hz, pronounced "hurts"), or cycles per second, and kilohertz (kHz), which is shorthand for "thousands of Hertz." The tuning note A 440 is 440 cycles per second. An octave above that A is 880 Hz; an octave below A 440 is 220 Hz. The open A string is 110 Hz. Human hearing ranges between 20 and 20,000 Hertz (20 — 20 kHz).

EQ units designed for guitars divide your instrument's signal into frequency ranges, called *bands*. The number of bands can vary, but EQs designed for guitars typically range between three and ten. Recording and sound reinforcement applications can use much larger EQs — for example, a graphic EQ with 31 or more bands. That level of precision is overkill for guitarists. Each band has a center frequency, which determines the part of the audio spectrum it affects.

EQs come in two basic types: graphic EQ and parametric EQ, but graphic EQs are much more common for guitarists.

Graphic EQ

Graphic EQs are easy to identify because the *sliders* that are used to control the individual frequencies form a graph on the surface of the EQ. Each band of a graphic EQ is fixed — it is permanently assigned to control a specific frequency range. These types of EQs are often called, logically enough, fixed-band graphic equalizers. The graphic EQ shown in Figure 15-4 has seven bands (plus a level control on the far right). Each band represents an octave in the sound spectrum.

You use the slider to *boost* (increase) or *cut* (attenuate) the gain of specific frequencies. When the slider is centered, the band is inactive (it neither boosts nor cuts). Pull the slider below the midpoint, or zero, and you're cutting that frequency range. Push the band above zero to boost that frequency. Boosting the higher bands makes your guitar sound brighter; boosting the lower bands makes it boomier and enhances the "thump" you need for hard rock. Boosting the mid bands will give you a thick, syrupy sound that's ideal for blues soloing. Cut the mid bands to create a scooped sound.

Filters

Although EQs are technically filters, guitarists usually reserve the use of the word for filters for specialized tone devices such as wah-wah pedals and auto-wahs (also known as envelope filters).

Figure 15-4:
The Boss
GE-7 EQ is a
seven-band
graphic EQ
that covers
the core of
the guitar's
frequency
spectrum.

Wah-wah

The wah-wah pedal (or just "wah," for short), such as the model shown in Figure 15-5, is one of the classic effects in rock music. Eric Clapton and Jimi Hendrix popularized it as a soloing tool back in the 1960s, while the funksters of the seventies made it an essential part of the R&B sound (not to mention *the* essential background for TV chase scenes).

A wah is an EQ filter with a variable frequency. As you rock the pedal up and down, the filter emphasizes specific frequencies and cuts others, creating a sweeping effect and giving your tone a vowel-like character.

You create the classic wah sound by moving the pedal back and forth in rhythm with the music (say, by rocking your foot in an eighth-note rhythm while playing quarter notes). Use more subtle movements to articulate specific notes. You can also create a mammoth-sized tone leaving the pedal in the center position. Hey — if it's fat enough for Slash of Guns N' Roses, it should work for you too.

Jimi Hendrix gave his wah a workout on his cover of Bob Dylan's "All Along the Watchtower."

Figure 15-5:
The Vox Wah-Wah powered many a psychedelic hit; it's still produced today.

There's a wah flavor for every taste. Some models offer variable bandwidth and frequency range, while others combine wah with additional effects, such as fuzz and volume.

Auto wah and envelope follower

Not all wahs are pedal operated. An auto wah, or envelope follower, sweeps through the frequency spectrum automatically. Two factors can determine the sweep:

- **Time:** The filter sweeps (or oscillates) over its range over a preset time period. This sweep occurs no matter what you play.
- **Dynamics:** The loudness of your playing affects the wah's sweep. Play harder, and the sweep widens, exaggerating the effect.

You can change the sensitivity and range of the filter to create subtle effects or radical *wacka-wacka* sounds, the ideal accompaniment for your upcoming tribute concert to *The Mod Squad.*

Getting Volume under Control: Other Volume Effects

Before moving on to the wacky world of modulation effects, I'll throw in two common volume-based effects that don't really alter a signal the way gain-based effects, such as distortion and compression (discussed earlier in the chapter), do but can provide a level of control of your signal that you can use for musical effect.

Volume pedal

A volume pedal isn't an effect per se, but it does alter your sound, letting you control your volume in real time without taking your hands off the guitar. Push the pedal forward to increase the volume, pull it back all the way to mute the signal.

You can use a volume pedal for mundane tasks such as turning your guitar down when the singer yells at you — and turning it up when your solo comes around — or for more creative moves, such as creating volume swells and reverse guitar effects.

 Combine a volume pedal with delay to create lush ambient sounds by increasing the volume only *after* you pluck a note. By burying the attack, you create a pick-less, violin-like sound. If you pull the volume back quickly as well, you can create the illusion of "backwards" guitar. Tie-dye T-shirt is optional.

Tremolo

James Bond might have the gun and the girl, but he'd never be as cool without the tremolo guitar that defines his theme song. Tremolo is a rapid and regular change in volume, like when you sing in front of an electric fan. Some people (including some notable amp designers) confuse tremolo with *vibrato*, a regular change in *pitch*. Tremolo was first heard on early tube amplifiers such as the Fender Vibrolux, but has since found its way into stompboxes and rack effects.

Tremolo effects include these two parameters:

- **Depth:** Controls the amount, or intensity, of volume change.
- **Rate:** Controls the frequency, or speed, of the volume change.

Making a Change: Modulation Effects

Modulation effects such as the chorus, flanger, rotating speaker, pitch shifter, octave divider, and phase shifter, or phaser, are mainstays of the modern guitar sound. Although each has its own distinct timbre and application, all three modulate (or change) your guitar's tone over time. They share some key parameters and controls:

✔ **Depth:** Determines the effect's intensity. Greater depth produces more noticeable results.

✔ **Rate (or Time):** Determines the speed of each sweep through the effects' range. With slow settings, the effect can seem almost static or shimmering; faster settings produce a more dramatic, vibrato-like effect.

✔ **Shape (some models only):** Governs the pattern, or waveform, the effect uses to change over time. A sine wave shape, which looks like a sideways S, and, as a rounded, regular pattern produces a smooth sound, while a triangle wave shape gives you a sharper, ramping effect.

TIP

Your pedalboard (see later in this chapter) might contain a number of different modulation effects, but you get better results by using only one at a time.

Chorus

Chorus is designed to make a single instrument sound like many. A chorus delays the signal by a small amount — usually between 10 and 30 *milliseconds* (ms), or thousandths of a second. When the delayed signal is mixed back with the original, it creates a thick, shimmering sound. Some chorus circuits also apply a small amount of pitch-shifting for a more pronounced effect. You can use a chorus such as the Boss CH-1, pictured in Figure 15-6, to make a mono guitar signal stereo by feeding each of the unit's outputs to its own amplifier.

Figure 15-6:
With two outputs, the Boss CH-1 Super Chorus can make a mono guitar signal stereo.

You can hear chorus on thousands of recordings. Andy Summers of the Police used the pedal to great effect on "Roxanne."

Flanger

The flanger traces its roots back to the late 1960s, when a recording engineer experimented by playing two tapes of the same material in sync with one another. As the old-style reel-to-reel tape decks played, the engineer pushed on the edge (or flange) of one of the tape reels. This slowed the tape slightly and made it go out of sync with its twin. When he let go, the tape would try to catch up. The subtle delay between the two tapes caused an audio phenomenon called *comb filtering:* As the comb filter swept across the frequency spectrum, the sound whooshed and breathed — just the thing for the tail end of the psychedelic era.

A pair of reel-to-reel machines would make your pedalboard a tad unwieldy, so designers came up with electronic *flangers,* which mate a delay to an oscillator. The unit feeds some of the delayed signal back into the original to intensify the effect. In addition to the core parameters of depth and rate, most flangers let you control *feedback* (the amount of signal being "fed back" into the input) and *resonance* (the emphasis of the filtering effect).

A flanger can create chorus-like effects (with slow rate, low depth, and moderate delay), metallic short-delay type effects, and noises that sound like a jet airplane taking off. Eddie Van Halen used one extensively on early recordings such as "Feel Your Love Tonight" from *Van Halen II.*

Phase shifter/phaser

A *phase shifter,* or *phaser,* such as the Boss PH-3 in Figure 15-7, applies an oscillator to an EQ filter and mixes the filtered signal with the original. As the filter moves up and down the tonal spectrum, some frequencies go out of phase and cancel each other out. While the effect is similar to flanging (some settings sound virtually identical), phasers usually sound thicker and creamier. Use them for funk and R&B rhythm work, or as an alternate to chorus and flange sounds in rock arrangements.

Rotating speaker or Leslie

The *rotating speaker* — also known as the *Leslie* after the company that made the classic models — was first designed for organs, but soon found its way onto the guitar scene. As the speaker rotates, it scatters sound waves around the room, causing a complex series of delays and phase cancellations.

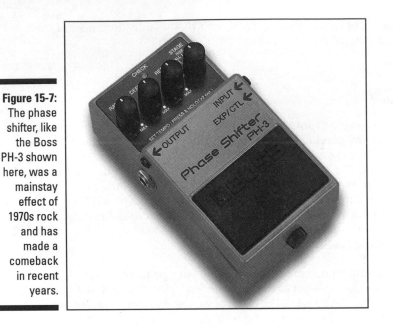

Figure 15-7: The phase shifter, like the Boss PH-3 shown here, was a mainstay effect of 1970s rock and has made a comeback in recent years.

Leslies sound amazing, but are bulky and delicate. Early chorus and phase pedals were designed in part to emulate the Leslie tone. They fell short, but produced some cool sounds in their own right.

Modern digital processors come closer to capturing the elusive Leslie sound. Look for a unit that offers both low- and high-speed rotation (the original devices could change speeds). An accurate Leslie simulation should also have a *crossover* that divides your guitar's signal into high and low frequency bands and processes each separately. One of the coolest aspects of the Leslie sound was the way the low notes shook while the high notes shimmered.

Eric Clapton's solo on the Beatles' "While My Guitar Gently Weeps" is the classic example of a guitar driving a Leslie.

Pitch shifters and octave dividers

As the name suggests, a *pitch shifter* alters the pitch of an incoming signal. The pitch-shifted signal is then mixed with the original, unshifted signal, creating a harmony. The number of harmonies depends on the number of *voices:* A one-voice pitch shifter adds one signal to the original; a two-voice shifter adds two voices to the original, and so on.

A pitch shifter has two principal parameters:

- ✔ **Pitch:** Determines the amount of pitch shifting. Sometimes, you find two separate pitch controls, one for larger intervals (usually measured in half-steps), another for fine-tuning, measured in cents (1/100th of a half step). Use small amounts of pitch shifting to dial up a chorus-like effect, and larger values to create harmonies and octave effects.
- ✔ **Mix:** Determines the blend between the original and shifted signal.

The pitch-shifting theme has a number of variations. Basic devices alter the pitch by a static interval. If, for example, you set the shifter for four half steps (the musical interval of a major 3rd), every note you play will be accompanied by a note four half steps higher. Although this is a cool effect, it has its limits — if you're playing a major scale, some of the harmonized note will fall outside the correct scale.

Intelligent pitch shifters (sometimes referred to as *harmonizers,* but that's a trademark name of the Eventide company) let you define the key and scale — the processor will adjust the interval accordingly.

Octave dividers produce a note that is one or two octaves above or below the input note. You can create octave effects with any pitch shifter, but some devices specialize in just octave production. Others combine octave effects with fuzz. Use an octave divider to imitate a 12-string guitar or combine with distortion to add extra low-end body to a solo tone.

Jimi Hendrix (his name comes up a lot when discussing classic guitar effects) used an octave divider extensively. Check out "Purple Haze" and "Foxy Lady" from *Are You Experienced?*

Putting Your Sound in Context: Ambient Effects

The class of devices known as *ambient effects* places your sound in an acoustic context or environment. When you listen to music, you hear it in a room or a concert hall. When music is recorded in a dry or dead environment, musicians and engineers try to put back some acoustic life into these sounds by adding electronic ambience. Virtually every recorded sound you hear has electronically applied ambience, from music on a CD to a spoken-voice radio commercial. Somewhere some engineer has applied some ambience, even if that ambience is the subtle hint that a speaker or musician is in a room of some kind. Rarely, if ever, do you hear the unadulterated sound of a

signal without ambience, either natural (a mike picking up the room reflec-
tions) or artificial (applied as an electronic effect). The two most common
electronic ambient devices, reverb and delay (echo), are related in that they
both simulate reflected and repeated sound, but musicians treat them as two
separate effects.

Delay or echo

Delay effects trace their roots back to early rock and roll. Recording engineers
created the first delays with tape machines, but the effect was quickly adapted
to portable devices. These days, almost all delays use digital technology,
although many are designed to emulate the tape delays (a delay using an
actual loop of recording tape, with one record head and multiple, staggered
playback heads) of yore. Figure 15-8 shows a popular digital delay model.

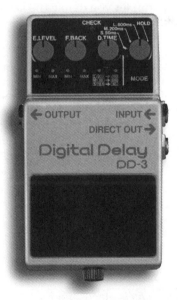

Figure 15-8:
The Boss
DD-3 is one
of the most
popular
digital delay
devices and
features
four
adjustable
parameters.

Some digital delays have three adjustable parameters and some have four.
The following list shows the four possible parameters:

- **Delay time:** The time between the original and the delayed signal. This
  is expressed in milliseconds or — if the delay can synchronize to an
  external tempo — musical values such as eighth note, quarter note, and
  so forth.

- **Feedback:** Determines the number of repeats. Low feedback provides
  one repeat; on some units, the highest settings produce infinite repeats.

> ✔ **Mix:** The blend between the original and delayed signals.
>
> ✔ **Tempo** (synchronizable delays only): Sets the reference tempo. Many delay units let you "tap" a tempo by tapping a footswitch in time with the music.

Delay devices are among the handful of "must have" effects because they can cover a number of sounds — from thickening to ambient echo to a doubling effect — and fit just about every musical style.

Slapback is the classic delay of early rock and roll and rockabilly. Although it sounds like deserved punishment for a lead guitarist with an attitude, the name describes a rapid and pronounced echo — it sounds like the sound is slapping back off of a nearby surface. Elvis' guitarist Scotty Moore used it on recordings such as "My Baby Left Me," and "Hound Dog." Vintage slapback effects were created with tape machines, but you can get the same sound by setting a delay to 100–132 milliseconds (ms) with low feedback. Go cat go.

Echo effects use longer delay times and — often — a greater number of repeats. An echo can range anywhere from 150 ms to 1 second or more, although settings in the 300–600 ms range are most popular. U2's The Edge is famous for his use of echo. Echo effects can be mono or stereo. On stereo delays, you can set each side to its own delay time — a cool way to create rhythmic effects.

Reverb

Reverb — short for reverberation — is the king of all effects for guitar, vocals, everything. Along with tremolo, it's one of the earliest effects ever included on a guitar amp. More important, reverb plays a vital role in classic guitar sounds of every style.

Although sometimes confused with echo, *reverb* is actually a more complex ambient effect that's designed to simulate a natural acoustic space.

The key parameters of a reverb unit include:

> ✔ **Reverb time:** The decay of the reverb. The longer the reverb time, the longer it takes the sound to dissipate.
>
> ✔ **Mix:** Controls the balance between the reverb and the original signal.

You use reverb for two main purposes: to give your guitar an otherworldly aura (spring reverb) and to create a natural ambient space around your guitar (digital reverb).

When you play live, use less reverb than you would in the studio.

Spring reverb

Early guitar reverbs, such as the ones found in Fender amps, consisted of a small metal tank filled with springs. As the signal passed through the tank, the springs became excited (hey — you would too, if you lived on the bottom of an amp). Spring reverbs are still widely used in guitar amps today. Their distinctly warm and full sound is the perfect complement to vintage guitar styles.

You can find examples of reverb on nearly all modern recordings. Classic spring reverb is one of the key elements of surf and British Invasion styles. Because a guitar amp's built-in reverb can be such an integral element of the guitar tone, many producers combine it with the subtler sound of room and hall reverb when recording.

Digital reverb

Digital reverbs are designed to sound like natural spaces. *Algorithms* — complex software routines that tell the processor how to behave — can emulate spaces such as rooms, halls, stages, and even cathedrals. There are also algorithms designed to sound like artificial reverbs, such as steel plates, chambers, and yes, spring reverbs.

When you're going for a natural sound, use a short to moderate reverb time. Set the pre-delay so that the reverb doesn't start immediately — this will give the listener a chance to hear the notes you're playing *before* they get washed away by the reverberations.

Designing a Signal Path

Back-scratching, real estate, and effects placement all subscribe to a common creed: Location is everything. The order of your effects — the path that the signal will follow — has a profound impact on your sound. For example, if a reverb follows a chorus, the reverb sound gets chorused — not the original signal. With rack and pedalboard type multi-effects units, you are sometimes limited as to how you can order things — the device orders them for you (though more and more modern multi-effects processors let you configure the order of the modules). But stompboxes are individual components, and you can place them anywhere you want. This can be a good thing (if you know what you're doing and appreciate the flexibility), or a bad thing (if you're clueless).

Unless you're using a multi-effect with internal signal routing, you must interconnect effects with patch cords. Unfortunately, many guitarists skimp on patch cords, and their tone suffers for it. Use the best patch cords you can afford, and use the shortest ones you can find — just make sure they can reach between the effects.

An effect device's physical construction should influence where you place it. Here are some tips for joining your effects:

- **Gain, EQ, and dynamics effects:** Most players prefer to put these effects early in the signal chain because they create the meat of the tone. These devices are designed to work on your guitar's direct output, so you should place them between your instrument and the amp's input.

- **Modulation and spatial effects:** These effects such as delay and reverb will work fine running into your amp's input, but may sound better patched into an effects loop (see Chapter 3). The loop inserts the effects after the amp's preamp and tone stages, put before the power-amp stage, which keeps more of your core tone intact.

- **Stompboxes:** Stompboxes are designed to go in-line (or between the guitar and the amp), so they will always work when feeding the amp input. You may choose to use a stompbox reverb in your amp's effects loop because you think it sounds better that way, but you don't have to.

- **Rack effects:** Because rack effects generally have a louder (or *hotter*) output than stompboxes, rack effects can overload your amp's inputs, causing distortion, a general loss in tone, and a feeling of existential angst. It's best to use them in an effects loop. Rack effects *designed specifically for guitar* can feed your amp's input or an effects loop, but the sonic results vary. If you're shopping, it's always best to test the effect with your own amp (or one with similar features).

Almost all effects add gain — or level — to your signal path. Be careful not to overload the input of sensitive devices such as digital delay by over boosting the effects in front of it. This won't damage the effect, but it can sound about as appealing as sharp fingernails across a blackboard on the day after a bachelor party.

If your signal starts to accumulate noise, due to the number of stompboxes you're adding, consider placing a noise gate somewhere toward the end of the chain.

Organizing Your Effects: Pedalboards

Pedalboards are not skateboards for overcoming inertia. Instead, they're units that let you organize your effects. The concept is simple — mount a number of effects pedals and their power supplies on a piece of wood or other sturdy and flat surface. You can then keep your effects connected *and* protected, saving setup time at the gig (not to mention reducing the risk that you'll forget the Hyper-Grunge Obliterator pedal you need to get through your command performance at Aunt Petunia's afternoon tea).

Although pedalboards can get pretty elaborate — some pros have digital switching matrixes that let them activate stompboxes stationed offstage, switch between amps, and start their sports car — you can build a board of your own with a scrap of plywood, some white glue, and some Velcro. There's no ideal design; just make sure the board is big enough to hold all your effects and power supplies, but not so bulky that you have to enroll in a gym just to carry it around. Spacing is important: you should be able to reach each effect without having to do the splits, but the individual switches should be far enough apart that you don't hit adjacent units by accident. A typical pedalboard is shown in Figure 15-9.

Figure 15-9:
You can arrange all of your effects (and their power supplies) on a pedalboard.

Battery access is another important consideration. If your effect's battery compartment is on the bottom of the device (most are), you need a way to get at it *after* the effect has been mounted on the board. (This is one reason you should use Velcro to attach your effects to the wood instead of something more permanent — such as glue). Better yet, invest in power supplies for your effects. Not only will this save you the hassle of changing batteries; you'll also be able to keep your effects "patched" together permanently without worrying about draining the batteries. Effects manufacturers make special power supplies for their individual effects; you can also buy commercial *universal* power supplies that are designed to work with several effects at once. Either way, make sure your power supply provides the correct voltage, polarity, and amperage for your individual effects units — power requirements vary, and the wrong power supply can damage your sound and your circuitry.

If you're not the home-improvement type, you can purchase a commercial pedal board. Look for a pedalboard that has enough room to fit and mount all of your effects — some models don't let you fit odd-shaped units — and provides a built-in power supply. Also, if you have a collection of pedals of different makes, be wary of pedalboards designed by manufactures to house only their own products.

You don't have to use stompboxes to take advantage of the pedalboard concept. Floor-mounted multi-effects are designed to function like pedalboards, where you can activate individual effects with footswitches.

If a rack effects unit is your aural weapon of choice, you can use an outboard foot controller to operate it like a pedalboard. Some devices come with specially designed footswitches, while others use a communication protocol called *MIDI* (Musical Instrument Digital Interface) controlled by a footswitch. With MIDI, you can activate individual effects, change presets, and even control individual parameters in real time. MIDI can be a little intimidating at first, but if you take the time to learn your effect's MIDI capabilities, you can harness its power and, eventually, rule the world, just like you've always wanted.

Chapter 16

The Care and Feeding of Your Electric Guitar

• •

In This Chapter

▶ Using guitar-adjusting tools

▶ Changing your strings

▶ Keeping your guitar clean

▶ Performing a setup

▶ Troubleshooting

▶ Storing your guitar and amp

• •

A guitar — like any other machine — is subject to wear and tear: The strings go bad, or they break; climate changes shrink and swell the wood; moving parts wear out, and so forth. These afflictions and deteriorations can prevent you from properly expressing yourself with your instrument and increase your tendency to express yourself in other, less printable, ways. If you want to keep your guitar on the straight and narrow, you should know how to perform some basic maintenance and repairs.

As you grow more comfortable playing the guitar, your sensitivity to its touch and response increases, so when little things go out of whack, you notice them more. Your ears develop too, so sometimes the guitar just won't sound right — even when it feels okay — and this too is a sign you may need to perform some adjustments. As you become more intimate with your guitar, you find its workings are demystified: You're no longer afraid to go, "This doesn't feel right. What if I turned this doohickey a notch . . . hey! It's better!" Gaining greater knowledge and increased confidence with the workings of your guitar as you play it is a natural process. You never know, however, when you might be stuck somewhere — or flat broke — and must or want to perform these guitar repairs yourself. And when you do the job yourself, you not only save money, but you gain a deeper understanding of the workings of your guitar. So put down your pick and pick up your tools! This chapter shows you what tool you need and how to use them.

Using the Tools of the Trade

Before attempting any tweaks on your guitar, you should acquire, lay out, or otherwise assemble certain tools specific to guitar maintenance and repair. Don't worry — you won't have to renovate your garage and find a new home for your car: The tools you need for the repairs described in this chapter should fit into a small pouch or the accessories compartment of a gig bag.

If you're at all uncomfortable with any of the procedures described in this chapter, stop, and take the instrument to a qualified repairperson.

The basics

You can use the tools shown in Figure 16-1 for the day-to-day maintenance tasks: changing strings, cleaning the guitar, and making minor setup adjustments (discussed later in this chapter). Don't leave home without the important items shown in the following list:

Figure 16-1:
Basic tools every guitarist should have (clockwise from top left): guitar polish, soft cloth, Allen wrenches, needle-nose pliers, reversible screwdriver, and string winder.

✔ **Soft cloth:** You use this for everything from wiping down the strings after you play to polishing the guitar. Keep the cloth clean and dry. You can use a cotton diaper, because it's absorbent, doesn't shed its fibers, and is tailor made for absorbing bodily fluids. But any absorbent material that won't shred and shed will suffice. Chamois (pronounced "shammy") is a traditional favorite for polishing-cloth material.

✔ **Guitar polish:** Although you can apply common furniture polish to your guitar's neck and body, the stuff tends to leave an oily film over the hardware and strings. You don't want your licks to be that slick. Guitar polish, available at most music stores, doesn't muck up the hardware, and still protects the wood. Plus, it comes in small containers that fit easily in your guitar case.

✔ **String winder:** Although not an absolute necessity, these plastic wonders save time when you must tighten or loosen strings with multiple wrappings. Most winders also double as a tool for removing the bridge pins on acoustic guitars.

✔ **Allen wrenches:** One of the most vital guitar adjusting tools is also one of the easiest to misplace — do yourself a favor and buy a multi-wrench set. You use Allen "keys" to adjust bridge saddles, fasten locking nuts and bridge pieces, and tighten or loosen neck truss rods.

✔ **Needle-nose pliers/wire cutters:** Use these for everything from cutting off old strings to tightening and loosening nuts and bolts.

✔ **Phillips and flathead screwdrivers:** You use a screwdriver to vary a pickup's height, tighten the tuning keys, adjust bridge saddles, and remove and replace parts like pickguards, jackplates, and pickup covers. A reversible screwdriver offers you both types of blades on one shank, but is often less versatile than a set of both kinds. If you keep your flathead screwdriver clean, it can also double as a cheese knife when the club owner lets the band visit the buffet table on their break, but doesn't provide silverware. (Most if not all musicians can operate cutlery when pressed.)

Power user tools

In addition to the kit described under "The basics," the well-equipped guitarist will want to add some or all of the following tools to his or her arsenal:

✔ **Soldering iron:** This is good for fixing and connecting electronic parts like pickups and potentiometers ("pots," for short, or just "controls" — the contraptions that sit under the knobs, switches, and jacks). A low-wattage soldering iron often works best, because it won't damage the surrounding components by overheating them. Most guitar wiring is very basic, so even if you've never soldered before, you can fix simple problems, such as a broken solder joint or a disconnected lead, without worrying too much that you'll cause any harm.

✔ **Rosin core solder:** It flows more easily than acid core solder, and makes a more solid contact with guitar parts. You don't need to know the specifics about its composition, so just look on the label or ask the hardware store clerk if you're not sure what to buy.

- **White glue:** You can use the familiar "white" glue (you know, the stuff with the cow on the bottle that you used in grade school) to fix a chipped nut (assuming you're lucky enough to find both pieces), or to fix a small wood chip in neck or body. Fixing a chip right when it happens will guarantee the best fit (wood changes over time). Be careful when gluing your guitar, though. Excess leakage on the finish can leave a nasty spot, if it's allowed to dry.

- **Spare wire:** Sometimes you can't work with the existing parts when a wire breaks, often because the lengths are too short or the repair area is inaccessible. So a length of insulated single-strand copper wire can often help you to create a makeshift shunt, or bridge.

- **Contact Cleaner:** Electronic parts, such as pots and switches, can corrode, and moisture, dirt and grime, which can result in crackling or other noise. Contact cleaner, available at your local electronic megastore, can rid your electronic components of pollution and improve their performance.

- **Flashlight and tweezers:** Carry a flashlight and tweezers, because these come in handy for any "surgical operations." Plus, you can take the splinters out of your drummer's feet when you play those summer gigs on the boardwalk.

- **Light vise or clamp:** Use this for holding individual components together while the glue dries or the solder sets. Most guitar parts are light, so a small portable vise or a clamp should do the trick. Having a vise around can also come in handy when you're renegotiating your contract with the record label.

- **Soldering accessories:** Stock up on alligator clips, sponges (for absorbing drips), and flux (a material that helps solder adhere to a surface). Every soldering surgeon keeps a supply of these. An alligator clip can hold together a broken-wire connection when you don't have time to break out the soldering kit.

- **Files:** You can use small files to make adjustments to the nut slots; you use larger files (with caution) to trim rough edges on frets or other metal parts. A file can also help you break out of the slammer after your raucous festival gig in Des Moines.

- **Sandpaper and steel wool:** Use this for smoothing out frets and other parts after filing. And there's no truth to the rumor that swallowing a sheet of 200-grit helps you sing like Rod Stewart.

Changing Strings

Most guitarists change their strings about as often as drummers change their socks — in other words, not often enough. Old strings can sound dull, go out of tune, and break more easily. An old saying goes, "There's nothing in the world better than an old guitar with new strings." So change your strings like a corrupt politician votes: early and often.

Choosing the right strings

Before you can change strings, you must decide what type of strings to use on your guitar. Strings come in various sizes (called gauges) and are made of a variety of materials. The chart in Figure 16-2 shows some typical sets. The first two strings (the high E and B) are always *plain,* or unwound — without a center core and a spiral wraparound material; the bottom three are always wound. The 3rd string can be plain *or* wound; rockers usually choose a plain 3rd because it's easier to bend, but there are styles — like authentic '50s rockabilly — where a wound 3rd works best.

Figure 16-2:
A chart showing different sets of electric guitar string gauges. The *w* stands for wound string.

String Set Name	1	2	3	4	5	6
Ultra Light	.008	.010	.015	.022(w)	.032(w)	.039(w)
Super Light	.009	.011	.017	.024(w)	.032(w)	.042(w)
Light	.010	.013	.017	.026(w)	.036(w)	.046(w)
Medium	.011	.014	.018	.028(w)	.038(w)	.049(w)
Medium Heavy	.012	.016	.024(w)	.032(w)	.042(w)	.052(w)
Heavy	.013	.017	.026(w)	.036(w)	.046(w)	.056(w)

The individual strings included in a set will vary by manufacturer — one brand might mate an .011 (pronounced "eleven") first string with a .015 ("fifteen") second, while another might use an .011 and a .014 for the same two strings. And brand names don't always tell the whole story: Some manufacturers call medium gauges things like "Power Gauge" and "Blues/Jazz Rock Gauge." Why? Wouldn't you rather be a power blues rocker than a medium? If you're unsure when presented with the gauge's name, you can ask for a set by naming just the manufacturer and the first string, as in, "I'd like a set of D'Addario elevens." Gauges for each string in a set are printed on the packaging, too.

Many rock-oriented electric guitars come from the factory strung with super-light strings, such as .009s ("nines"). Lighter-gauge strings make the guitar easier to play, which is a good thing on the sales floor. If you have a light touch and like to bend the strings, the .009s will serve you well; for an even lighter touch, you might try .008s.

Change 'em now!

Here are ten reasons why you need to change your strings *now:* (1) Guitar sounds dull; (2) Guitar won't stay in tune; (3) Intonation — the guitar's ability to produce the correct pitch at various points on the neck — is off, even though the neck is correctly aligned; (4) Strings are hard to play; (5) Strings break; (6) Strings show fraying around the winding. This can lead to breakage, which always occurs at the climax of your show-stopping solo; (7) Strings are mismatched: maybe you had to use a heavier E string than your string set calls for — that's okay for one gig, but now that you're home, it's time to change the lot of 'em; (8) You can't remember the last time you changed your strings; (9) Strings have become dirty or rusted; (10) Your strings are older than your lead singer.

But heavier strings offer a more powerful tone — and they stand up better to aggressive playing. You can compensate for the increased string tension (the heavier the string, the tighter they feel to your fingers on the neck) by tuning the guitar down by a half or whole step. Stevie Ray Vaughan used heavy strings and tuned down — his top string was a .013, and he tuned down a half step to E♭ though his reasons were certainly musical, not tactile. Other players who tuned down include Jimi Hendrix, Guns N' Roses, and heavy metal rockers Pantera and Korn — who often tune down a whole step or more.

When you change the string tension on your guitar, as you do when putting on a different-gauge string, you may have to adjust the intonation, action, and truss rod (discussed in detail later in the chapter). If you're inexperienced — or if this is the first time the guitar has undergone a radical string-tension change — take the guitar to a professional repairperson.

Removing the old strings

Before you can put on new strings, you must first remove the old. This statement may seem obvious, but still it raises a few questions that you must answer before you begin.

What kind of bridge does your guitar have?

Electric guitars come with a variety of bridges: both fixed and floating. A fixed bridge, as its name implies, doesn't move. A floating bridge allows you to move it up or down, by pressing down or pulling up an attached arm or bar. With a floating bridge you can create pitch-wavering effects that can range from subtle, shimmering vibrato to dramatically wide vibrato and "dive-bomb" effects. For some styles of music, like heavy metal, a floating bridge is essential. (Steve Vai is considered to be the master of modern whammy bar technique.) But as far as changing strings, what type of bridge you have can influence your approach to taking off the strings.

A *fixed bridge* doesn't mean that it "ain't broken," but that it stays in place at all times, so feel free to take all the strings off at once. This makes it easier to clean and inspect the fingerboard, frets, and other hardware. Guitars with fixed bridges include Telecasters, "hardtail" Stratocasters, and many Gibson models, like the Les Paul, SG, Explorer, and Flying V.

Floating bridges fall into two categories: tension and vibrato (also erroneously called "tremolo," probably because the abbreviation *trem* sounds cooler than *vib*). In either case, the strings play a role in holding the bridge in the correct position. Change strings one at a time unless you plan to give the guitar a thorough cleaning. Here are the differences between the two types of floating bridges:

- *Tension* bridges are similar to the ones found on violins — the bridge sits freely atop the body, held down by the downward tension of the taught strings passing over it. If you remove all the strings at once, the bridge will come off the guitar. This won't damage the bridge or the guitar, but — assuming your guitar was set up correctly in the first place — you must put the bridge back exactly where it was *before* you removed the strings. Otherwise, the intonation and action will go out of whack.

- *Vibrato* (or *whammy*, or *tremolo*) bridges are secured to the body by a combination of screws and springs. The bridge rocks on a fulcrum (the center point of a lever), its movements adding or reducing string tension (and increasing or decreasing the pitch). The springs offset the string tension so that the bridge can rest in a neutral position. It's like a tug of war — if one side pulls too hard, you'll find yourself in the mud. Floyd Rose is a designer who created a popular floating bridge system that bears his name. A Floyd Rose is the bridge of choice great for manic metal manipulations.

When you remove a string (or worse, *break* one in the middle of a set) on a floating bridge, the springs pull the bridge back, closer to the body, making the rest of the strings go sharp. If you replace and retune the missing string right away, this isn't much of a problem — the guitar will regain its balance, so to speak. But if you remove more than one string at a time, or replace the old string with one of a different gauge, you can be in for some serious tuning problems. Strings that are way out of tune — or purposely detuned — will also displace the tension, putting the guitar out of tune.

If you simply *must* take off all the strings on a vibrato-type floating bridge, use a shim between the bridge and body to keep the bridge stationary. This keeps the bridge more or less in position while you clean the neck and frets, and then restringing doesn't become a tuning nightmare. If you change the string gauge (thickness), you'll have to adjust the spring tension — tighter if you increase the gauge, looser if you decrease the gauge. I cover that adjustment in more depth in the section on setup later in this chapter.

Not all vibrato systems use a floating design. Some, like the Bigsby (found on many old Gretsch models), have a fixed bridge with spring-loaded tailpiece. The vibrato bar moves the tailpiece to change the pitch. Bigsby-type systems don't offer the same range of pitch changing as their floating counterparts, but when you change strings, you can treat them like a conventional fixed bridge.

What kind of tuning system does your guitar have?

Not all guitar tuners and tuning systems (which can involve the nut and/or the bridges as well) work in the same way, so your technique for removing strings will vary. Restringing may not seem like a "technique" when you're in your living room, but if you break a string in the middle of a set, you'll find that your "string-winding chops" are just as important as your vibrato. Following is a list of two different tuning systems:

- **Standard (non-locking) tuner system:** Unwind the string part way — after it's loose, you can usually pull it away from the headstock by grabbing the string with your right hand and yanking it off the post. You can also snip old strings off with a wire cutter.

- **Locking system:** With a locking system you must "unlock" the string before you can remove it. Locking systems come in two types: 1) The *locking nut/bridge systems*, such as the Floyd Rose, which clamp down on the strings at the bridge and the nut. You must loosen the clamps in both places (usually with an Allen wrench or a screwdriver) to replace the string. 2) *Locking tuners,* such as the ones shown in Figure 16-3, are simpler because they use standard, non-locking bridges. A small clamp inside the tuning machine keeps the string in place so you don't have to wind the string multiple times around the post to keep it from slipping. A thumbscrew on the back of the tuner opens and closes the clamp. Provided you have opposable thumbs, no additional tools are required.

Figure 16-3:
A Sperzel locking tuner uses an internal vise-like clamp to hold the string in place.

Putting on the new strings

Attaching new strings requires three steps:

1. Threading the string.
2. Wrapping the string.
3. Winding, tuning, and stretching out the string.

Threading the string

With most electric guitars, you start by threading the string through the tailpiece, or — if the bridge and tailpiece are combined into one unit — the bridge.

On some models, such as the Fender Stratocaster shown in Figure 16-4, you thread the string through the back of the guitar. Others, like the Gibson SG shown in Figure 16-5, have a tailpiece mounted on the top of the guitar. Although you encounter many variations on both string-through and surface-mounted bridges, the procedure for threading the string is similar on all of them.

Figure 16-4:
Many guitars — such as the Fender Stratocaster pictured here — have string-through-body designs. You must insert new strings through the back of the guitar.

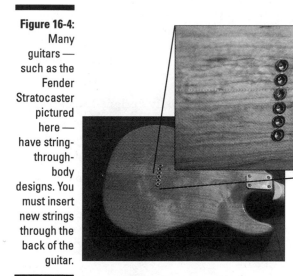

The string goes in plain-end first; a cylinder at the other end (called a *ball*) fits into a slot in the tailpiece. The ball holds the string in place and prevents it from slipping through.

Figure 16-5:
A Tune-O-Matic bridge (A) with a stop tailpiece (B).

Locking bridge systems, such as the Floyd Rose, require a different stringing technique. Rather than passing the string through a tailpiece, you must clamp it down at the bridge, using a screw mechanism. Then you pass the string through a locking nut, which uses another clamp system. Though stringing with the locking system is more complicated and requires more time, because the string is locked in two places — at the nut and at the bridge — it also offers the highest tuning stability. For music that involves dramatic or wild whammy-bar antics, a locking system is the only way to go.

The following list shows the stringing process in a locking bridge system step by step:

1. **Snip off the ball end (you can also buy specially designed strings that have no ball ends).**

2. **Clamp the string in the bridge, using the appropriate tools (usually Allen wrenches, but these will vary depending on the actual model).**

3. **Loosen the nut clamp, and pass the string through the nut to tuning machine.**

4. **Wrap the string.** Tighten it until it's close to the desired pitch. Then set the micro tuner — a small tuner that's mounted on the bridge — to a half-way position, so that you'll have some leeway in fine tuning the guitar.

5. **Clamp the nut closed.** Use the micro tuner to finish getting the guitar in tune. Repeat Steps 1–5 for each string. Once you're clamped off, the micro (or *fine*) tuners are the only way to tune the string without loosening the nut clamp.

The micro tuner allows you to make only minor adjustments in pitch. If you've turned the micro tuner all the way in either direction and your string is *still* out of tune, you need to unclamp the string at the nut, adjust the tuning by using the headstock tuning keys, and re-clamp the string. Don't forget to reset the micro tuner to its midpoint before completing your tuning process with the tuning machines.

Some locking bridge systems use a modified pass-through design, instead of the "clip and clamp" configuration mentioned earlier. These offer a special slot at the end of the bridge that accommodates the ball end of the string, so you don't have to snip the ball off, which saves you a step.

Wrapping or winding the string

The method for winding, or wrapping, the string around the tuning peg is simple but vital. A good winding technique is critical to ensure tuning stability in your guitar.

For conventional tuning machines follow these steps:

1. **Pull the string from the bridge toward the tuning machine.** Pull tight, ensuring that the ball end is secure in the bridge or tailpiece, with no slack at the bottom end.

2. **Guide the string to the correct tuning peg and inset the string through the post hole.** Leave enough slack so that the string can wrap around the tuning post. With thicker, wound strings, two inches should suffice; with thinner unwound strings, leave about four inches. If the string has too little slack, it won't grip the post properly. Too much slack (especially on wound strings) causes the string to overlap the post, which may result in slippage.

3. **Bend the string at the tuning post.** You actually *kink* (fold or crease) the string in the opposite direction you wind it. Correct winding direction depends on the type and position of the tuning machines. For inline, or six-on-a-side, tuners like the ones in Figure 16-6a, the strings go counterclockwise around the peg as you face the headstock. For split, or three-by-three tuners like the ones in Figure 16-6b, the bass side tuners go counterclockwise, while the treble side tuners go clockwise.

4. **Turn the tuning key to wrap the string.** Use your free hand to hold the string in place near the tuning key. Allow for moderate tension in the string between the post and your hand as you wind the tuner. This creates a tighter wrap and prevents slippage.

5. **As the string tunes up, guide it into the nut slot.** Keep applying pressure.

Figure 16-6:
(a) Six inline tuners, where all the strings wind in a counter-clockwise direction. (b)Three-by-three tuners, where the bass strings wind counter-clockwise, the treble strings wind clockwise.

6. **Stretch out the string.** Slippage is one of the leading causes of tuning problems. The string seems tight on the post, but there's actually some hidden slack that can cause the string to go out of tune when you play (especially if you bend the strings or use a vibrato bar). Prevent this by stretching out the string. Pull firmly but gently along the length of the string, raising it directly above the fretboard. After a couple of solid, steady pulls, check the tuning. If the string is flat, retune and repeat. After several tries, the string will stop going flat when you pull it. Congrats: You've removed all the slack. You are now free to beat your guitar to death without worry (at least with regard to tuning, that is).

7. **Clip the excess string.** Go as close to the tuning peg as possible. Alternately, you may leave a small amount of excess and wrap this around the string.

Cleaning the Parts of Your Guitar

You may not want to hear this, but the most destructive force your guitar wil encounter is you. Your hands sweat, depositing moisture, oil, corrosive chemicals, and — unless you have Howard Hughes's compulsion for hand washing — dirt on the strings, wood, and hardware. That's not to mention environmental hazards like dust, beer, cigarette smoke (which, despite your own clean-living habits, are unavoidable if you play gigs), and drool from the bass player. Fortunately, basic guitar cleaning is easy and fast. Most jobs take just a couple of minutes, and restore your guitar to a like-new luster.

You can minimize dirt/drool buildup by always storing the guitar in its case. And whenever you put the guitar in its case, always close the lid and engage at least one of the clasps.

The strings

Use a soft cloth to wipe down the guitar after each performance. As you do, take a moment to check the nut and bridge pieces for grunge. Wipe each string individually all the way around — this will prolong its life. Do this every time you play.

The body, fingerboard, and hardware

With the strings on, apply guitar polish to a soft cloth and rub liberally on the body, neck, and fingerboard (you can slip the cloth under loosened strings to get better contact with the wood). Use a dry portion of the cloth to buff the guitar. You can also clean the hardware with the soft cloth; use a Q-Tip to reach crevices, like string slots and the area under the string saddles. Try to avoid getting polish on the strings; it can make them feel as oily as a politician's handshake.

The frets

Remove the strings. Wipe down the frets with a soft cloth. To remove grime and other buildup, use a piece of light (0000) steel wool and carefully push the wool over each fret, horizontally across the neck. Use a light touch to avoid wearing down the fretwire

Be careful not to scratch the wood with the steel wool. Always sand in one direction, and proceed very slowly, so that your hand doesn't slip and brush against the wood.

Inspect the frets for pits and gouges. You can rub out small pits with the steel wool or light sandpaper. Deeper gouges are best left to a qualified repairperson.

The constant pressure of the string pressing against the fret wears a groove in the fret. When the fret surface is perfectly flat, the string hits it in random (although in a small area) places, spreading the "damage" around. After a groove develops, however, the string goes for that place every time — like your tongue finding the hole of a newly missing tooth — hastening the wear. So filing out dips — before they become grooves — is essential for prolonging fret life.

The electronics

Dirty switches, jacks, and pots can make your guitar sound like a bowl of Rice Krispies — snap, crackle, and pop. You can often eliminate these unwanted noises with a good cleaning.

Cleaning pots

Follow this simple three-step process and you should be able to eradicate most minor problems caused by dirt or rust:

1. **Remove the outer knob.** Plastic knobs are usually held on by just friction. Use a flathead screwdriver to gently pry the knob off its post. Metal knobs are often held in place by a small screw. Loosen the screw and pull the knob off.

2. **Spray contact cleaner into the pot.**

3. **Turn the pot back and forth a few times to spread the cleaner over the contact.**

Cleaning switches and jacks

Switches and jacks are not always as accessible as pots. On some guitars, you must remove either the pickguard or the jack plate to get at the switch. After you have accessed the part, though, the cleaning technique is the same: Use only as much contact cleaner as you need to get the job done.

Optimizing Your Guitar's Performance: The Setup

It's a well-guarded secret, but guitars are made primarily of wood. As time goes by, various factors — moisture, temperature, string tension, and even your playing — make the wood expand and contract, warp, and move around. Your guitar's performance suffers as a result. Before you play it again, Sam, it's time for a *setup*, a thorough adjustment over of your guitar's key components. You can have a professional repairperson do your setup for you, but you can also perform many of the tasks involved in a setup yourself. This way, you get to learn a little more about what makes your guitar tick — and how to set that ticker just how you like it.

Warning signs

You know it's time for a setup if the:

- Intonation is off.
- Action is too high.
- The guitar buzzes when you fret a note.
- Strings "fret out" — stop vibrating and buzz as you bend them.
- Frets feel sharp along the edges.
- Neck appears warped.

Fortunately, you can solve many of these problems yourself.

Intonation

Intonation is often confused with tuning, but accurately used, intonation refers to a guitar's pitch accuracy up and down the neck (not the strings' open-tuning status, which is a function of tuning). You can test intonation by playing a harmonic at the 12th fret, then fretting a note in the normal fashion at the same place. Use a tuner to measure the difference between the notes (for more on using tuners, see Chapter 4). When you perform the harmonic test, one of three things will occur:

- The two notes match, meaning the string is intonated correctly.
- The fretted note is *sharper* than the harmonic, meaning the string is too "short." Use a screwdriver or Allen wrench to move the saddle *away* from the nut (usually a clockwise turn).
- The fretted note is *flatter* than the harmonic, meaning the string is too "long." Use a screwdriver or Allen wrench to move the saddle *closer* to the nut.

Most electric guitars let you adjust intonation for each string separately, although some (like the vintage Telecaster) put two or more strings on one saddle. Turn the screws carefully — the screws can strip easily, especially when the saddle is under tension from the string.

If you've reached the end of the screw and the string is *still* not intonated correctly, it's time to call in the cavalry (or in this case, your guitar tech).

Action

Action refers to the height of the strings relative to the fretboard. You may want a high-action social life (that's why you took up the guitar in the first place, right?), but most guitarists prefer low or moderate action on their instruments.

Low action is best for a light touch because it takes less effort to fret the strings — thus facilitating speedy playing. But low action can make the guitar buzz under a heavier hand (because the strings come into more contact with the frets), which is why many blues players opt for higher action. Slide players who rarely fret the guitar with their fingers prefer very high action, which lets the side move freely without interference from the frets.

Whether your action is low, high, or somewhere in the middle, it should be consistent up and down the neck. Measure the action by placing a ruler on the frets in several places on the neck. The distance between the string and the fret should be about the same at each point you measure. A standard measurement for low action is 5/64" at the 12th fret.

If you want to measure the action of the guitar independent of the nut's influence, capo the first fret, and then measure the string's distance from the fretboard at various places. The capo removes the nut's contribution to the action and can help you better isolate the location of a problem in your action.

The easiest way to adjust the action is by raising and lowering the bridge (or individual string saddles). Some bridges, such as the Tune-O-Matic shown in Figure 16-7, have thumbscrews on the bass and treble sides instead of individual saddle screws. These let you raise overall action but offer less precise control over individual strings.

If your bridge has individual saddles, use an Allen wrench to turn the screw clockwise to raise the action, counterclockwise to lower it. Be sure to raise both sides of the saddle to the same height.

The position of a floating tremolo bridge can also affect the action. Adjust the bridge tension *before* you adjust the string saddles.

If the action is too high at the nut, adjusting at the bridge may not solve the problem. You can use a small file to trim down the string slots in the nut. If action is too low at the nut, you may need to adjust the neck or replace the nut.

Unlike adjusting bridge saddles, filing the nut is a destructive act that can't be undone. If you're in doubt, take the guitar to a qualified tech.

Figure 16-7:
Adjust the
action on a
Tune-O-
Matic
bridge with
side-
mounted
thumb-
screws.

Truss rod

If the action is higher or lower in the middle of the neck than at either end, the neck is probably warped, or curved. This sounds ominous, but it's not uncommon — especially during seasonal changes. A change in string gauge can also cause the neck to warp.

When the neck warps, you can straighten it with an adjustment of the truss rod — the metal rod that runs inside your neck from the headstock to the body. A simple quarter turn with an Allen wrench in either direction (tightening the truss rod to correct a curve away from the strings, loosening the rod to correct a curve into the strings), is fine to alleviate slight misalignments, but beyond that, and unless you know what you're doing, a truss rod adjustment is best left to a professional.

Bridge spring tension

Correct spring tension is one of the keys to getting the best performance out of a floating bridge system. The springs counteract the pull of the strings, holding the bridge in a neutral position. For most players, the ideal bridge position is 1/4"–1/2" off the guitar's body, because this allows you to both raise and lower the pitch with the vibrato arm.

If the springs are too loose, the bridge will sit too high, adversely affecting intonation and action. If the springs are too tight, the bridge will make contact with the body. When the bridge is in this position, you can't raise the pitch with the bar.

Some players actually prefer a little body contact with their bridge because they feel that it improves tuning stability.

Anytime you change string gauges, you must adjust spring tension by removing the backplate.

The following list describes the procedure for adjusting spring tension:

1. **Turn the guitar over and unscrew the backplate that covers the springs and bridge.** (Most guitarists leave this off permanently because the backplate can get in the way when you change strings.)

2. **The springs are attached in two places: at the *claw* at the top of the cavity, and to holes at the back of the bridge, as shown in Figure 16-8.** The claw is attached to the body with two screws. Tighten the screws to increase string tension by turning clockwise. Loosen tension by turning the screws counterclockwise.

These screws can be very tight; be careful not to strip them.

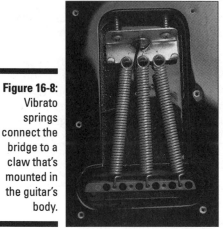

Figure 16-8: Vibrato springs connect the bridge to a claw that's mounted in the guitar's body.

You can further increase tension — and change the feel of your vibrato bridge — by adding or subtracting springs. Most bridges can take from two to five springs. The more springs, the tighter the bridge. You'll have to apply more energy to your vibrato bar, but there is a benefit: a loose bridge can move when you rest your hand on it, or when you bend a string with your fretting hand (causing the rest of the strings to get out of tune). If this happens, add a spring.

Fixing minor wiring problems

Rock and roll is about a half-century old, and the electric guitar's basic wiring hasn't changed much since the days of "Rock Around the Clock." Buddy Holly's tech (if he even had one) could probably fix your Strat without so much as a look at the owner's manual. With some basic soldering chops, you should be able to repair most minor wiring problems yourself.

Output jack

The output jack is one of the first things to break on a guitar (it sees a lot of action, after all). Fortunately, it's also the easiest to repair. Use a socket wrench to unscrew the jack and check for loose wires.

Pots, pickups, and switches

Pots, pickups, and switches can also go bad. They're harder to get at than the output jack, but they're usually easy to repair. If your guitar has rear-mounted controls (you'll find these on Les Pauls and other models), you can access the connections without removing the strings and pickguard. Sadly, Strats and other models with front-mounted controls require that you take off the strings before working on the electronics. Although the connections can vary depending on the specific capabilities of the individual components, you should be able to find your way around with an assist from a good wiring diagram (when in doubt, contact the guitar or pickup manufacturer).

Repairing Amps and Effects

Hard-core amp repair is best left to a qualified repairperson (you can damage your amp and yourself). There are, however, some maintenance routines you can do yourself. Just remember to unplug the amp — and leave it off for a while — before trying any of them.

Replacing the fuse

Most amplifiers are equipped with a Slo-Blo fuse that you can access at the back panel by unscrewing the cover that holds the fuse in place. External factors — like faulty wiring at a club — can cause your amp's fuse to blow, shutting down all power. Unless you're in a major emergency (such as the middle of a gig) always replace the fuse with one of the same value. The fuse is designed to blow at the first sign of trouble to protect the rest of your amp's circuits; if the replacement is too heavy, the fuse won't blow — your amp will. If your amp's fuse blows frequently, this is a sign of trouble. Take it to a tech immediately.

Cleaning and replacing the tubes

Symptoms of dirty and/or worn out tubes include crackling, whistling, ringing (*microphonic feedback* that has no identifiable cause), diminished output, and (unwanted) distortion.

Your amp uses different kinds of tubes in the preamp and power amp stages. The power amp tubes burn hotter and wear out more quickly than the preamp tubes do — if you use your amp regularly, you should replace the power amp tubes about once a year or so. Always use the types of tubes specified with the amp — alternate tubes may fit the socket, but they won't work with your amp's circuitry and can harm the amp.

Speakers

An amp is only as good as its speakers. You can damage your amp by feeding a speaker rated for low wattage with a high-powered amp or simply by careless handling of your amp or speaker cabinet as you move from venue to venue. Blown or damaged speakers can sound distorted or may produce nothing at all. Running an amp into one or more bad speakers for a prolonged period can also damage the circuits. Fortunately, speakers are easy to replace. You simply unscrew them from the *baffle* (that piece of wood the holds them in place), lift them off their mounts, and put the new ones in their place.

If you have a closed-back speaker cabinet (such as a Marshall 4x12), you need to unscrew the back of the cabinet in order to access the speakers.

Follow these two simple rules when replacing speakers:

- ✔ **Check connections:** Sometimes the problem isn't the speaker, but the wire going from the amp to the speaker. Always check this first.

- ✔ **Always replace a speaker with one of the same impedance (a rating involving electrical resistance, measured in ohms):** Although professional amp technicians can find ways around this rule, in general, mismatched impedance in your speakers can diminish your amp's performance and damage its circuitry.

Troubleshooting Guide

Many seemingly insurmountable problems often have a simple and quick solution. The troubleshooting guide in Table 16-1 should cover most of the basic problems. I won't offer the obvious troubleshooting standbys like

"Make sure your guitar is plugged in" and "Make sure your amp is turned on," because I know you don't need to hear them. (Snuck those by you, didn't I?)

Table 16-1	Troubleshooting Guide	
Symptom	*Possible Cause*	*Solution*
Buzzing	Action too low	Adjust bridge saddles Adjust truss rod Adjust action at the nut
High action on the upper frets	Bridge saddles set too high	Lower bridge saddles
High action in the middle or top of neck	Neck is warped	Adjust truss rod
Guitar won't stay in tune	Strings too old	Replace strings Replace cheap tuners
Floating bridge up too high	Spring tension is too loose	Tighten vibrato bar springs
Floating bridge too close to guitar body	Spring tension too tight	Loosen vibrato springs
No output	Bad output jack	Remove jack, check wiring
Scratchy output	Bad volume or tone pots or switches	Spray pots and switches with contact cleaner
Amp has no output	Bad connection between guitar and amp Blown fuse Bad tube Blown speaker	Replace guitar cable Replace fuse Replace tube Replace speaker
Amp whistles, rings, or sounds distorted	Bad tube Blown speaker	Replace tube Replace speaker
Crackling sound, signal cuts out	Bad cable or patch cord	Replace
Low output, diminished sound, unwanted distortion	Bad battery or power supply (effects)	Replace battery

Storing Your Guitar

You can take great care of your guitar while it's with you, but all of your due diligence will be for naught unless you store the guitar properly. As I mention earlier in this chapter, wood is sensitive to changes in the environment, and these changes can cause some serious problems for your guitar. The following steps should save you from quite a few headaches — and repair bills.

✔ **Always store the guitar in its case.** Gigbags are fine for short-term storage, but nothing protects the wood, hardware, and strings like a good hard-shell case, which can keep the neck stable and blocks dust, moisture, and your adorable nephew who got your guitar confused with his soccer ball. Remember to latch the case — otherwise, you (or your nephew) may pick it up and spill your guitar to the floor.

✔ **Avoid temperature extremes.** Store your instrument in a temperate space (like your house) and avoid places that can get very hot or very cold, like the trunk of your car, an unheated garage, attic, or warehouse (like those self-storage facilities), your fridge, or your oven.

✔ **Keep the guitar in moderate humidity.** Spaces that are too damp can make the wood swell. Spaces that are too dry can make the wood shrink and crack. Both factors affect intonation, playability, and tone. You can combat dampness by inserting desiccant (available at most hardware stores) in your guitar case. Combat dryness with a humidifier or a moist sponge. You don't have to loosen the strings when storing the guitar or checking it on an airplane, as is commonly believed.

✔ **Check your guitar regularly.** Even if your instrument (or your playing career) is in hibernation for a while, it's a good idea to look things over every now and then. Who knows — the sight of your well-preserved guitar may inspire you to play.

Part VI
The Part of Tens

The 5th Wave — By Rich Tennant

"That's the third time tonight that's happened. They start out playing the blues, but by the end, everyone's playing a polka. I blame the new bass player from Milwaukee."

In this part . . .

I know, I know, if this is rock and roll, how come the Part of Tens doesn't go to eleven? But that's okay, this part has lots of impressive trivia for you to wow your friends and family with. Check out the ten rock guitarists who changed history, the ten must-have rock guitar albums, and the ten classic rock guitars. Turn to Chapters 17, 18, and 19 to get the scoop using that famous *For Dummies* top-ten treatment.

Chapter 17

Ten Rock Guitarists Who Changed History

Some names on this list are household names, and one or two may not be familiar to you (or someone you know). But read on, and you'll see why these ten are considered some of the brightest stars to ever light up the rock guitar universe.

Chuck Berry

A pioneer of '50s rock, Chuck Berry helped turn the guitar from a country and blues instrument into a dangerous rock 'n' roll one. His clever songs laid down the blueprints for early rock guitar, especially with his fast, "double-stop" solo licks. Berry's songs are also among the most universal in rock history — indeed, just about every guitarist on the planet can play a Chuck Berry song. His signature tunes include "Johnny B. Goode" and "Maybellene."

Eric Clapton

Between 1964 and 1970, Eric Clapton carved out a stunning career path, blazing a trail from the Yardbirds to John Mayall's Bluesbreakers to Cream to Blind Faith and finally to the legendary Derek & the Dominos — all before the age of 25. Clapton's role in rock history was to take the electric Chicago blues style of Buddy Guy and Otis Rush and translate it into a rock context with deafening volume and a distorted tone. Never a speed demon, he concentrated more on a perfectly articulated wrist vibrato or singing string bends than trying to be the flashiest player in town. Even today, as a wildly popular solo artist, he remains one of the most influential players in rock history. A couple of his signature tunes are "Crossroads" and "Layla."

Jimi Hendrix

Perhaps the greatest guitarist in rock history, Jimi Hendrix synthesized blues, pop, rock, soul, proto-funk, jazz, and '60s psychedelia into his own unique style and vision. Armed with a Fender Stratocaster (which he flipped over to play lefty), Marshall amp, and then-new effects such as a fuzzbox, wah-wah, and Octavia (a stompbox that added a lower-octave note), Hendrix blew the roof off rock guitar with 1967's *Are You Experienced?* and never looked back. Although his career only lasted four years, he constantly pushed the envelope of electric guitar, virtually inventing techniques such as whammy-bar dives and controlled feedback. He remains a legend in every sense of the word. His signature tunes include "Purple Haze" and "Voodoo Child (Slight Return)."

Jeff Beck

One of the most formidable lead players ever, Jeff Beck's career has spanned over 35 years and shows no sign of letting up. In the '60s, he got his start in the Yardbirds (replacing Eric Clapton) before leading the Jeff Beck Group, a progenitor of heavy metal. In the '70s, he helped pioneer jazz-rock fusion on solo albums such as *Blow by Blow* and *Wired*, and has spent the last 20 years investigating various mixtures of heavy-rock and electronic dance music. His solos are unpredictable and wild, always willing to push the frontiers of sound and style. Indeed, Jeff Beck may be the best electric guitarist alive today. Some of his signature tunes are "Cause We've Ended As Lovers" and "Blue Wind."

Jimmy Page

Where Clapton and Beck shone as lead players, Jimmy Page proved himself to be the consummate studio master, using the recording studio like a giant musical instrument to make his guitar tracks shine even more. During his 12 years leading Led Zeppelin (1968–80), he produced some of rock's great guitar tracks, while also fathering the style known as "heavy metal." His studio tricks included prolific overdubbing of tracks to create a huge "guitar army" sound, as well as mixing gentle acoustic parts with crunchy electric ones to generate a highly dynamic sound. Both as a player and producer, Jimmy Page was years ahead of his time. His signature tunes include "Heartbreaker" and "Stairway to Heaven."

Eddie Van Halen

By the late '70s, the bluesy riffing of Clapton and Page, to most audiences, had become dull and stagnant. Into the void stepped a young California kid who single-handedly rewrote the heavy-metal guitar book. In addition to blues scales, Eddie Van Halen infused his lead guitar work with exotic scales, speedy flatpicking, fast hammer-ons, and two-handed tapping licks. On cuts such as "Eruption" and a cover of the Kinks' "You Really Got Me," he burned up the fretboard of his guitar like it was covered with napalm, pushing it even further with a blistering tone. Suddenly, every kid in the United States wanted to buy a modified Strat like Eddie's and to tap the fretboard in meek imitation of the master. Until well into the '80s, Eddie Van Halen was the most influential guitarist on the planet with signature tunes such as "Eruption" and "Spanish Fly," both unaccompanied guitar solos.

Stevie Ray Vaughan

Blues guitar was all but dead when Stevie Ray Vaughan released his first album as a solo artist in 1983 (*Texas Flood*). A few years later, blues-rock music was alive 'n' well, thanks to Stevie's smoldering Stratocaster solos. Heavily influenced by Jimi Hendrix and "the Kings" (Albert, B.B., and Freddie), the Texas guitarist was unapologetically bluesy, even during this period of techno pop, and won a huge following as a result. His tone is similarly legendary, a combination of a vintage guitar with heavy strings and high action, and a veritable wall of great tube amps. A single note from Stevie blew most '80s "shredders" away in an instant. Vaughan's signature tunes include "Texas Flood" and "Crossfire."

Eric Johnson

Another Texan, but one with a completely different style than Stevie Ray Vaughan's, is Eric Johnson. A child of the '70s jazz-rock movement, Johnson developed a singular lead style. Fast, precise, and highly melodic, the guitarist was, for over a decade, considered the best unknown guitarist in the United States (indeed, he turned down offers to work with stellar acts such as Stanley Clarke, UK, and the Dixie Dregs, preferring to stay solo). After releasing his first major-label album in 1986, he won an instant cult following, and scored a national audience with the release of 1990's smash, *Ah Via Musicom*. For taste, tone, and flat-out speed, few players can match the guitar prowess of Eric Johnson whose signature tunes include "Cliffs of Dover" and "Righteous."

Steve Vai

What Eddie Van Halen started, Steve Vai took to the next level . . . *and then some*. Vai first popped up as the second guitarist in Frank Zappa's band, but he turned heads with his first, self-financed solo album, *Flex-able*. Tracks such as "The Attitude Song" and "Call It Sleep" were radical revisions of metal-guitar style and technique, mixing brilliant chops with a daring sense of harmony. He also reversed the overused whammy "dive-bomb," now using the bar to bring notes and chords *up* to the stratosphere. In the mid-'80s, Vai finally achieved mass success as a member of ex-Van Halen singer David Lee Roth's band and, a few years later, joined Whitesnake for an album. His masterpiece, though, was his 1990's solo set, *Passion & Warfare*. Filled to the brim with hot instrumentals (including the classic "Blue Powder"), the album pushed Vai to guitar superstardom. Indeed, at that time, he was simply the state-of-the-art rock guitarist.

Kurt Cobain

In many ways, Nirvana's Kurt Cobain was rock's "anti-guitar hero." After 25 years of guitar adulation by the masses, Cobain's riffing on "Smells Like Teen Spirit" (from the wildly successful album *Nevermind*) proclaimed the *oeuvre* dead, ushering in the '90s grunge era. Eschewing solos and flashy pyrotechnics in favor of crude power chords and queasy string bends, his playing was a reaction against the glossy "shred" style of the 1980s. Whereas other guitarists were measured by how fast or soulful a player they were, Cobain's angst-ridden riffs set a new standard for garage-band guitarmanship and influenced players for the rest of the decade. What he lacked in panache, he more than made up for in style and innovation in such signature tunes as "Smells Like Teen Spirit" and "Lithium."

Chapter 18

Ten Must-Have Rock Guitar Albums

*Y*ou don't necessarily need to acquire the exact-named record listed in chronological order at the beginning of this chapter (unless you're a collector), because you can readily purchase "greatest hits," anthologies, and complete collections that offer most or all of the songs contained in any individual album by one band, plus many more of their hits. From a *historical* standpoint, however, each of these albums' release had some major significance attached to it. Anthologies do sometimes scramble the original album's order, so if you're really a purist, get yourself the original and experience it the way listeners did back in the day.

The Beatles, Rubber Soul (1965)

A turning point both in the Beatles' career and in rock music as a whole, *Rubber Soul* was Lennon and McCartney's answer to Bob Dylan's *Highway 61 Revisited*. Instead of straight-ahead pop, this album brought in acoustic folk influences, as heard in "In My Life" and "Michelle." An exotic Indian sitar rings out in "Norwegian Wood" and George Harrison finally got a writing credit with the breezy "If I Needed Someone." It would only be about 12 months later that the Fab Four would be in the studio recording *Sgt. Pepper's Lonely Hearts Club Band,* but you can see the roots of that masterpiece right here in *Rubber Soul.*

The Jimi Hendrix Experience, Are You Experienced? (1967)

Released around the same time as the Beatles *Sgt. Pepper's,* Jimi Hendrix's debut album helps put the stamp on psychedelia, as well as usher in a whole new world of rock guitar playing. Far from the twangy guitar of just a few years earlier, Hendrix's playing on "Purple Haze" and "Foxy Lady" was funky, bluesy, heavy, and absolutely out of this world. He had taken Chicago blues guitar and put in a whole new musical context — it was innovation in every sense of the word and rock 'n' roll would never be the same again.

Led Zeppelin, Led Zeppelin II (1969)

Cream, Hendrix, the Jeff Beck Group, and the Who had all hinted at heavier things to come in the late '60s, but Led Zeppelin virtually invented "heavy metal" on their first two albums. The second, *Led Zeppelin II,* was a sonic onslaught of distorted guitars, deep bass, and thundering drums. From the thudding riff of "Whole Lotta Love" to the unprecedented solo in "Heartbreaker," Jimmy Page set a new standard in heavy guitar playing and influenced rock players for the next decade. Page's production values were revolutionary, too, featuring a massive bottom end that was unheard of in other rock recordings of the day.

The Who, Who's Next? (1971)

The Who always walked their own line, mixing blunt hard-rock riffs with politically charged lyrics and innovative arrangements. Their studio album *Who's Next?* was recorded far better than its predecessor, *Tommy,* and proved to be another huge hit for the band. "Baba O'Riley" and "Won't Get Fooled Again" both broke ground for their use of then-novel electronic synthesizers and the hard-edge fury of Pete Townshend's power chords. In fact, the whole album rocked: "Goin' Mobile," "My Wife," and the finale of "Behind Blue Eyes" were testaments to the guitar power of the Who. It's no surprise that they quickly became one of the top rock bands of the '70s.

The Rolling Stones, Exile on Main Street (1972)

With a number of gold albums already racked up, the Rolling Stones were on a hot streak in 1972 and then topped it off with *Exile on Main Street.* A sprawling two-album set, *Exile* was a masterpiece in every sense, overflowing with great performances, production, and Jagger-Richards compositions. On guitars, Keith Richards and Mick Taylor also made up one of the best 6-string duos in rock (even though Keith only played with five strings!), with Keith laying down rock-solid rhythms and Mick adding his bluesy solos on top. Key guitar moments include the hit "Tumblin' Dice," the slide guitar of "Happy," and the kick-ass rocker "Rocks Off." Then, as today, it's one of the greatest rock 'n' roll albums of all time.

Jeff Beck, Blow by Blow (1975)

Ten years into his career, Jeff Beck took a turn towards instrumental rock with *Blow by Blow* and was rewarded with the biggest hit of his career. Fueled by period albums from the Mahavishnu Orchestra, Billy Cobham, Roy Buchanan, and Return to Forever, Beck jumped feet first into the world of jazz-rock fusion and revolutionized rock guitar playing in the process. Instead of backing up a lead vocalist, he put the guitar out front, creating dizzying melodies and deeply soulful solos. His take on Stevie Wonder's "Cause We've Ended as Lovers" set a new standard for guitar ballads, while "Highway Jam" took the concept of the '70s boogie to new levels of groovedom. To boot, the album was orchestrated by Beatles producer George Martin, who mixed Beck's guitar with orchestral strings in "Diamond Dust" to absolutely brilliant effect. Breaking all previous barriers, *Blow by Blow* peaked at #4 on the album charts.

Van Halen, Van Halen (1978)

The most influential metal album of the late '70s, *Van Halen* threw out the blues-rock riffing of Ted Nugent and Foghat and created a whole new lexicon of heavy rock. With Eddie Van Halen power chording and soloing like a demon (replete with everything from hammer-ons and pull-offs to two-handed tapping to violent whammy-bar dives), tracks such as "Jamie's Crying" and "Ain't Talkin' 'Bout Love" were pure sonic assaults, driving concert audiences of the day crazy. The album went platinum in an instant and set the stage for a long string of multi-platinum Van Halen discs to come. To this day, though, no one — not even Eddie Van Halen himself — has been able to recapture the guitar sound and fury of that first album.

Joe Satriani, Surfing with the Alien (1987)

Joe Satriani was the whiz kid of '80s rock guitar. He brilliantly mixed the tapping tricks of Van Halen with the scalar legato of Allan Holdsworth and metal attack of Michael Schenker, in the process creating something very new and exciting. *Surfing with the Alien* was a guitar junkie's dream come true, a power packed album that was full of expert guitar from end to end. And nowhere was this evident than in the title track, which sports a loopy wah-wah melody and a barn-burning solo. It was the quintessence of '80s "shred" guitar.

Metallica, Metallica (The Black Album) (1991)

In the 1980s, Metallica invented the sound of "thrash" heavy metal, but come the '90s, a fresh approach was needed. Recognizing the need to evolve, the quartet streamlined the jarring rhythms of their earlier albums, while frontman James Hetfield began to actually sing melodies, rather than simply scream and croak into the microphone. The album's first single, "Enter Sandman," had a ferocious riff and thundering drum beat that captured the metal world's attention. Later in the track, Kirk Hammett chimed in with a sinfully greasy guitar solo. Another track, "Unforgiven," was a dramatic power ballad that, in a rare turn, had acoustic guitars and a bluesy solo from Hetfield. In short order, Metallica became the United States' favorite metal band, a position they held for over a decade afterward.

Korn, Issues (1999)

Spearheading the fusion of heavy metal and hip-hop, Korn became one of the most radical rock acts of the turn-of-the-century, tossing out preconceived notions of "what metal is" and playing by their own dark, twisted rules. The album, *Issues,* spews rage at every corner, all anchored by the 7-string insanity of guitarists Munky and Head. Unlike vintage guitar teams, these two players are more likely to lock into an intricate, off-the-wall rhythm pattern than take a traditional solo. On cuts such as "Falling Away from Me" and "Trash," they mix the deep bassy thump of their Ibanez 7-strings with miscellaneous scrapes, buzzes, and sickly melodies to create the distinctive Korn sound. Clearly, this is not your father's heavy metal band.

Chapter 19

Ten Classic Guitars

*W*ithin the universe of available electric guitars, you can choose from hundreds, if not thousands, of makes and models in assorted shapes, configurations, and colors. All of them, however, owe a debt of inspiration to one of the ten presented in this chapter. Each of these makes and models has appeared on some classic recording, or helped one of your favorite artists achieve musical immortality in some way or another.

Fender Telecaster

The first mass-produced "solidbody" electric, Leo Fender's original Telecaster was designed for country and jazz players, but quickly evolved into a dangerous rock 'n' roll machine. With its bright, twangy tone (created by its ash or alder body, simple electronics, and bolt-on maple neck), the Tele became a rock workhorse, able to withstand a beating from live work but still deliver a great tone night after night. Indeed, it sometimes seems that the more abuse a Telecaster gets, the better it sounds.

Gibson Les Paul

Named for pop pioneer and inventor Les Paul, the Gibson Les Paul model grew into one of the premier rock solidbodies. It was produced for eight years in the '50s but was then discontinued. Ten years later, Eric Clapton, Jeff Beck, and Jimmy Page revived interest in Les Pauls — particularly the flame-top Standards made from 1958–1960 — and the guitar's place in history was set. With a single-cutaway design and fat, bassy tone, it became the guitar of choice for hard rock and heavy metal guitarists of the 1970s. Les Pauls have also become excellent investments. Original '50s Les Pauls regularly command thousands of dollars, with mint 1959 Standards fetching upwards of $100,000!

Fender Stratocaster

The best-selling electric guitar in history, the Stratocaster appeared in the mid 1950s with a space-age shape, tremolo bar, and comfortable body contours — clearly it was a guitar designed to be played standing up. Championed by the likes of Buddy Holly, Eric Clapton, Jimi Hendrix, and Stevie Ray Vaughan, this solidbody grew into the standard by which all electric guitars are judged and remains so, nearly 50 years after its birth.

Gibson ES Series

Trying to straddle the jazz and pop worlds, Gibson invented the ES line of "semi-hollow" guitars in the 1950s. These thinbody electrics had f-holes and hollow wings but also a solid block of maple running under the bridge and pickups to its built-in neck. Guitars such as the ES-335, ES-345, and ES-355 later wound up in the hands of such masters as Chuck Berry, blues great B.B. King, Alvin Lee of Ten Years After, Rush's Alex Lifeson, and LA studio giant Larry "Mr. 335" Carlton. For guitarists who crave versatility, the Gibson ES has long added a touch of elegance to the world of electric guitars.

Gibson Flying V

There was no mistaking the intent of the Gibson Flying V: this was a guitar that was meant for gigging. With a daring, windswept body shape and arrowed-tipped headstock, the Flying V looked like a supersonic jet about to take off. Ironically, the guitar bombed when released in 1958 — clearly, its design was a few years ahead of its time. But in the 1960s, players such as the

Kinks' Dave Davies and Jimi Hendrix revived interest in the guitar. In the following decade, the Flying V finally found its own, as metal and glam-rock heroes such as UFO's Michael Schenker, Randy Rhoads, and T. Rex's Marc Bolan rocked out onstage with Vs. Over 40 years old, this classic electric guitar continues to be a radical to this very day.

Mosrite Ventures Model

In the early 1960s, instrumental rock became the rage and no band was greater than the Ventures. With their simple melodies, Ventures' songs such as "Walk, Don't Run" became instant garage-band classics. Not surprisingly, the Ventures inked a deal to put out their own line of guitars through the Mosrite Company. The instruments were hardly top-of-the-line, but their funky appeal turned the guitars into classics. Today, original Mosrite Ventures models are highly sought after by guitar collectors.

Rickenbacker 360/12

As pop music exploded in the mid 1960s, one sound was ubiquitous: the chiming tone of a Rickenbacker 360/12. This electric 12-string added a ringing folk dimension to the records of Beatles and Byrds, as well as their horde of copycats. Taming its trebly tone was a semi-hollow construction, which added a touch of warmth to its sound. Later, this Rickenbacker sound was lovingly appropriated by Tom Petty, Marshall Crenshaw, R.E.M., and many other modern popsters who grew up on the "Rick sound."

Ibanez Iceman

In the tradition of radical guitars like the Gibson Flying V and Explorer, Ibanez issued their own wildly shaped guitar in the mid 1970s — the Iceman. Made for live performance, this guitar featured a solid mahogany body and neck with an ebony fingerboard. Like some razor-blade company trying to take technology to absurd heights, some models even sported unusual triple-coil pickups (not that they made the guitar sound any better, but it was a good marketing gimmick). The Iceman finally found fame in the hands of Kiss guitarist Paul Stanley, who played a custom black Ibanez with a mirror pickguard. This guitar was perfect for Kiss's outrageous live performances and, even today, when the name "Iceman" is mentioned, players instantly think of the alluring PS10 Paul Stanley Model.

"Super Strats"

Thanks to the arrival of Eddie Van Halen, guitarists everywhere wanted a Stratocaster-style guitar with humbucking pickups (as opposed to the classic single-coil configurations Strats had been known for) and a locking whammy bar. In the breach came a slew of '80s guitar makers offering "Super Strats" to meet the demand. Charvel was one of the first companies to offer these sleek Super Strats, but soon Jackson, ESP, Ibanez, Yamaha, and Kramer joined the fray. Often these instruments sported custom graphics or eye-popping paint jobs to further indicate that they were custom instruments. At the same time, traditional electrics from Fender and Gibson were at an all-time low point in popularity. As "hair bands" lost popularity at the end of the decade, however, so, too, did the Super Strat, fading away into another fascinating chapter of guitar history.

Paul Reed Smith

A true phenomenon in recent guitarmaking has been the rise of Paul Reed Smith (PRS) guitars. Originally a lone luthier in Annapolis, Maryland, Smith created his own modern version of the venerable Les Paul — a solidbody electric with mahogany body and neck, two humbuckers, and a hand-carved, arched top. By keeping the emphasis on superb workmanship and construction, PRS guitars eventually gained a favorable reputation. It didn't hurt that master guitarists from Al Di Meola to Carlos Santana to Alex Lifeson of Rush swore by their PRS guitars, and newcomers such as Creed's Mark Tremonti are jumping onboard. By the 1990s, Paul Reed Smith had become one of the most successful musical-instrument companies in the United States, finally cracking the Gibson/Fender stranglehold on traditional-style electric guitars.

Appendix

Using the CD

• •

*E*very music example in *Rock Guitar For Dummies* is performed on the CD that comes with this book — over 140 examples! This makes *Rock Guitar For Dummies* a true multimedia experience. You have text explaining the techniques used, visual graphics of the music in two forms — guitar tablature and standard music notation — and audio performances of the music, complete with the appropriate tonal treatment (massive distortion for heavy metal, mild overdrive for blues-rock, and so on) and the appropriate accompaniment settings.

One fun way to experience *Rock Guitar For Dummies* is to just scan the text by music examples, looking at the printed music in the book and listening to the corresponding performances on the CD. When you hear something you like, read the text that goes into detail about that particular piece of music. Or go to a particular chapter that interests you (say, Chapter 11 on rock guitar playing), skip to the appropriate tracks on the CD, and see if you can hack it. A little above your head at this point? Better go back to Chapter 4 on barre chords!

Relating the Text to the CD

Whenever you see written music in the text and you want to hear what it sounds like on the CD, refer to the box in the upper-right hand corner, which tells you the track number and start time (in minutes and seconds).

Use the *track skip* control on your CD player's front panel or remote to go to the desired track (indicated in the track label) and then use the cue button of the *cue/review* function (also known as the "fast forward/rewind" control) to go to the specific time within that track (also indicated in the track label in minutes and seconds). When you get on or near the start time, release the cue button and the example plays.

If you want to play along with the CD, "cue up" to a spot a few seconds *before* the start time. Giving yourself a few seconds head start allows you to put down the remote and place your hands in a ready position on the guitar.

Count-offs

All of the music examples are preceded by a *count-off,* which is a metronome clicking in rhythm before the music begins. This tells you what the tempo is, or the speed at which the music is played. It's like having your own conductor going, "A-one, and a-two . . ." so that you can hit the downbeat (first note of music) in time with the CD. Examples in 4/4 time have four beats "in front" (musician lingo for a four-beat count-off before the music begins); examples in 3/4 have three beats in front.

Stereo separation

I've recorded some of the examples in what's known as a *stereo split.* In certain pieces, the *backing,* or accompanying, music appears on the left channel of your stereo, while the featured guitar appears on the right. If you leave your stereo's balance control in its normal position (straight up, or 12:00), you'll hear both the rhythm tracks and the featured guitar equally — one from each speaker. By selectively adjusting the balance control (turning the knob to the left or right) you can gradually or drastically reduce the volume of one or the other.

Why would you want to do this? If you have practiced the lead part to a certain example and feel you've got it down good enough to where you want to try it "along with the band," take the balance knob and turn it all the way to the left. Now only the sound from the left speaker comes out, which is the backing tracks. The count-off clicks are in *both* channels, so you'll always receive your cue to play in time with the music. You can reverse the process and listen to just the lead part, too, which means you play the chords against the recorded lead part. Good, well-rounded guitarists work on both their rhythm *and* their lead playing.

Always keep the CD with the book, rather than mixed in with your rack of CDs. The plastic envelope helps protect the CD's surface from scuffs and scratches, and whenever you want to refer to *Rock Guitar For Dummies* (the book), the CD will always be right where you expect it. Try to get in the habit of following along with the printed music whenever you listen to the CD, even if your sight-reading skills aren't quite up to snuff. You absorb more than you expect just by moving your eyes across the page in time to the music, associating sound and sight. So store the CD and book together as constant companions and use them together as well for a rich visual and aural experience.

Tracks on the CD

Here is a list of the tracks on the CD along with the figure numbers that they correspond to in the book. Use this as a quick cross-reference to finding more about tracks that sound interesting on the CD. The first part of the figure number equates to the chapter in which we explain how to play the track. Then just flip through the captions and songs in order until you find the track you're interested in playing. To ease matters a bit, the exercises also contain the track numbers (and times, if appropriate) to help you find just the track you need.

Track	(Time)	Figure Number	Song Title/Description
1			Tuning reference
2		4-5	Strummed E chord
3		4-13	Progression using E- and A-based major power chords
4		4-15	Progression with alternating E- and A-based forms
5		5-1	E chord in one bar of four quarter notes
6		5-2	Eighth-note progression using right-hand downstrokes
7		5-3	4/4 eighth-note strum using down- and upstrokes
8		5-4	Strumming to convey different levels of intensity
9		5-5	Medium-tempo progression using 16th notes
10		5-6	Eighth-note shuffle in G
11		5-7	Bass-chord pattern in a country-rock groove
12		5-8	Bass-note-and-chord treatment
13		5-9	Moving bass line over a chord progression
14		5-11	Rock figure using eighth-note syncopation
15		5-12	Rock figure using eighth- and 16th-note syncopation

(continued)

Track	(Time)	Figure Number	Song Title/Description
16		5-13	Eighth-note strum employing left-hand muting
17		5-14	Rhythm figure with palm mutes and accents
18		5-15	Eighth-note 5-6 progression
19		5-16	Fingerstyle arpeggios played with right-hand fingers
20		5-17	4/4 groove in the style of the Eagles
21		5-18	Two-beat country groove with bass runs
22		5-19	Medium-tempo funky groove in a 16-feel
23		5-20	Heavy metal gallop using eighths and 16ths
24		5-21	Reggae backup pattern highlighting the offbeats
25		5-22	Song in 3, featuring a moving bass line
26	(0:00)	6-1	Quarter-note melodies on each of the guitar's six strings in open position
	(1:12)	6-2	Quarter-note melody played across different strings
27	(0:00)	6-3	One-octave C major scale, ascending and descending
	(0:14)	6-4	Two-octave G major scale, ascending and descending
	(0:35)	6-5	One-octave A minor scale
	(0:49)	6-6	Am7 arpeggio
28	(0:00)	6-7	Rocking low-note melody
	(0:11)	6-8	Low-note melody in moving eighth notes
	(0:26)	6-9	High-note melody in open position
29		6-10	Two-octave G major scale in 2nd position
30		6-11	Classic walking-bass boogie-woogie riff in G
31		6-12	Neck diagram showing the pentatonic scale in 5th position

Track	(Time)	Figure Number	Song Title/Description
32	(0:00)	6-13	Descending eighth-note C pentatonic major scale
	(0:11)	6-14	Solo in C major over a medium-tempo 4/4
	(0:35)	6-15	Minor solo over a heavy backbeat 4/4 groove
	(0:52)	6-16	Blues solo over an up-tempo shuffle in A
33		6-17	Slow blues shuffle in A
34	(0:00)	7-1	Powerful-sounding riff using only half notes and whole notes
	(0:11)	7-2	Quarter-note riff, with one eighth-note pair
	(0:19)	7-3	Eighth-note riff, with one quarter note on beat 2
	(0:27)	7-4	Boogie shuffle in quarter notes
	(0:37)	7-5	Steady-eighth-note riff in E minor with chromatic notes
	(0:45)	7-6	Two-bar riff in steady eighth notes
	(0:57)	7-7	Riff that steps through quarter, eighth, and 16th notes
	(1:12)	7-8	Hard rock/heavy metal gallop riff
	(1:23)	7-9	Fast 16th-note-based riff in a hard-rock style
	(1:33)	7-10	Eighth-note riff with beat 1 anticipated, or tied over
	(1:46)	7-11	Eighth-note riff with anticipations on beats 1 and 3
	(1:58)	7-12	Highly syncopated eighth-note riff
35	(0:00)	7-13	Moving double-stop figure, used as a chordal device
	(0:10)	7-14	Double-stop figure on non-adjacent strings
36		7-15	Hard rock progression mixing chords and single notes

(continued)

Track	(Time)	Figure Number	Song Title/Description
37	(0:00)	8-1	Open-position chord forms
	(0:13)	8-2	Moving double-stops over an A pedal
38	(0:00)	8-8a	Melodic figure that shifts on the 5th string
	(0:08)	8-8b	Shifting melodic figure on the 2rd string
	(0:16)	8-9	Lateral and longitudinal motion
39		8-11	Pentatonic melody in all five positions
40	(0:00)	8-12	Short blues lick in 5th position and 7th position
	(0:09)	8-13	Lick that dips down from 5th to 2nd position
	(0:18)	8-14	Ascending line with three position shifts
41	(0:00)	8-15	Riff in 7th-position G major pentatonic
	(0:08)	8-16	F major lick with an added flat 3 in 7th position
	(0:18)	8-17	Low riff in 1st-position F minor pentatonic
42	(0:00)	9-1	Hammer-on from a fretted note
	(0:07)	9-2	Various hammer-ons in a blues-rock groove
	(0:16)	9-3	Two kinds of pull-offs to fretted notes
	(0:23)	9-4	Several different types of pull-offs
	(0:34)	9-5	Slides connecting two notes
	(0:41)	9-6	Various slide techniques
43	(0:00)	9-7	Bends on the 3rd string, 7th fret
	(0:07)	9-8	A bend in rhythm and an immediate bend
	(0:16)	9-9	Bend and release in rhythm
	(0:23)	9-10	Using a bend and release over chord changes

Track	(Time)	Figure Number	Song Title/Description
44	(0:00)	9-11	Vibrato executed with left-hand fingers
	(0:07)	9-12	Natural harmonics on the 7th and 12th frets
	(0:16)	9-13	Pinch harmonic concluding a melodic phrase
	(0:25)	9-14	Two different kinds of bar moves
	(0:36)	9-15	"Just an Expression"
45		10-1	The "Bo Diddley Beat"
46		10-2	Bluesy double-stop riff
47		10-3	I-vi-ii-V in D, in 12/8 time
48		10-4	I-vi-IV-V with a heavy backbeat
49		10-5	Single notes and chord in a I-vi-ii-V shuffle
50		10-6	Classic, driving rockabilly rhythm figure
51		10-7	5-to-6 rhythm figure in a 12-bar blues
52		10-8	Chuck Berry-style double-stop solo
53		10-9	Surf chord progression and lead solo
54		10-10	Progression using all open-position chords
55		10-11	Melodic, song-inducing riffs
56		10-12	Low-note/high-note riff
57		11-1	Extended riff-based figure in A
58		11-2	Chord progression with embellishments
59		11-3	Dynamic all-chord rhythm part
60		11-4	Simple low-note riff
61		11-5	Chordal riffing inside assorted left-hand chord forms
62		11-6	Blues-based lead solo in the style of Eric Clapton
63		11-7	Hendrix-style lead featuring bent notes and whammy bar moves

(continued)

Track	(Time)	Figure Number	Song Title/Description
64		11-8	Heavy low-note riff, followed by a blues-based solo riff
65		11-9	Minor-key, Latin-flavored lead line
66		11-10	E pentatonic major passage in southern rock style
67		11-11	Southern-flavored funky riff
68		11-12	Blues-based boogie riff, with pinch harmonic
69		11-13	Stevie Ray Vaughan-style rhythm figure and lead
70		11-14	Funky single-note riff
71		11-15	Eagles-style country-rock solo
72		11-16	Arpeggiated rhythm figure in the style of U2's The Edge
73		12-1	Dark, menacing heavy-metal power chords
74		12-2	Rock and Baroque music blended into a formidable whole
75		12-3	Classic mid-'70s metal riff
76		12-4	Big Boston-style strummed chords on electric
77		12-5	Two-handed tapping lick in Van Halen style
78		12-6	Straight-ahead blues-rock
79		12-7	Mixolydian-based riff
80		12-8	Polished metal riff of 1980s metal
81		12-9	Diminished scale over a dominant-7th
82		12-10	Speed metal blends heavy rock with punk
83		12-11	Harmonic "trick" using Floyd Rose whammy bar
84		12-12	Moody grunge lick
85		12-13	Hip hop-inspired metal riff

Track	(Time)	Figure Number	Song Title/Description
86		13-1	Jazzy lick using two-string double-stops
87		13-2	Unique melody accented with a whammy bar
88		13-3	Lick involving notes that slide
89		13-4	Bluesy lick placed within a progressive format
90		13-5	Haunting arpeggio of simple chords
91		13-6	Chords that use ringing open strings and full strumming
92		13-7	Heavy rock riff
93		13-8	Combination of slurs, chromatic licks, and bluesy bends
94		13-9	Lick that blends jazz and funk
95		13-10	Single-note picking over major and minor chords
96		13-11	Lead lines with full- and half-step bends
97		13-12	Flamenco-style lick requiring precise flat-picking
98		13-13	Progressive riff in the style of Jeff Beck

If you have trouble with the items on the CD, please call the Hungry Minds, Inc. Customer Service phone number at 800-762-2974 (outside the U.S.: 317-572-3993) or send e-mail to techsupdum@hungryminds.com.

Index

Hungry Minds, Inc.
End-User License Agreement

READ THIS. You should carefully read these terms and conditions before opening the software packet(s) included with this book ("Book"). This is a license agreement ("Agreement") between you and Hungry Minds, Inc. ("HMI"). By opening the accompanying software packet(s), you acknowledge that you have read and accept the following terms and conditions. If you do not agree and do not want to be bound by such terms and conditions, promptly return the Book and the unopened software packet(s) to the place you obtained them for a full refund.

1. **License Grant.** HMI grants to you (either an individual or entity) a nonexclusive license to use one copy of the enclosed software program(s) (collectively, the "Software") solely for your own personal or business purposes on a single computer (whether a standard computer or a workstation component of a multi-user network). The Software is in use on a computer when it is loaded into temporary memory (RAM) or installed into permanent memory (hard disk, CD-ROM, or other storage device). HMI reserves all rights not expressly granted herein.

2. **Ownership.** HMI is the owner of all right, title, and interest, including copyright, in and to the compilation of the Software recorded on the disk(s) or CD-ROM ("Software Media"). Copyright to the individual programs recorded on the Software Media is owned by the author or other authorized copyright owner of each program. Ownership of the Software and all proprietary rights relating thereto remain with HMI and its licensers.

3. **Restrictions On Use and Transfer.**

   (a) You may only (i) make one copy of the Software for backup or archival purposes, or (ii) transfer the Software to a single hard disk, provided that you keep the original for backup or archival purposes. You may not (i) rent or lease the Software, (ii) copy or reproduce the Software through a LAN or other network system or through any computer subscriber system or bulletin-board system, or (iii) modify, adapt, or create derivative works based on the Software.

   (b) You may not reverse engineer, decompile, or disassemble the Software. You may transfer the Software and user documentation on a permanent basis, provided that the transferee agrees to accept the terms and conditions of this Agreement and you retain no copies. If the Software is an update or has been updated, any transfer must include the most recent update and all prior versions.

4. **Restrictions on Use of Individual Programs.** You must follow the individual requirements and restrictions detailed for each individual program in the "Using the CD" appendix of this Book. These limitations are also contained in the individual license agreements recorded on the Software Media. These limitations may include a requirement that after using the program for a specified period of time, the user must pay a registration fee or discontinue use. By opening the Software packet(s), you will be agreeing to abide by the licenses and restrictions for these individual programs that are detailed in the Appendix and on the Software Media. None of the material on this Software Media or listed in this Book may ever be redistributed, in original or modified form, for commercial purposes.

5. **Limited Warranty.**

(a) HMI warrants that the Software and Software Media are free from defects in materials and workmanship under normal use for a period of sixty (60) days from the date of purchase of this Book. If HMI receives notification within the warranty period of defects in materials or workmanship, HMI will replace the defective Software Media.

(b) **HMI AND THE AUTHOR OF THE BOOK DISCLAIM ALL OTHER WARRANTIES, EXPRESS OR IMPLIED, INCLUDING WITHOUT LIMITATION IMPLIED WARRANTIES OF MERCHANTABILITY AND FITNESS FOR A PARTICULAR PURPOSE, WITH RESPECT TO THE SOFTWARE, THE PROGRAMS, THE SOURCE CODE CONTAINED THEREIN, AND/OR THE TECHNIQUES DESCRIBED IN THIS BOOK. HMI DOES NOT WARRANT THAT THE FUNCTIONS CONTAINED IN THE SOFTWARE WILL MEET YOUR REQUIRE-MENTS OR THAT THE OPERATION OF THE SOFTWARE WILL BE ERROR FREE.**

(c) This limited warranty gives you specific legal rights, and you may have other rights that vary from jurisdiction to jurisdiction.

6. **Remedies.**

(a) HMI's entire liability and your exclusive remedy for defects in materials and workmanship shall be limited to replacement of the Software Media, which may be returned to HMI with a copy of your receipt at the following address: Software Media Fulfillment Department, Attn.: *Rock Guitar For Dummies*, Hungry Minds, Inc., 10475 Crosspoint Blvd., Indianapolis, IN 46256, or call 1-800-762-2974. Please allow four to six weeks for delivery. This Limited Warranty is void if failure of the Software Media has resulted from accident, abuse, or misapplication. Any replacement Software Media will be warranted for the remainder of the original warranty period or thirty (30) days, whichever is longer.

(b) In no event shall HMI or the author be liable for any damages whatsoever (including without limitation damages for loss of business profits, business interruption, loss of business information, or any other pecuniary loss) arising from the use of or inability to use the Book or the Software, even if HMI has been advised of the possibility of such damages.

(c) Because some jurisdictions do not allow the exclusion or limitation of liability for consequential or incidental damages, the above limitation or exclusion may not apply to you.

7. **U.S. Government Restricted Rights.** Use, duplication, or disclosure of the Software for or on behalf of the United States of America, its agencies and/or instrumentalities (the "U.S. Government") is subject to restrictions as stated in paragraph (c)(1)(ii) of the Rights in Technical Data and Computer Software clause of DFARS 252.227-7013, or subparagraphs (c)(1) and (2) of the Commercial Computer Software - Restricted Rights clause at FAR 52.227-19, and in similar clauses in the NASA FAR supplement, as applicable.

8. **General.** This Agreement constitutes the entire understanding of the parties and revokes and supersedes all prior agreements, oral or written, between them and may not be modified or amended except in a writing signed by both parties hereto that specifically refers to this Agreement. This Agreement shall take precedence over any other documents that may be in conflict herewith. If any one or more provisions contained in this Agreement are held by any court or tribunal to be invalid, illegal, or otherwise unenforceable, each and every other provision shall remain in full force and effect.

FOR DUMMIES
BOOK REGISTRATION

Register This Book and Win!

We want to hear from you!

Visit **dummies.com** to register this book and tell us how you liked it!

- ✔ Get entered in our monthly prize giveaway.

- ✔ Give us feedback about this book — tell us what you like best, what you like least, or maybe what you'd like to ask the author and us to change!

- ✔ Let us know any other *For Dummies* topics that interest you.

Your feedback helps us determine what books to publish, tells us what coverage to add as we revise our books, and lets us know whether we're meeting your needs as a *For Dummies* reader. You're our most valuable resource, and what you have to say is important to us!

Not on the Web yet? It's easy to get started with *Dummies 101: The Internet For Windows 98* or *The Internet For Dummies* at local retailers everywhere.

Or let us know what you think by sending us a letter at the following address:

For Dummies Book Registration
Dummies Press
10475 Crosspoint Blvd.
Indianapolis, IN 46256

FOR DUMMIES ™

BESTSELLING BOOK SERIES